With tips on everything from nutrition to finding p
a science-packed and incredibly practical guide t
Highly recommended for anyone who wants to fe

Laurie R. Santos, P
Professor of Psycho[illegible] University
Host, The Happiness Lab podcast

PAVING the Path to Wellness has been an incredible tool for me personally and professionally. Being in corporate wellness for 25-plus years, I have utilized many tools to bring lifestyle medicine into workplaces but nothing compares to the benefits of this program in targeting the root causes of employees' mental and physical illnesses. Beth, Michelle, and Amy are powerhouses in this topic, as well as in the field of lifestyle medicine. They are transforming healthcare and corporate wellness with this tool. Improving health outcomes requires that people become aware of their present state in many important areas, such as social connection, purpose, sleep, stress resilience, and more. This is the first step in order for employees and patients to make sustainable and long-term lifestyle changes that can positively impact their health and well-being, and consequently contribute to a decrease in healthcare cost and an increase in employee engagement. Chronic diseases are the leading causes of death, disability, and healthcare costs in the U.S. The status quo is no longer acceptable or sustainable. Companies must start doing what truly works, and *PAVING the Path to Wellness* is it!

Valeria S. Tivnan, MPH, MEd
Employee Benefit Solutions (EBS)
Director, Population Health Strategy and Well-being

Whether you are trying to manage your chronic health condition or you are just trying to improve your physical, mental, and emotional wellness but feel overwhelmed with the quantity of information and different, sometimes contradicting advice from diverse sources, this book is for you. Addressing the six pillars of body, mind, and soul well-being, this workbook offers sound, scientifically tested information and interventions that work together to address all aspects of human health and wellness. Use this workbook as a guide to designing your own wellness experiments and crafting your individualized path to health and flourishing. Having used principles of PAVING Steps program in a stroke survivor wellness program, I can attest to the value and satisfaction that both patients and their caregivers derived from this program and improvements many of them made in their overall health and quality of life.

Irena Matanovic
MA Clinical Psychology
Certified Health and Wellness Coach

I was introduced to the amazing Dr. Frates and the PAVING course thanks to the charity SameYou, as part of my rehabilitation from a brain injury. The PAVING blend of science, psychology, culture, and ancient wisdom, and not to mention Beth's own family story, means there is something to inspire everyone to start on their own journey to wellness. The practical steps of the PAVING course went from being a tool for rehabilitation to an everyday guide to help me to be the best me. This practical and inspiring approach to well-being is a gift that can benefit everyone at whatever stage they are in their journey in life.

Mark Robinson
PAVING Program Participant

PAVING the Path to Wellness Workbook is an evidence-based plan to help individuals utilize the power of daily habits and actions to improve their health and quality of life by lowering the risk of chronic disease. Written and tested by three acknowledged physician experts in lifestyle medicine, *PAVING the Path to Wellness Workbook* provides an easy-to-follow road map for individuals to improve their health, happiness, and well-being.

James M. Rippe, MD
Founder and Director, Rippe Lifestyle Institute

PAVING THE PATH TO WELLNESS WORKBOOK

A Guide to Thriving With a Healthy Body, Peaceful Mind, and Joyful Heart

Beth Frates, MD
Michelle Tollefson, MD
Amy Comander, MD

ISBN: 978-1-60679-550-7
Book layout: Cheery Sugabo
Cover design: Cheery Sugabo
Front cover photo: pr2is/Shutterstock.com

Healthy Learning
P.O. Box 1828
Monterey, CA 93942
www.healthylearning.com

ACKNOWLEDGMENTS

We would like to thank all the students and patients who helped us create this workbook. Irena Metanovic was the student who created the first PAVING manual for participants in the PAVING the Path to Wellness program at Spaulding Rehabilitation Hospital in 2015. The first few participants in the program requested a copy of the program slides so that they could take the material and information home with them. They wanted to refer to it in weeks and months to come. We are grateful for their enthusiasm.

We would also like to thank our family and friends who have supported us in our endeavor to craft this workbook to be as impactful as possible. We met each week for 2-3 hours every Friday morning. We are grateful to have such supportive spouses and families.

FOREWORD

PAVING the Path to Wellness guided me towards a more fulfilling medical career. Sitting wearily in Stanford Physical Medicine & Rehabilitation (PM&R) Grand Rounds early one morning as a second-year resident in 2013, I felt energized as Dr. Beth Frates enthusiastically explained how she used lifestyle medicine—nutrition, exercise, stress, sleep, substance moderation, social connection—to help patients manage a broad range of health conditions. She would effectively serve as a coach: exercising with patients, connecting with them emotionally, and empowering them to make healthy decisions for themselves. Her patients saw big improvements, and Beth clearly loved her role; now this was meaningful medicine!

Beth was particularly excited about a new program called *PAVING the Path to Wellness,* which she had just started for post-stroke patients at Harvard. She led small group discussions and group walks that not only emphasized the foundations of healthy living, but also provided a forum for meaningful social interaction. And it was fun! Though the program was in its infancy, patients seemed to walk more, eat more vegetables, feel less stressed, and even stop smoking. Over the next few years, I sought Beth out as a mentor. I listened to her lectures, observed her work, and attended her Harvard extension-school course on Lifestyle Medicine, which dove in-depth to the PAVING STEPSS program.

Backing up a little, I was first exposed to the power of lifestyle medicine as a fourth-year medical student at UC San Francisco while studying at Dr. Dean Ornish's Prevention Medicine Institute. Groups of patients with heart disease (heart attacks, unstable chest pain, etc.) would gather weekly to exercise, cook healthy foods, do yoga, and engage in group support discussions. I had a deep appreciation for technology (indeed, I'd worked in software for eight years prior), but this simple program worked better than any other intervention I'd seen in medical school. Research showed reduced symptoms, significant improvement in all biomarkers (cholesterol, blood pressure, etc.), and even reversal of atherosclerosis. Not only that, but the patients felt better and loved the program—one group I witnessed had been meeting on their own accord for 25 years!

Because the underlying disease that causes heart attacks (cardiovascular disease) is essentially the same as that which causes strokes (cerebrovascular disease), the potential for applying Ornish's program to stroke patients seemed obvious, especially in light of Beth's early success with PAVING. I had seen many post-stroke patients fall into a vicious cycle of worsening health and increased repeat-stroke risk due to fatigue and musculoskeletal changes, poor diet, social isolation, and stress. While the healthcare system typically provides medications and therapy to address acute needs, it focuses very little on helping patients with the fundamental, long-term healthy behaviors that can break this cycle, thereby dramatically improving recovery and preventing the next stroke.

Our vision was to turn PAVING into a comprehensive lifestyle medicine program for stroke patients, and in 2018, this became a reality at the Veteran Affairs Palo Alto Hospital. We introduced a three-month intensive outpatient program that included weekly exercise, cooking, mindfulness, group support, education, and coaching. While only a few cohorts completed the program prior to the COVID outbreak, the results were very encouraging. Participants improved their fitness—as measured by $\dot{V}O_2max$ (the best measure of cardiopulmonary fitness)—to a degree that roughly correlates to a 10 to 40 percent decreased mortality risk and 17 percent decreased stroke risk. Without medication changes, they also improved their blood pressure (the #1 risk factor for stroke) along with their endurance, walking speed (six-minute walk test), standing ability (30-second sit to stand), grip strength, and balance. And just as Dr. Ornish and Dr. Frates had found, patients loved participating—overall satisfaction scores were > 9.6 out of 10, attendance was nearly 90 percent, and many patients continued to participate in alumni and mentor programs. Results were published in the *American Journal of Lifestyle Medicine* in January 2021,[1] and we hope to continue our work following the pandemic.

While PAVING has clearly benefited patients following stroke, it can really help anyone to enhance their level of wellness. These principles are foundational for treating many health conditions, ranging from diabetes, obesity, and hypertension to rehabilitation from cancer, musculoskeletal conditions, and spinal cord injuries. The *PAVING the Path to Wellness Workbook* shares perspectives from three experienced physicians, provides a wealth of important facts, and offers many practical self-reflection exercises. The PAVING questionnaire in the workbook helps with assessment, while the various chapters guide readers to take concrete steps to lead them on their path to wellness. It can be used by individuals, or adapted for use by clinicians with their patients—indeed, I wish I had had this workbook a few years ago!

Many thanks to Drs. Frates, Tollefson, and Comander for putting together such a valuable resource. I hope that the material has the same positive impact on you that it has had on my patients and me.

Jeffrey Krauss, MD, DipABLM, DipABPMR
Chief Medical Officer, Hinge Health
Staff Physician, VA Palo Alto Health Care System
Clinical Assistant Professor (affiliated), Stanford School of Medicine, PM&R Division

1. Krauss J, Frates E, Parekh M, et al. (January 2021). Comprehensive lifestyle medicine program improves fitness, function, and blood pressure in poststroke veteran cohort: a pilot study. *American Journal of Lifestyle Medicine.* doi:10.1177/1559827620988659

CONTENTS

PREFACE

What is the secret to healthy living and reaching optimal wellness? No matter what your age, phase of life, or stage of recovery from a health setback, like a heart attack, stroke, diabetes diagnosis, or cancer treatment, or even a life setback, such as a change in work, loss of a loved one, divorce, or house fire, this workbook is intended to be a helpful resource.

After decades of reviewing the medical literature, listening to patient stories, reading countless books, attending multiple courses, and working directly with people helping them adopt healthy lifestyles, we are aware that change is possible, but it is not a one-size-fits-all process. In fact, it takes paying attention to 12 specific steps, which involve the body, mind, and spirit. Whether people are wanting to lose weight, become more fit, quit smoking, wean off sleeping pills, or are trying to get back on their feet after what they consider an earth-shattering setback, these 12 steps empower people to reach their goals and enjoy a happier and healthier life.

Live and Learn: Dr. Beth Frates

It was 1986, when I became passionate about living a healthy life and preventing heart attacks and strokes. Heart disease has been the number one killer of individuals worldwide for many decades. That's not why I focused on it though. I focused on it because of a patient whom I knew. I'd like to share the story of that patient with you now. Many people see themselves, a friend, a colleague, or a family member in this particular patient. He has a common story.

This gentleman was 52 in 1986. He was an overworked, overstressed, overweight New York City businessman who walked fast, talked fast, and ate fast. And, he often walked, talked, and ate all at the same time. He dined almost exclusively on fast foods, burgers, French fries, cakes, cookies, ice cream, and hard candies, which he stored in the middle drawer of his desk at work. He managed his stress with eating comfort food and perhaps a little yelling. At this point in his life, he had teenage children and a wife, but he rarely saw them, as he was at work 7 a.m. to 9 p.m. or later most days of the week. Many Sundays, he would head into work after church and family brunch. When he was at home, he was not actually present, as his mind was off wondering and worrying about his clients.

He and his brothers took over the family accounting business in New York City, which was started by their father. They were desperate to keep the business thriving. His job was his life. He wanted to help people get mortgages, help them pay for college for their kids, and reach other joyful milestones in life. For this reason, he was devoted to his work. In fact, he rarely slept more than a couple hours, as he often had great ideas at night, which he felt that he needed to immediately write down. Furthermore, he was hungry in the middle of the night too, often eating at 2 or 4 a.m.

As you may guess, exercise was not part of his daily or even weekly routine. He was an athletic guy growing up, a star basketball player and baseball player. At this point in his life, however, he did nothing. Well, that's not entirely accurate. He did do one activity. He did this sporadically—no special day of the week, and it may not occur each week.

But, when it did happen, it happened at the exact same time 11:07 pm—on the dot. And the activity was sprints. Yes—fast running, as fast as he could. At 11:07, this man sprinted from his office to Grand Central Station to catch the last train home. He knew exactly how long it took to get from his office to the train. He was desperate to catch that last train home, because if he did not make it, he was forced to return to his office and sleep on the cot he had at work. While this happened occasionally, it was not comfortable.

On one of these mad dashes to the train station, this gentleman experienced some pressure, some pain in his chest. One of his favorite mottos was "No pain, no gain," so he forged forward and made that train. By the time he reached his home station, he felt as if an elephant were resting on his chest. He was sweating and short of breath. Also, he was experiencing numbness and tingling down his left arm into his fingertips.

When his wife, who was a schoolteacher, arrived to take him home, she noticed his pale, sweaty, grimacing face and immediately drove him to the local emergency room. There he completed his myocardial infarction, a heart attack, and his subsequent right middle cerebral artery infarct, a stroke, leaving him paralyzed on the left side. One day this man was fine, and the next he was not.

I know this patient's story very well, better than any other patient's story. That's because this patient I am describing is my father. I was 18 when this happened. In fact, I was planning to major in economics. I was a freshman at Harvard at that time. My plan was to take the family business into a third generation of thriving. But my dad's heart attack and stroke changed everything for me—changed the way I looked at life, at work, at career, at family, and at health.

My father made a complete recovery, except for fine motor movements in his left hand. This meant that manipulating coins at the grocery store could be an issue. He also made a complete lifestyle change. He sought out intensive lifestyle programs and participated in them with my mom who was eager to do whatever she could to help her husband enjoy a full and happy life. He attended Pritikin Programs and learned about healthy eating, the importance of exercise, and how to manage stress.

My father changed. He was 52, and he changed. Often, my father said that his heart attack and stroke helped him to live the best years of his life. Sure, initially, he was mad, bitter, angry, and confused as to how and why this happened to him. He went through all the stages of loss, as he lost his old life and the way things were. Ultimately, he ended up wiser, healthier, and more joyful. He was fully present when he was with friends and family.

Personally, I noticed a huge difference, not just with me, but also with my brother and mother too. My dad changed his work schedule so that he spent more time at home. He bought a stationary bicycle and rode it five days a week for one half an hour at a time. He was often watching financial news shows or listening to them on the radio as he cycled, but he cycled. He also took walks with my mom. This was part of his stress reduction plan as well. His social connections became more important to him. He prioritized his relationships. In fact, it was after dad's health setback that I witnessed him kiss my mom for the first time. This was the first time I saw that public display of affection between them. I can still see my dad quietly, calmly, and sweetly approaching my mom from behind her, as she sat at the kitchen table with me. Then, he gently kissed her right cheek. They both smiled, and I did too.

In addition, dad's diet completely changed. He had vegetables, whole grains, and fish on his plate for the first time. Desserts were fruits. No more cookies or candies for him. Needless to say, my diet changed too. I was having salads, green beans, asparagus, peas, carrots, eggplant, and other vegetables that I had never eaten before. We all changed our diets.

When my dad put his mind on accomplishing a goal, he put 100 percent of his energy into it. In this case, it was being healthy! My dad's health setback changed him and me in profound ways.

His new healthy lifestyle saved my dad's heart. He lived 27 more wonderful, joyful years. We were grateful for every single one. Dad was diagnosed with high blood pressure, high cholesterol, congestive heart failure, and atrial fibrillation at the time of his heart attack and stroke. Due to his changes in his lifestyle, he was able to thrive despite his health setback.

Right after my father's heart attack and stroke, I knew my calling. It was medicine. I wanted to help people prevent heart attacks and strokes. So, I changed my major at Harvard. We call the major a concentration. I then concentrated in biology and psychology. I loved it. I so enjoyed my studies. The pre-med courses were challenging, but I knew they were an important part of my journey to medical school.

I particularly loved my psychology courses. In my sophomore year, I was lucky enough to be in a tutorial in which B.F. Skinner joined us for a class. The twelve of us could not believe we were sitting at an oval table with THE B.F. Skinner. I will never forget it.

My senior thesis was on how stress impacts the heart. I was part of a research project that tested how serial-seven subtraction influenced the EKG and muscle contractions of the heart. We found that this type of mental stress involving asking patients to subtract the number 7 from 100, and then subtract 7 from the answer and on and on, could cause stress severe enough to change people's heart electrophysiology and create changes in their EKGs that were noted with ischemia (lack of oxygen due to low blood supply) to the heart muscle cell.

At Stanford Medical School, I knew I wanted to perform research in cardiology and heart health. I was part of labs that examined the effect of a high nitric oxide diet on the endothelial cells (cells that line the blood vessels). We found that diets rich in nitric oxide were healthier for the endothelial cells than those with high cholesterol levels. I was fascinated by this work.

After Stanford, I went to Massachusetts General Hospital (MGH) for my internal medicine transition year before my residency in physical medicine and rehabilitation at Spaulding Rehabilitation Hospital, a Harvard Affiliate. I selected this specialty, because it is the one that takes care of stroke patients long term. My passion and purpose was to help stroke patients make a full recovery to a full life, and to help their family members along the journey.

This mindset led me to write a book on ways to prevent a second stroke. This is when I dove into exercise, nutrition, stress, and the other pillars of lifestyle medicine. Shortly, after writing that book, I became one of the first physicians trained and certified in health and wellness coaching in 2008. I loved the coach approach. I loved empowering people to make and sustain lifestyle changes. Since that time, I have completed four coaching programs and a motivational interviewing certificate. And, now I help teach medical students and practicing physicians how to empower patients to make and sustain lifestyle change.

Subsequently, I became deeply involved with the American College of Lifestyle Medicine. In 2018, I co-authored the *Lifestyle Medicine Handbook* with Jonathan Bonnet, Richard Joseph, and James Peterson. I loved sharing the information on healthy living for patients and providers alike. I am honored to report that the book is on the list of the Best Medicine Books of All Time by Book Authority. The second edition was released in 2020. I use all the principles in the book when I counsel a patient to adopt and sustain healthy habits.

When I first started working with patients to help them reach their optimal health and wellness, I focused on exercise and nutrition, mostly. My clients made adjustments to the way they moved their bodies and performed physical activity, if that was walking, jumping rope, or playing tennis. They also paid close attention to what they were eating. Nourishing the body with delicious and nutritious foods is a great way to lose weight.

We also set weekly SMART goals (specific, measurable, action-oriented, realistic, and time-sensitive) for my patients. Most of my clients were overweight or obese by the body mass index (BMI).

By the end of our sessions together, my clients were happy, and they lost weight. They felt great! However, months later, a stressful event may have occurred in their lives, like a job change, a relationship change, a move, selling a home, a new baby, the death of a parent, or an argument with a friend, creating a rift in the relationship.

These stressful events threw people off. They often went back to old habits. Fortunately, many of them called me. We worked together again and focused on stress resilience. Learning deep breathing, meditating, focusing on the things in their control, and making plans to address the stressful event in a productive, creative, calm manner helped tremendously. During these stressful times, sleep was often severely disrupted. As a result, we also worked together to set them up for sound sleep on a regular basis, with some critical changes to their behaviors and night time routines.

As you can see, I started with physical activity, nutrition, and goals. Then, I quickly added stress resilience and sleep basics to my coaching. With time, I also noticed I was using attitude adjustments and encouraging clients to look at mishaps and setbacks as opportunities to learn and grow, adding gratitude to their daily thoughts, and working on using their strengths to help them enjoy the state of "flow" more often.

In addition, I noticed the way I used experimentation each week, asking the clients to try new things and take note of how they worked. They were using their curiosity and investigating different parts of their lifestyles. Since no one can merrily do the same thing every day for hundreds of days or eat the same thing for hundreds of days, I encouraged clients to use variety with exercise, diet, stress resilience techniques, and friendships, too.

It is clear that we all need a sense of belonging, connection, and social support. Working with clients to help them connect with family and friends helped increase the success and the joy of the PAVING the Path to Wellness program. Cultivating high-quality connections is key to sustaining and enjoying a healthy lifestyle.

Most people focus on time management and neglect the concept of energy. I noticed this with client after client. Not only do people feel time pressure when they are stressed, but they also feel exhausted, fatigued, and lack energy. Thus, I made sure to have a focus on energy management and energy optimization. Part of this is learning to take time-outs, to take breaks in order to gain perspective, to relax, and to restore energy. Time-outs are actually empowerment moments. They help us gain perspective and restore energy.

Finally, research and my experience with clients over the past decade demonstrated that a sense of purpose is a key component of a joyful life and longevity. It also helps prevent burnout. Identifying a sense of purpose and having a reason for getting up in the morning is an integral part of the PAVING the Path to Wellness program.

The PAVING program is a whole person, holistic lifestyle medicine body, mind, soul program that adds years to your life and life to your years. It has 12 important steps as you can now appreciate. This is not "eat less and exercise more!" It is so, so much more. It's deep, meaningful, heartfelt, and life changing.

The Twelve Steps of PAVING the Path to Wellness Program

P = Physical Activity

A = Attitude

V = Variety

I = Investigations

N = Nutrition

G = Goals

S = Stress Resilience

T = Time-outs

E = Energy

P = Purpose

S = Sleep

S = Social Connections

The First Step

Your first step is to decide where you want to start. There is no right answer. Follow your heart. Whatever is pulling you, may it be stress resilience, social connection, nutrition, attitude adjustment, or movement, start where you want to start. You oversee this unique journey. We are honored to serve as your guides and share our PAVING the Path to Wellness program with you through this workbook.

"A journey of a thousand miles begins with a single step."

—Lao Tzu
Ancient Chinese
Philosopher and Writer

Allinone/Shutterstock.com

SECTION I
THE BASICS

DavigGyung/Shutterstock.com

CHAPTER 1
YOUR HEALTH MATTERS

You're likely reading this workbook because you're concerned about your health. If you're not, a considerable amount of evidence-based research indicates that spending time on your own health and following healthy habits are important for longevity, well-being and joy. Without question, personal health is a universal issue.

What is health? In its most basic definition, health is occasionally defined as the state of being free from illness or injury. Several years ago, the World Health Organization (WHO) offered a more nuanced view of health: Health is a state of complete physical, mental, and social well-being, as opposed to merely the absence of disease or infirmity.

Regardless of how anyone might define health, however, a review of America's health-related statistics paints a dire image. Not only is the number of individuals who are suffering from a health-related problem increasing at an alarming rate, but also the amount of money spent on healthcare exceeded $4 trillion in the past year.

Leading drivers of healthcare costs are chronic diseases (a disease that persists over a long period of time). Chronic diseases are also the most common causes of death and disability in the United States. A list of the (11) most common chronic diseases in the United States is detailed in Figure 1-1.

- Alzheimer's
- Arthritis
- Asthma
- Cancer
- Diabetes
- Heart disease
- High blood pressure
- High cholesterol
- Lower back pain
- Migraine headaches
- Stroke

Figure 1-1. The most common chronic diseases in the United States (Centers for Disease Control)

Individuals with chronic conditions account for the vast majority of spending on healthcare in the U.S. In fact, almost 60 percent of the U.S. population (over 190 million) has at least one chronic disease. Equally disturbing is the fact that chronic diseases are responsible for 7 out of 10 deaths in the U.S., killing more than 1.7 million Americans annually.

Not only are chronic diseases relatively common, but most are also highly preventable. Research shows that the lifestyle-related choices a person makes account for more than 80 percent of the premature deaths in the U.S. In other words, a definitive link exists between how you choose to live your life and the health-related outcomes you experience. In that regard, positive choices lead to positive health outcomes (i.e., a healthier you).

What is a healthy lifestyle? According to the American College of Lifestyle Medicine, a healthy lifestyle entails six pillars: adhering to a healthy eating pattern; engaging in physical activity on a regular basis; the ability to manage stress; avoiding risky substances; getting a sufficient amount of sleep; and forming and maintaining relationships. As such, the decisions you make concerning each pillar will have a dramatic impact on the quality of your life, as well as your level of risk of becoming yet another chronic disease statistic.

The knowledge of and the ability to make sound lifestyle choices are critically important. This factor is especially relevant for you, given that healthy choices are within your personal purview. The underlying focus of this workbook is to provide you with a practical tool—the PAVING STEPSS wheel (see Chapter 2)—that enables you to readily and easily ensure the degree to which the choices you are making in your daily life are consistent with the need to minimize your risk of experiencing a health-related problem. Of note, following these 12 steps will bring more joy into your life, or in some cases help to bring the joy back to your life, at work and at home.

CHAPTER 2
A TOOL FOR EVERYONE—THE PAVING THE PATH TO WELLNESS PROGRAM

The PAVING the Path to Wellness program is designed for anyone who wants to take stock of their current lifestyle and make a positive change. In that regard, this workbook is a practical tool to help guide you on your journey to a happy and healthy life that fulfills your body, mind and soul. In step-by-step fashion, the book helps you identify the lifestyle-related changes you can consider undertaking, what those changes entail, and what actions will help to facilitate your fun-filled journey to a healthier, happier you.

This workbook is a hands-on resource to help you design a strategy that will enhance your lifestyle and level of wellness, by applying the evidence-based information and suggestions presented to you. The strategy encompasses several interrelated parts, including an overview of 12 steps (six basic lifestyle-related habits and six steps for sustaining the core habits) that are key to successfully completing your wellness journey; a PAVING the Path to Wellness questionnaire to help you determine how your lifestyle currently aligns with those steps; a PAVING STEPSS wheel that, when completed, offers a visual image of how you are doing with the 12 essential habits; a series of "Live and Learns" interspersed throughout most of the chapters in this workbook in which the co-authors and several of their patients share their personal stories concerning their wellness journeys; and a variety of techniques to help you pinpoint information essential to your journey, such as employing the MOSS™ strategy (motivators, obstacles, strategies, and strengths) and specifying habit-specific goals that adhere to the tenets of SMART goal-setting.

THE PAVING THE PATH TO WELLNESS PROGRAM COMPONENTS

The PAVING Mnemonic

First consider the PAVING the Path to Wellness program PAVING mnemonic, which is designed to help you remember the following six core habits:

- P for physical activity
- A for attitude
- V for variety
- I for investigations
- N for nutrition
- G for goals

The first habit is regular physical activity. In this instance, physical activity entails moving your body around. This could be in the form of a structured exercise activity, like going to the gym, riding a stationary bicycle, or swimming laps in a pool. Or it could also be in the form of lifestyle-related exercise, such as riding your bike to work or taking the stairs at work instead of the elevator. Regular refers to making exercise a routine part of your life, hopefully every day.

Exercise has numerous benefits. Why not reap these rewards daily? Scientific studies show multiple benefits to exercise, including increased concentration, decreased anxiety, better stress management, improved mood, and better sleep. Accumulating 150 minutes of moderate-intensity physical activity each week should be your goal. Performing strength training twice a week on non-consecutive days is another physical activity-related objective. Doing balance exercises, as well as flexibility exercises, is also important.

Physical activity helps you not only to look good, but also to feel good. But, how do you incorporate it into your daily routine? That is the million-dollar question. This issue is addressed in Chapter 4—physical activity.

The next aspect of the program is one that is often ignored in typical diet and exercise books—A for attitude. If you want to feel content, there are certain attitudes and mental exercises that you will need to practice, including expressing gratitude, savoring the moment, celebrating success, being optimistic, being mindful to your current task, reframing situations, and refraining from multitasking.

Much of what our parents and grandparents taught us is accurate, and research exists to prove it. For example, "Try to see the glass as half full instead of half empty," "Find the silver lining to the situation," and "Be grateful for each day."

Words really do make worlds. What you appreciate, appreciates. If you are always talking about how much you love cookies or how much you hate to exercise, you will keep those thoughts close to your heart.

On the other hand, if you look for opportunities to talk to yourself in a positive, compassionate way, reminding yourself of your strengths, you are far more likely to feel confident and empowered to make small changes in your daily routine. Utilizing the "growth mindset," as outlined by Dr. Carol Dweck, a renowned Stanford psychologist and researcher in the field of motivation, and working to use mistakes as opportunities to grow, rather than as opportunities to punish yourself relentlessly with automatic negative thoughts, is essential to PAVING. The specifics of attitude are covered in Chapter 6.

The next component of the PAVING mnemonic is variety, which is an important factor in all aspects of life. The V in PAVING stands for variety. Sometimes, you might need something new to keep you interested in exercise or healthy eating. Perhaps a new pair of sneakers might do the trick. Adding a new exercise, like Zumba, might be the spice you desire. Trying new types of exercises like yoga, hiking, exercising with a physioball, or skiing, if you are so *inclined*, is key to keeping yourself entertained while being physically active. Cross training is another viable option for exercising to incorporate variety.

Working just one set of muscles in one specific way, like jogging, can be rewarding and even meditative. On the other hand, a runner also needs to work on their flexibility and upper-body strengthening in order to be balanced and healthy. Ideally, a jogger enjoys participating in other activities besides running, such as yoga, hiking, bicycling, swimming, dancing, and maybe even team sports like softball.

Variety in the kitchen is just as important. While arguably it is great if you eat carrots every day, the recommendation is for you to consume a daily rainbow of fruits and vegetables so that you can consume all the phytonutrients, vitamins, minerals, and disease-fighting natural substances you possibly can. The specifics of variety are detailed in Chapter 6.

The next part of the PAVING mnemonic is I, which stands for investigations. As physicians, we, three, are lifelong learners. One of the underlying goals of this workbook is to help you be lifelong learners too.

Some part of you likely enjoys learning now, or you did as a kid. It's delightful to let your curiosity lead you to exploration and investigation, as a child and as an adult. It is a joy to learn new information each day. Constant curiosity is a gift. What is new in medicine? What is working well with your body now? What foods do you enjoy? What is your resting heart rate? How many steps are you taking each day? When do you like exercising—in the morning or in the evening? What is your blood pressure now that you have been exercising for six months?

Experiencing joy from learning more about yourself and wanting to better understand your body is a substantial part of your wellness journey. This is not about shame, blame and guilt. It's about learning and growing. Furthermore, what was working for you at age 30 might not be working at age 60. If that is the case, then it is time to investigate. Chapter 7 looks at the topic of investigation.

The next element of the PAVING mnemonic is N, which stands for nutrition. There are thousands of nutrition books available in the marketplace. Furthermore, there are numerous myths, misunderstandings, and misrepresentations concerning nutrition that are equally widespread. What is fact and what is fiction? Whom do you trust? What should you believe?

This workbook reviews different diets and diet recommendations. Common threads among the healthiest diets are identified and discussed. A whole-food. plant-based diet, the Mediterranean Diet, the Mayo Clinic Diet, and the Full Plate Diet are highlighted. The importance of eating for health and letting food be your medicine are addressed.

People make choices each day as to what they put in their mouths. By showing you the guidelines for healthy eating, you are provided with the framework for choosing what eating pattern works best for you. Knowing what to eat is one thing, but setting up a plan to eat healthy foods each day and implementing that plan is the focus of the chapter on nutrition, Chapter 8. Whether you want a step-by-step, cookbook approach or a more relaxed follow-the-guidelines approach, this information is designed to help you find the comfort and strength to address your eating habits and move along in your wellness journey.

The sixth habit in the PAVING mnemonic is creating goals, which is represented by the letter G in PAVING. When you create goals, they need to be SMART goals. In other words, they are specific, measurable, action-oriented, realistic, and time-sensitive. For example, a SMART goal is not "I will lose 20 pounds." Rather, a SMART goal is "I will walk for a half an hour five days a week in the morning right after I wake up in the morning."

Taking small steps forward is the key to this journey. Small successes lead to larger successes. Setting yourself up for success will help you gain confidence and increase your level of wellness. Having long-term goals, such as "In a year, I will be eating a plate that is half vegetables and fruits, a quarter protein, and another quarter complex carbohydrates for lunch and dinner every day" is an appropriate tactic.

Identifying long-range goals like what you want to accomplish in a year is a sound strategy. Setting a vision of yourself further in the future, 10 or 20 years from now, can help you see where you want to be years from now. Then, use three-month goals, monthly goals, weekly goals, and even daily goals to keep you on track. Having a to-do list also works for many people. Just having certain expectations for yourself and following specific guidelines each day will help you to reach your optimal level of wellness. Chapter 9 reviews goal-setting in greater detail.

The STEPSS Mnemonic

After the initial first six steps, there are six more. The second set of six steps is critical to sustaining the first six habits. All the steps are important, but without these next six steps, change is not likely to become a way of life. The six sustaining steps are represented by the mnemonic STEPSS, are:

S = Stress management

T = Time-outs

E = Energy appraisal

P = Purpose identification

S = Sleep

S = Social support

The underlying root cause of many illnesses is excessive stress and a corresponding lack of healthy ways to manage stress. This seventh habit—stress reduction and resiliency building—is represented by the initial S in the second mnemonic STEPSS. A little stress can be a motivator and an instigator. However, too much stress can lead to chronic alterations in the body and mind that result in failure to thrive and even to disease.

Understanding the purpose of stress, the fight-or-flight response, as well as the parasympathetic nervous system (which enables you to rest and digest), is a critical part of the wellness puzzle. How can you turn off the stress response and turn on the relaxation response? Deep breathing is one of the easiest and most effective techniques to utilize in times of stress. There are different ways to accomplish relaxation with deep breathing, many of which will be explored in Chapter 10. Beyond breathing, there is reframing and positive self-talk that can help put things in perspective. What appears to be a crisis might only be a small slip-up that can be fixed or worked through with relative ease. Identifying your stressors, tracking them, and learning about methods you can employ to de-stress comprise the bulk of this chapter.

The next sustaining habit is time-outs. This refers to everything from taking short breaks, empowerment moments, to breaks from sitting for over an hour, as well as a break in which you unplug from work in all ways. It is important to know that excessive sitting is a risk factor for heart disease. Many people view it as the new "smoking." This information might be new to you. Ideally, this chapter and every chapter will open your eyes to something new–a new fact, a new way of looking at something or a new strategy to help enhance your sense of well-being.

The action you need to do to avoid excessive sitting is taking time-outs from prolonged sitting. You might use the tool of a timer and set a timer to go off each hour. Then every hour, stand up and move, e.g., walk in place, jump rope, balance on one leg, or whatever suits you, just as long as you move your large muscles and propel blood through your body. The skill, in this instance, will be finding a break activity that you can do daily or identifying a variety of break activities that will keep you on your toes every hour. These time-outs will not only help your body but also your brain.

What about vacation? The Danes take their full six weeks, and they live in one of the happiest countries in the world. Americans, in contrast, tend to hoard their vacation time. It's somewhat unclear why people don't take their vacation time. Perhaps, they think that they can pass the time off to their children, like an inheritance after they die. Some people say that they're storing up their vacation time so that they can use it when they get sick. Someone made this previous comment after a PAVING the Path to Wellness workshop conducted by Dr. Frates. In response, Dr. Frates asked the person, "What if taking your vacation time and relaxing would help you to stay healthy?" The participant said she hadn't thought of it that way. New knowledge, skills, and attitudes concerning the need for and value of taking breaks periodically are addressed in Chapter 11 on time-outs.

Chapter 12 focuses on the third element of the STEPSS mnemonic–energy... natural energy and artificial energy. What brings you energy naturally? When you are with certain friends and colleagues, do you feel happy, confident, and energized? These are energy-givers. What about other colleagues who demean you, use you to get work done, and make you feel useless? These are energy-zappers. As a good friend once told Dr. Frates in the early 2000s, "Beth, it's time for you to get rid of your leeches and cultivate your lilies!" He was specifically speaking about some colleagues who were draining her of time, resources, and energy.

Looking into your natural forms of energy, such as exercise, a steady supply of glucose from a healthy diet, as well as at least seven hours of nightly sleep, is also critical. For example, if you are using coffee for energy, how much are you using? Do you know what receptor caffeine binds to and how it works? What is its half life? The answers to these questions are in this book. Other questions to ponder are: When are you drinking coffee? Why are you drinking it–to stay up another hour past midnight? If you are using other drugs to stay awake or be more energized, evaluate the need for those items now!

What is the purpose of your life? This is a relatively deep question, one that will be explored in Chapter 13. How do you find purpose? What if you don't think there is a larger purpose to your life? In fact, there is great purpose in being a loyal friend, a loving mother, a good cook, and an honest person. This was the purpose for Dr. Frates' Greek Grandmother's life. Grandma Rose emigrated from Greece at age 18 and had an arranged marriage with a family friend in Greece. Grandma Rose raised a loving family that adored her. Her priorities of family, friendship, and love were her purpose in life. We all have a purpose. Sometimes that purpose changes with changing opportunities and circumstances. We can all find a reason for being, a reason for getting up each morning and a way to make the world a better place in some small way, each day. Some of us will be curing cancer and flying to the moon in this lifetime, but not all of us. However, all of us have a part to play and a unique way of contributing to the greater good.

Some people want to cure ALS and other deadly diseases; others need to make money for their family to have food and shelter. Taking a step back and considering your own strengths and how to use them daily to make the world a better place, will help you to find your purpose. Other exercises in finding your purpose in life include writing your own obituary and discussing your strengths with friends. The topic of purpose is explored in detail in Chapter 13. The work of Holocaust survivor and renowned psychiatrist Viktor Frankl is highlighted in this important chapter.

Chapter 14 reviews the power of sleep. Sleepless nights reduce our productivity and reaction time the next day. They impact our ability to learn. Driving while drowsy, for example, is a significant problem and a major cause of accidents. Being overtired impacts the way we see the world and our mood. In addition, a lack of sleep can make it difficult to maintain a healthy body weight and can cause carbohydrate cravings. Furthermore, sleep disorders are associated with several diseases, for example, sleep apnea (snoring episodes associated with a temporary cessation of breathing), which can lead to suffering a stroke.

Chapter 14 examines the basics of sleep, as well as the physiology of sleep. A variety of subjects, such as the sleep-wake cycle, are addressed in this chapter. An explanation of exactly how caffeine keeps you up when you are tired is included. The tenets of healthy sleep hygiene and how much sleep is recommended at certain ages and stages in life, are also covered. The key point that is emphasized is that sleep is a natural restorative force, which should not to be taken for granted. Do you know how much sleep is recommended for a healthy body and mind? Are you sleeping the recommended number of hours? What can you do to get a sound sleep? Chapter 14 will answer these questions.

The final aspect of the sustaining mnemonic (STEPSS)—social connections and the importance of selecting specific people for your support team along your lifelong wellness journey—is covered in Chapter 15. There are certain criteria that your support team members should meet to help keep you accountable to your goals and purpose in life. This team could have members who help you in person, on the phone, or online. They could be family, friends, coaches, teachers, doctors, fellow health seekers, or pets, like dogs and cats. Learning how to cultivate high quality connections is key to leading a joyful and fulfilling life. We can't enjoy high quality connections with everyone we meet, but it's essential to cultivate these types of connections at home and work when possible. Research shows that social connections can have far-reaching consequences. For example, if a friend of yours gets happier, you get happier. This basic support is one of the keys to sustaining healthy habits.

PAVING the Path to Wellness Questionnaire

This workbook also includes a PAVING the Path to Wellness questionnaire to help guide you on your wellness journey (Figure 2-1). There are five questions for each of the 12 steps for a total of 60 questions. The questions are all based on a scale of 1 to 5, with 1 representing "I never do this" and 5 representing "This is part of my routine." The questions are based on the current evidence-based guidelines for the steps, including exercise, nutrition, and sleep. Questions for steps, such as goal-setting, purpose, time-outs, investigations, variety, energy, attitude, social connection, and stress management, are based on research and accepted guidelines for healthy living.

PAVING the Path to Wellness

Measuring your Overall Wellness Using the PAVING Wheel

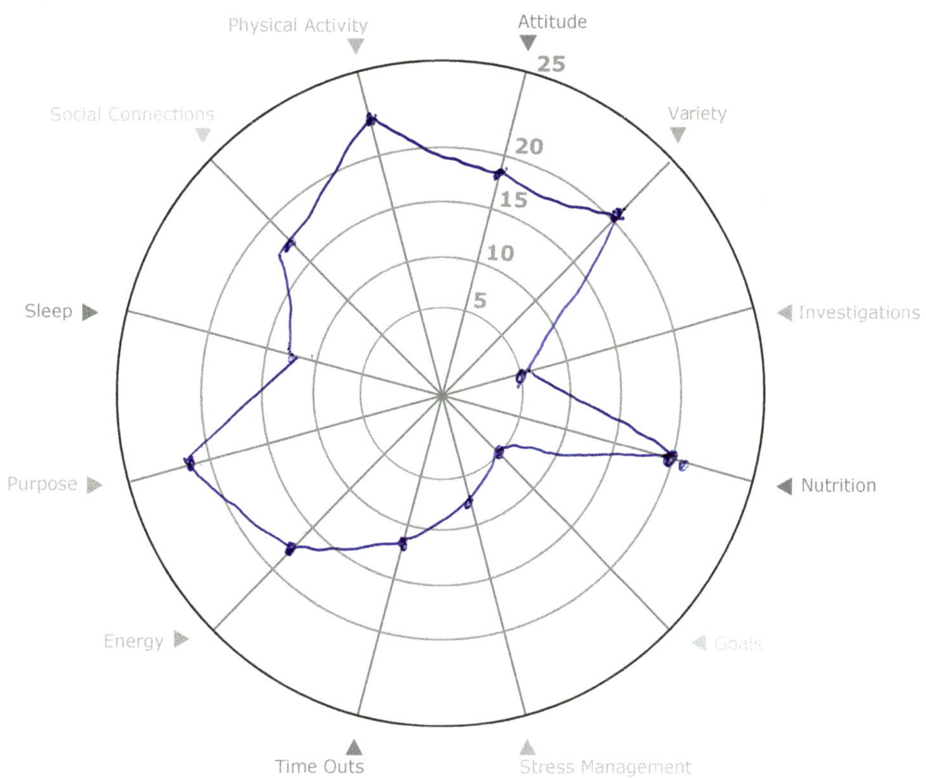

HOW TO USE THIS PAVING WHEEL

SCORE Plot your total scores for each component of the PAVING Wheel.

CONNECT Connect your scores.

EVALUATE Use the resulting PAVING Wheel (see example to the right) to evaluate areas where you may want to improve and consult the corresponding Module for more guidance.

RE-EVALUATE regularly by re-using this PAVING Wheel whenever you want to gauge your overall wellness and areas where you may want to improve.

EXAMPLE

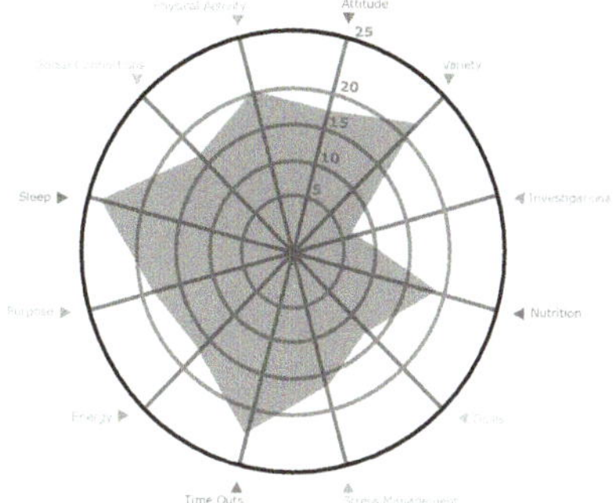

There are no right or wrong answers. No scores are good or bad. Using the PAVING Wheel is for you alone to assess your Wellness and identify areas to improve your own personal Wellness.

1

Figure 2-1. PAVING the Path to Wellness questionnaire

INSTRUCTIONS

Rank each item on a scale of 1-5. The Key is below. Calculate the subtotal of each of the 12 sections and plot them on the PAVING Wheel on page 1.

1 **Never** do this **2** Only **rarely** do this **3** **Sometimes** do this **4** **Often** do this **5** Do this regularly as **part of my routine**

	MODULE 1 Physical Activity
3	I exercise 5 days in the week for about a half an hour.
5	I enjoy myself when I exercise.
5	I perform strength training exercises twice a week.
5	I perform flexibility exercises routinely.
5	I perform balance exercises routinely.
	Physical Activity Total: 23

	MODULE 1 Stress
1	I have learned about stress and its effect on the mind and body.
1	I am familiar with stress reduction techniques, and I use at least one when I feel that I am anxious, annoyed, or worried.
1	I know about stress resiliency, and I practice enhancing my resiliency on a regular basis.
4	I don't get angry easily.
1	I meditate, take deep breaths, practice yoga, or do mindfulness based stress reduction (MBSR) regularly.
	Stress Total: 8

	MODULE 2 Attitude
4	I use mistakes as opportunities to learn and grow.
3	I write thank you notes or express my gratitude verbally.
2	I celebrate success when it happens.
4	I concentrate on the task at hand fully without distraction.
5	I am optimistic about the day.
	Attitude Total: 18

	MODULE 2 Time outs
5	If I sit for over an hour, I stand up and take a break for five minutes each hour.
1	If I feel frustrated and annoyed, I take a few deep breaths to calm down.
3	I take my vacation every year.
2	When I am at home, I make sure to turn off my computer and put my work projects away at least for an hour at dinner time.
1	After working on the same project for a few hours, I step away from it to get perspective on it.
	Time Outs Total: 12

	MODULE 3 Variety
5	I do a variety of different exercises.
5	I try to have a rainbow of colors on my plate.
5	I enjoy a variety of fruits and vegetables.
2	I like to try new activities.
3	I spend time and connect with a wide range of friends.
	Variety Total: 20

	MODULE 3 Energy
3	I have a friend who I know energizes me.
5	I have identified at least one activity that brings me joy and energy.
4	I am able to avoid situations and people that drain my energy.
5	I only drink two cups of coffee a day.
1	I don't rely on sugar/sweets or cookies for a quick energy fix.
	Energy Total: 18

	MODULE 4 Investigations
1	I perform mini experiments on myself regularly.
1	I am curious as to what foods are good for my body.
1	I am curious as to what effect physical activity has on my body.
1	I read about the latest research findings in medicine, nutrition, sleep, stress management, and/or exercise.
1	I talk about health with family and friends.
	Investigations Total: 5

	MODULE 4 Purpose
5	I feel that I have a clear purpose in life.
3	I am able to prioritize my activities and projects easily.
5	I make sure that my activities and projects are in alignment with my values.
5	I have identified the people and activities that are most important to me.
3	I am using my strengths to fulfill my purpose.
	Purpose Total: 21

	MODULE 5 Nutrition
4	I eat 4 fruits a day.
4	I eat 5 or more vegetables a day.
4	I know proper portions for protein, carbohydrates, and fats, and I eat those portions.
4	I think about the food that I eat and ask myself if it is good for my body.
4	I view food as fuel, as medicine, and enjoyment too.
	Nutrition Total: 20

	MODULE 5 Sleep
3	I sleep 7-8 hours a night.
5	I don't drink coffee after noon time.
1	I have a bedtime routine in which I relax before bed.
1	I don't sleep with my phone on in the bedroom.
1	I take 20 minute naps when I am over tired.
	Sleep Total: 11

	MODULE 6 Goals
1	I set long-term goals for myself, share them with someone, and review them.
1	I set three-month goals for myself, share them with someone, and work toward them.
1	I set monthly goals and share them with someone.
1	I set weekly goals and share them with someone.
1	I set daily goals for myself and keep myself accountable for them.
	Goals Total: 5

	MODULE 6 Social
5	I can name at least one person who brings me strength.
1	I am involved with a group (activity, exercise class, art class, religious affiliation or the like)
2	I visit with friends on the phone or in person at least 5 times a week.
5	I have a healthy relationship with my spouse, partner, or best friend.
5	I have a pet or plant that I can nurture and spend time with every day.
	Social Total: 18

Figure 2-1. PAVING the Path to Wellness questionnaire (cont.)

It is recommended that you take the questionnaire before reading Chapters 4-15. By taking the questionnaire, you are performing your first investigation. You are finding out where you are right now regarding these 12 well-being-related steps. Self-awareness is a critical part of your wellness journey. No one is perfect. No one needs to be perfect. Perfection is not the goal. Progress is the goal. In fact, perfection is often the enemy of progress. Wellness is a journey an individual takes step by step, day by day, and in some cases moment by moment.

PAVING the Path to Wellness Wheel

After filling out the PAVING the Path to Wellness questionnaire, you can use the number totals for each step to complete the Wellness Wheel radar plot (see Figure 2-1). This provides an overall visual of where you are with each of the 12 steps. Some steps will have lower scores than others. That is fine. It is all fine. What is, is. You need to accept things for what they truly are. This undertaking is information-gathering and is intended to inform you about how to proceed. The goal is not to have a "perfect" wheel all the time with 25 on every step. Most people are going to have areas in their life that are working well for them and others that are not working as well. It's all a matter of balance.

When you complete the wheel, you are learning about yourself at this snapshot of time in your life. The wheel changes year to year, month to month, and sometimes week to week. The wheel acts as a guide so that you can decide where you want to devote time and energy on yourself and self-care.

Ultimately you are striving for a healthy body, peaceful mind, and joyful heart, which can be experienced with a variety of wheel radar plots. It does not have to be a full

circle. In fact, you can feel inner peace without having a full circle radar plot at 25. This is a learn-and-grow process, in which there is no shame, blame, or guilt involved. You will not be graded on your wheel. It is not meant for judging. It is meant for learning.

After looking at the wheel and the radar plot, see if you gravitate to any one step on the wheel. It might be a step where you are doing fairly well, or it might be a step where you need a lot of work. The best place to start is where you want to start. What aspect do you feel motivated to address? Consider tackling that one initially.

Educational Material

The chapters are meant to provide you with up-to-date, research-based information and guidelines, as well as food for thought. Ideally, you will read and digest the material. There will also be space for you to write down your thoughts. This workout is an active process.

Charts, figures, and images are included to help you remember the material in this workbook. We hope this book is an easy read. It's meant to be enjoyable. In some places, you may be challenged or even uncomfortable as you either ponder your purpose in life at this point or work to identify solutions around obstacles you may be facing. In some instances, the workbook details the most common obstacles and then offers viable options for solutions to address them. In time, you may come up with your own potential ways forward that work for you. There is space in each chapter to develop your own answers and strategies for ways forward.

When appropriate, key terms are defined in each chapter. Obviously, some of you are experts on these topics, while others are being introduced to these concepts for the first time. Accordingly, the workbook attempts to accommodate readers who are at various stages of knowledge while also supporting different learning styles, with lists, graphics, examples, and questions. We hope this book makes you think!

Questions

Each chapter of this book includes questions to ponder while you're reading the material. These questions invite you to think, think deeply. Just as with the questions on the PAVING Wheel, there is no right or wrong answer. You are encouraged to take your time with these questions and to answer them honestly. Write what comes to mind. Remember, these questions neither are being graded nor do they need to be shared with anyone. They are meant to help you advance on your wellness journey.

If you notice initial hesitation around answering a question, ask yourself why. It may be a particularly sensitive topic, or you may want to explore this topic further with a health/wellness professional or a trusted companion. It may not be the right time for you to explore this topic. Remember, these questions are meant to support your journey, and you can use them however is best for you. You may find that you want to share your thoughts about these questions with your colleagues and friends.

Live and Learns

The chapters also provide you with personal examples, which are called Live and Learns. In some cases, real patients share their stories, many of which are very personal examples. In other chapters, one of the co-authors openly reflects upon their own struggles and successes. When you read these Live and Learns, you are invited to think about your own journey and what you have learned from your experiences. Life presents countless opportunities to learn from circumstances and challenges, if you are willing to reflect.

MOSS Strategy

Many of the topics in this book are explored by using the MOSS™ strategy. MOSS™ stands for motivation, obstacles, strategies, and strengths. Dr. Frates created this strategy over a decade ago. It is a helpful way to address any sticky situations that arise in your life at home or at work whenever you are making a change.

- *Motivation:* What motivates you to want to make a particular health behavior change?
- *Obstacles:* What obstacles are preventing you from making that change or embracing a particular health behavior?
- *Strategies*: What strategies could you use to overcome those obstacles?
- *Strengths:* What strengths do you have that you could use to help you make the health behavior change?

Establishing Habit-Specific SMART Goals

For each of the 12 habits reviewed in Chapters 4-15, you are asked to specify a habit-specific SMART goal. SMART is a mnemonic acronym that offers the following criteria for setting a particular objective: specific, measurable, action-oriented, realistic, and time-sensitive. Ideally, these goals provide you with guidance, direction, and focus as you proceed on your wellness journey.

Getting Involved With This Workbook

The following Live and Learns penned by the three co-authors of this workbook help illuminate how each of them decided to become ambassadors for the PAVING the Path to Wellness program:

❏ Beth Frates, MD, DipABLM, FACLM

I was working with people and was focusing mainly on nutrition and exercise. This was great because it helps people, but it wasn't quite enough.

I developed the PAVING the Path to Wellness model in 2012. I have been using this model to work with patients and clients in my lifestyle coaching practice ever since. I work 1:1 with patients, as well as conduct group lifestyle medicine sessions with 6-12 participants. The initial positive feedback was heartwarming and encouraging to me. For example, in the first pilot study using this program at Spaulding Rehabilitation Hospital, a Harvard Medical School affiliate, the participants reported walking more minutes each week, eating more vegetables each week, and feeling less stressed. In fact, one participant had set a quit date for smoking after participating in a 4 week PAVING the Path to Wellness group intervention for stroke survivors and caregivers.

Since that time, I have run groups annually for stroke survivors and their caregivers. Over the years, the format has changed, as I have investigated and experimented with a variety of options for delivering the PAVING the Path to Wellness program. Most recently, PAVING the Path to Wellness has been virtual, due to the COVID pandemic. To my surprise, it has worked extremely well online. There is a different feeling during the in-person sessions, but the virtual groups provide the space for learning and connecting in a deep way, as all the participants have attested.

Since there has been no PAVING the Path to Wellness workbook until now, participants were using a version of the workbook, which was a compilation of the PowerPoints from my PAVING the Path to Wellness presentations. In 2018, when the *Lifestyle Medicine Handbook* was published, participants also used that for their reading materials. This is still a great resource in addition to this workbook, but it is not required.

Originally, I started working with stroke patients and their caregivers with the PAVING the Path to Wellness groups at Spaulding Rehabilitation Hospital. My passion and dedication to this population comes from deep within my heart. In fact, when I was 18, my father suffered a heart attack and subsequent stroke, which left him paralyzed on his left side. He was 52 years young. This was a life-changing event for everyone in the family (see the Preface for additional details).

This experience when I was 18 served as the impetus for me to continue working to find ways to empower people to adopt and sustain healthy living at any age or stage of life. As luck would have it, I connected with Dr. Comander and Dr. Tollefson about a decade ago. Our journey with the PAVING programs and lifestyle medicine has brought me great joy. Our collaboration birthed this PAVING the Path to Wellness Workbook and has sparked my passion for promoting these programs to a diverse group.

Dr. Comander and Dr. Tollefson helped me realize that this program can empower and equip everyone (not just Stoke Survivors) with the knowledge, tools, and strategies to reach their optimal wellness, be their best selves, and thrive, no matter what their age or stage in life. These amazing women have inspired me in many personal ways too. In fact, Dr. Tollefson's personal story inspired me to run a marathon and Dr. Comander's devotion to her patients gave me the opportunity to get a number for the Boston Marathon (which I completed virtually in 2020). These strong women inspire me daily. Working with them is a joy. Together, our goal is to disseminate the PAVING The Path To Wellness program philosophy and teachings far and wide. We have visions of holding PAVING workshops on the Greek Islands one day. Perhaps you will join us in person for those!

❏ Michelle Tollefson, MD, DipABLM, FACLM

I spent the first 30 years of my life giving little thought to healthy lifestyle behaviors. As a child, I ate family dinners that my mom cooked with ingredients from my dad's garden; I took dancing lessons and played on the tennis team, and routinely exchanged sleep for late night studying.

During medical school and my obstetrics and gynecology training, these home-cooked meals were replaced by diet soda to stay awake during morning rounds, free lunches from drug representatives, and middle-of-the-night visits to McDonald's in our hospital basement where I joined patients pushing their IV poles in line. I usually got the fruit and yogurt parfait, trying to be somewhat healthy. I no longer had time to exercise and only ran when a nurse called me for an emergency delivery. I routinely worked 24-hour shifts and sleeping more than six hours per night was a luxury I rarely had.

When I had my daughter near the end of residency, I naively thought, when I'm in private practice, then I'll have time to prioritize my health. However, I struggled to maintain a work-life balance, never really learned to cook, and felt successful if I could quickly heat a frozen dinner in the microwave that my husband and daughter would eat at the end of a long day. While studying for my medical board exams, I don't even remember nutrition, exercise, sleep, or stress resilience being mentioned. When patients asked how they could eat healthier or improve their overall health, I didn't have much wisdom to offer.

Over a decade ago, I was introduced to the Harvard Institute of Lifestyle Medicine and became a guest faculty member. The more I learned about nutrition, physical activity, sleep, and stress and the more I embraced healthier lifestyle behaviors myself, the better I felt. While I was noticing all of the benefits of healthy living, I eagerly shared this knowledge with my patients and anyone who would listen. It was like I had found a secret superpower in healthy lifestyle behaviors that I had not been taught during my medical training.

My expertise in the field of lifestyle medicine grew. After a decade of work in academia, I founded a Bachelor of Science in lifestyle medicine at Metropolitan State University of Denver in Colorado that launched in 2019. I volunteer at a local non-profit clinic where I focus on women's health lifestyle medicine. I co-founded the Women's Health Member Interest Group of the American College of Lifestyle Medicine (ACLM) as well as the Lifestyle Medicine Pre-Professional Education Member Interest Group with Dr. Beth Frates.

When I met Dr. Frates, I knew she was a kindred spirit. We were two of the first physicians trained as wellness coaches almost 15 years ago, and we had both been teaching lifestyle medicine courses at our respective universities. I had even heard her speak at Harvard Lifestyle Medicine conferences I had attended and was impressed by her expertise and ability to share the evidence in a way that motivated people to change their health trajectory. She was passionate and purpose driven.

Over the past few years, I've had the opportunity to learn from Dr. Frates and to collaborate with her on a variety of education-related initiatives, including the creation of LM101 curriculum, based upon her Harvard Extension School class. Over the course of one year, we met weekly and worked collaboratively. The experience led us to a close bond as friends and to a fantastic finished product the Lifestyle Medicine LM 101 Curriculum offered for free to the American College of Lifestyle Medicine members. After that successful collaboration we embarked on a second one—to bring lifestyle medicine to teenagers. We worked with a team to develop PowerPoint decks for school teachers to use in health and wellness classes, a teacher's manual and a Teen Lifestyle Medicine Handbook co-authored by Dr. Frates, Dr. Plaven, Dr. Watts, Dr. Agarwal, Dr. Dalal, and my daughter Kaitlyn. Dr. Frates and I have synergy that makes working on projects a joy and this PAVING Program has proven to be another opportunity for us to share our passion for healthy living with others on a much larger scale. Dr. Frates has become a real mentor and dear friend, and I am grateful to serve alongside her on the ACLM Executive Board, our professional organization that has about 7,000 members.

From a health standpoint, I was feeling somewhat invincible, as I had no major medical problems and no significant risk factors for cancer. I even considered delaying my mammogram at age 42, but a reminder on my phone's calendar encouraged me to schedule this routine screening. Even though I knew that breast cancer was a possibility for anyone, I had no symptoms and still had the mindset that my healthy lifestyle behaviors would protect me from a breast cancer diagnosis.

The mammogram found an invasive breast cancer hiding against my chest wall. Initially I thought, "why me." My thought quickly shifted to, "why not me." One in eight women in the U.S. will be diagnosed with invasive breast cancer, and many will have had no known risk factors. What do we do with this knowledge? What do we do when a diagnosis leaves us feeling powerless? I did what I believe many lifestyle medicine physicians would do... I decided to fight this aggressive cancer with everything evidence-based medicine had to offer, lifestyle medicine included!

I made an appointment with my oncology center's dietitian, purchased new pink running shoes, joined the ACLM Cancer Member Interest Group, and got ready for battle. Even though I knew the basics of healthy lifestyle practices during breast cancer treatment, I sought an "all-star" team to learn the most current information. Luckily, my health system has a wellness center that offers an oncology-specific exercise program and nutrition and cooking classes, as well as many other treatments aligned with the pillars of lifestyle medicine.

When discussing my recent breast cancer diagnosis with Dr. Frates, she offered to connect me with her friend and colleague, Dr. Amy Comander, due to her expertise. In addition to reassuring me about my treatment plan of a bilateral mastectomy and chemotherapy, my visit with Dr. Comander helped me feel empowered by the capacity of lifestyle medicine to optimize treatment.

My transition from active treatment to surveillance was challenging and anxiety-provoking. Cancer had changed my life so dramatically that I found it difficult to resume some of my normal activities. I joined a local breast cancer support group but quickly dropped out, as it left me feeling disempowered and with a heightened awareness of what breast cancer had taken from me.

Dr. Frates encouraged me to join Dr. Comander's PAVING the Path to Wellness for Breast Cancer Survivors group, which had just transitioned to an online format due to the pandemic. Although I didn't believe that I really "needed" a group to connect with, I was eager to learn more about the program that Dr. Frates had created and that Dr. Comander was leading.

As the weeks went by, I transitioned from being a spectator within the group to fully embracing the PAVING process. The program provided opportunities for enhanced wellness beyond physical well-being. Through the weekly sessions, I developed a renewed enthusiasm for embracing lifestyle medicine as a breast cancer survivor (and thriver). As our 12-week sessions came to an end, I was surprised by the emotion I felt and the deep appreciation I had for being invited into this group of amazing women. As a lifestyle medicine-focused physician, I knew much of the content that was presented. However, being part of the group inspired and empowered me to embrace life more fully through the meaningful connections I made, as well as the insight shared by Dr. Comander and the participants.

When Drs. Frates and Comander asked if I would like to lead the first PAVING the Path to Wellness group outside of Massachusetts, I was honored and thrilled by the opportunity. To partner with these two amazing women through the creation of this workbook has been a gift to me. It is my hope that you will embrace the content in this workbook and that it will support your continued growth, regardless of wherever you are at on your wellness journey.

❑ Amy Comander, MD, DipABLM

You might think that physicians know how to counsel patients on how to exercise, eat healthy, and lose weight. There I was, feeling fortunate to have finished training in some of the best medical institutions in the country, with my patients looking at me and asking these simple questions like: "I am so tired; how can I resume an exercise regimen?" "What type of diet should I follow?" "How can I get back to my healthy weight?" These were not casual questions.

These were women who were recently handed some of the most difficult news anyone can receive—that they have cancer. The stakes are high, and I was supposed to be the expert with answers. But I did not know the answers. Managing chemotherapy? No problem. Reducing symptoms such as nausea and vomiting? Again, no problem. Counseling about nutrition and wellness after cancer treatment? Not taught, no training, no practice.

Well, one of the things you DO learn in medical training is to recognize when you don't know something, and how to figure out where to learn what you need. Fortunately, I attended a Harvard Medical School course entitled, "Lifestyle Medicine: Tools for Promoting Healthy Change," where I met Dr. Frates!

This conference was my first introduction to the field of lifestyle medicine. When I met with Dr. Frates, I learned about her passion for lifestyle medicine, and the innovative program (PAVING the Path to Wellness) she had started at Spaulding to help stroke survivors and their caregivers. I wanted to start a similar program to help women following completion of treatment for breast cancer.

Subsequently, we began a collaboration, and I started by leading group sessions with patients at the MGH Cancer Center at Newton Wellesley. The first PAVING group, held in the Fall of 2019, involved 14 women, and this was my first experience as a facilitator for a group intervention. I was amazed by the participants' engagement in each topic, their support for one another, and the deep social connections that formed over the course of 12 weeks.

The program was a hit, not because of me, but because the material is so incredibly useful. The PAVING program is now growing quickly, and now conducted over Zoom, due to the pandemic, with increasingly larger enrollment. Scaling the teaching of these "secrets" to a larger audience was the motivation to write this book, for you and anyone else looking to enhance your health and wellness.

I have noticed that the participants in the PAVING courses appreciate when the facilitator describes how she puts the lessons into practice, and you probably do as well. I can share with you how I made changes in my life, and how those changes have made a positive impact on my health, as well as the health of my family. I became a vegetarian. I stepped up my exercise regimen, from running a couple times a week, to training for marathons. (Hey, I might have lost a few of you there, but let me tell you, I never thought I would be able to do that, either!) Now my passion is running the Boston Marathon to support charitable causes. I have had a blast organizing events to raise funds for cancer survivorship programs at our hospital, including the PAVING the Path to Wellness Program.

Because it has been important for me to broaden my knowledge of lifestyle medicine, I recently pursued board certification in lifestyle medicine to solidify my expertise. I am learning about the science of plant-based nutrition. I was also fortunate to have another physician join my PAVING class—none other than the amazing Dr. Michelle Tollefson! Her participation in the PAVING program has grown into a beautiful partnership, as you will read in Michelle's Live and Learn. I joined ACLM and am now the founding co-chair of the Breast Cancer committee. Most recently, I have been training other colleagues at the MGH Cancer Center to run PAVING groups, so we can offer this transformational experience to a larger group of breast cancer survivors.

CHAPTER 3
STARTING YOUR JOURNEY

"When your habits don't line up with your dream, then you need to either change your habits or change your dream."

—John C. Maxwell
American Author

As someone who sincerely has decided to make a change in their lifestyle, this workbook can help you achieve your dream of being healthy. In that regard, this workbook guides you through 12 steps to enhance well-being, productivity, and joy in your life.

Everyone can benefit from this book no matter their age, gender, global geographic location, educational level, or socioeconomic background. As such, regardless of your current health status or physical limitations, this workbook can help you start or continue your wellness journey to thriving and enjoying your unique life. You may be working to prevent a heart attack, diabetes, or a stroke, based on your family history. You may be attempting to reduce your risk of cancer or optimize your health during cancer survivorship. You may even be recovering from a mastectomy from breast cancer, colon resection for a newly diagnosed colon cancer, or a recent hospitalization. Or perhaps, you have experienced a recent divorce, loss of job, or the death of a loved one that has sparked a renewed commitment to healthy living.

In one way or another, everyone is a survivor of the struggles, obstacles, mishaps, and difficult times that life has tossed their way. Whether you are a single working mom, a dad recovering from prostate cancer, a grandfather with a history of stroke, an obstetrician-gynecologist balancing work and family demands, a teacher juggling the needs of students, a middle-aged divorced person looking to start a new chapter, someone who has lost a loved one too young, or anyone struggling to find inner peace, this workbook is designed to help you. It will help guide you on a path to uncover your own true beauty and inner wisdom, allowing you to thrive in this one precious life you've been given.

Using This Workbook

Initially, you need to decide where you want to start. There is no right answer. Follow your heart. Whatever is pulling you, may it be stress resilience, social connection, nutrition, attitude adjustment, or movement, start where you want to start. You are in charge of your unique journey. Use this workbook as your guide as you navigate your way through this PAVING the Path to Wellness program.

- Consider looking at your PAVING Wheel to see which step is most compelling for you in the moment. Skip to that step and read about it, or you can progress through this book, chapter by chapter, at a pace that works best for you. You don't have to read this book cover to cover. You can jump around. You can always come back to any particular chapter for further exploration.
- Although you may want to use this book independently, consider working with a friend, relative, or colleague who is interested in improving their well-being. You may use this book in a work setting if you are working on elevating your health at your worksite. Perhaps, you have a partner who wants to join you on your wellness journey through using this workbook as a guide. The possibilities are endless. It's fun to have people join you on your journey.
- Remember to reach out for support from your physician, primary care provider, mental health experts, and/or health/wellness professionals as you use this book, as needed.
- Be aware that this workbook is not intended to replace the medical advice of your healthcare team. Rather, it is intended to support your wellness journey, as you partner with them to address your health concerns and needs.

Making Your Plan a Reality

This workbook is a tool that you can utilize to become the best possible you. As such, you can use it as a roadmap to plan your future course of action. In other words, this is your opportunity to take the time to consider why you want to enhance your health, what will be required on your part to achieve that, how you plan to accomplish that, and when do you plan to undertake the necessary steps.

By deciding in advance what to do, how to do it, and when to do it, you are bridging the gap from where you currently are to where you want to go in the future. Not only will this factor resonate with and encourage you to be proactive concerning your health, it will enable you to achieve the life you expect, need, and deserve.

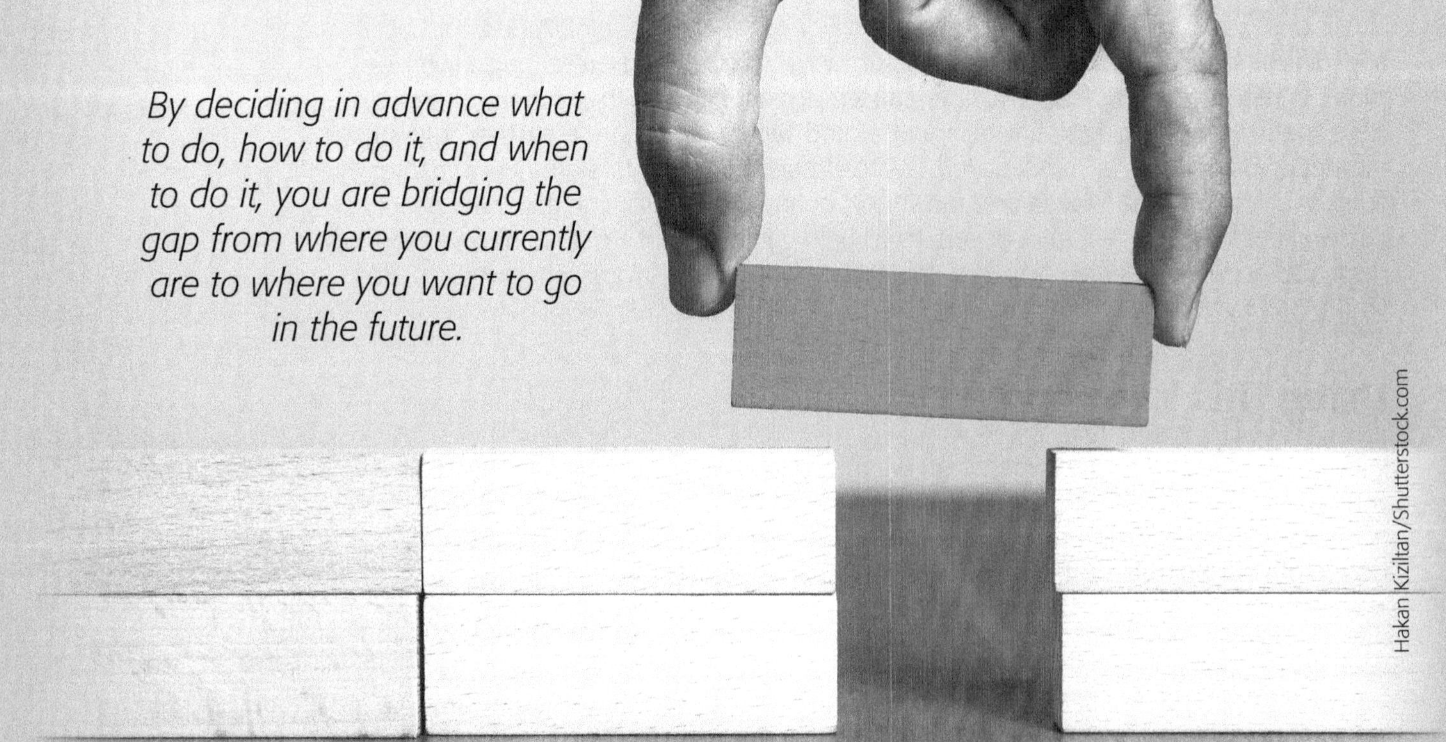

SECTION II
UNDERSTANDING THE BASICS

CHAPTER 4
PHYSICAL ACTIVITY

"Exercise not only changes your body, it changes your mind, your attitude, and your mood."

—Anonymous

PAVING the Path to Wellness: Questions for Physical Activity

For each of the following five statements, choose the number on the frequency scale that best relates to you (frequency: 1= never, 2= rarely, 3= sometimes, 4= often, 5= routinely).

- I exercise five days in the week for about a half an hour at a time.___
- I enjoy myself when I exercise.___
- I perform strength training exercises twice a week.___
- I perform flexibility exercises routinely.___
- I perform balance exercises routinely.___

Subtotal—physical activity:____

wavebreakmedia/Shutterstock.com

Live and Learn: Dr. Michelle Tollefson

As a child and throughout adolescence, I loved tap dancing and spent countless hours taking dance lessons and tapping to big band songs. As academic achievement became my priority in college, I no longer felt I had time to make dancing a priority. As a result, my tap shoes gathered dust in the closet. On the other hand, I knew that exercise was "good for me" and my New Year's resolutions often involved starting a new exercise regimen at the college fitness center. However, the gym resistance-exercise machines intimidated me, the classes left me feeling uncoordinated, and spending time on the treadmill felt like a punishment.

Throughout college, medical school, and residency as a new physician, my sedentary time increased and attempts to exercise made me feel like a failure. As a young obstetrician-gynecologist, I told my colleagues that the only time I ran was if a baby was going to be born imminently.

Gradually my weight increased, my energy decreased, and the literature supporting the connection between physical activity and health continued to grow. After a knee injury and surgery, my physical therapist told me what I already knew, if I wanted to be healthy, I needed to move more and to continue regular exercise indefinitely.

I started slowly by going on brief morning walks, worked with a personal trainer to overcome my intimidation to resistance-exercise machines at my gym, and purchased a recumbent bicycle that is just feet from my bed. As I moved more, I felt better physically, emotionally, and cognitively. When I was diagnosed with breast cancer last year, I was encouraged to learn that physical activity could help combat chemotherapy-related fatigue. Movement became a priority for me, while recovering from my mastectomy, multiple surgeries, and going through chemotherapy. My cancer center's oncology physical therapist encouraged me to "listen" to my body, modify my exercise regimen, and to truly use exercise as medicine. Whether playing basketball with my sons, doing water aerobics with my mom, or encouraging others to learn how to use the strength training machines that no longer intimidate me, I'm on a mission to help others experience the health benefits that come through movement.

Physical Activity Timeline

Write out or draw what you liked to do for physical activity, playtime, movement, or exercise during each of these phases of your life: childhood, adolescence, early adulthood, middle adulthood, older adulthood.

❏ Reflection Time:

Reflect on your relationship with exercise and physical activity throughout your life, including what influenced your view of exercise. Describe what type of relationship you have or would LIKE to have with physical activity. How does your current health and lifestyle impact what you do for physical activity?

❏ Reflection Time:

What would you love to do for physical activity if all barriers were removed, including physical ability, financial resources, and time? What are you hoping or wishing that you could try? This concept will be discussed later in the chapter, using the MOSS framework.

Movement

Regular physical activity provides tremendous health benefits and decreases the risk of chronic diseases, such as heart disease, stroke, osteoporosis, hypertension, dementia, depression, and some cancers. According to the World Health Organization,[1] one-in-four adults don't meet the physical activity recommendations. Insufficient activity is associated with a 20-30 percent increased risk of early death compared to others who get the recommended amount of physical activity.

The human body is beautifully designed to move! It's easy for someone to take their body's ability to move for granted, until they struggle with a health condition or challenge with movement.

For some people, discussing physical activity is associated with feelings of shame or guilt, not fitting cultural health norms, past exercise discomforts, or weight loss attempts. The underlying goal of this workbook is to support you wherever you are at with your current physical activity level, so that you can take the next step along the PAVING the Path to Wellness journey. If you've struggled with "exercise" in the past, you may want to use the words "physical activity" or "movement," instead, which are more inclusive and aligned with the focus of this chapter. Exercise is structured, planned movement of the large skeletal muscles, whereas physical activity includes any movement of your body.

Physical Activity Benefits

Research continues to highlight the benefits of physical activity for physical, emotional, and cognitive health. As you read the list of the following benefits, consider how physical activity currently influences (or could improve) your health and well-being.

❑ Health Benefits of Regular Physical Activity:

- Improves cardiovascular fitness.
- Helps prevent cardiac disease and stroke.
- Reduces blood pressure.
- Controls blood glucose.
- Controls weight and helps prevent obesity.
- Helps prevent bone loss.
- Reduces cholesterol.
- Dulls pain sensation.
- Improves sleep.

❑ Emotional (Mood) Benefits of Regular Physical Activity

Your emotional (mood) level is impacted by your level of physical activity. Not engaging in regular physical activity can act as a depressant. In contrast, physical activity helps to elevate mood, while decreasing stress, depressive and anxiety symptoms. During exercise, the "feel-good" chemicals, serotonin, dopamine, and endorphins are released. Physical activity is associated with both short- and long-term elevation of mood, self-esteem, and motivation to accomplish goals. If your mood could use a boost, consider moving more.

❑ Cognitive, Memory, Learning, and Focus Benefits of Regular Physical Activity

Physical activity increases blood flow to your brain, so that it receives more oxygen and nutrients, while removing waste products. Regular physical activity protects brain cells from damage, helps repair injured cells, and even promotes the creation of new brain cells. Brain scans show that with exercise, the hippocampus, which is involved with learning and memories, grows. If you want to enhance and maintain your cognitive abilities, mental alertness, and ability to concentrate, you'll need to incorporate movement into your daily routine. In order to have a healthy brain, you need to move!

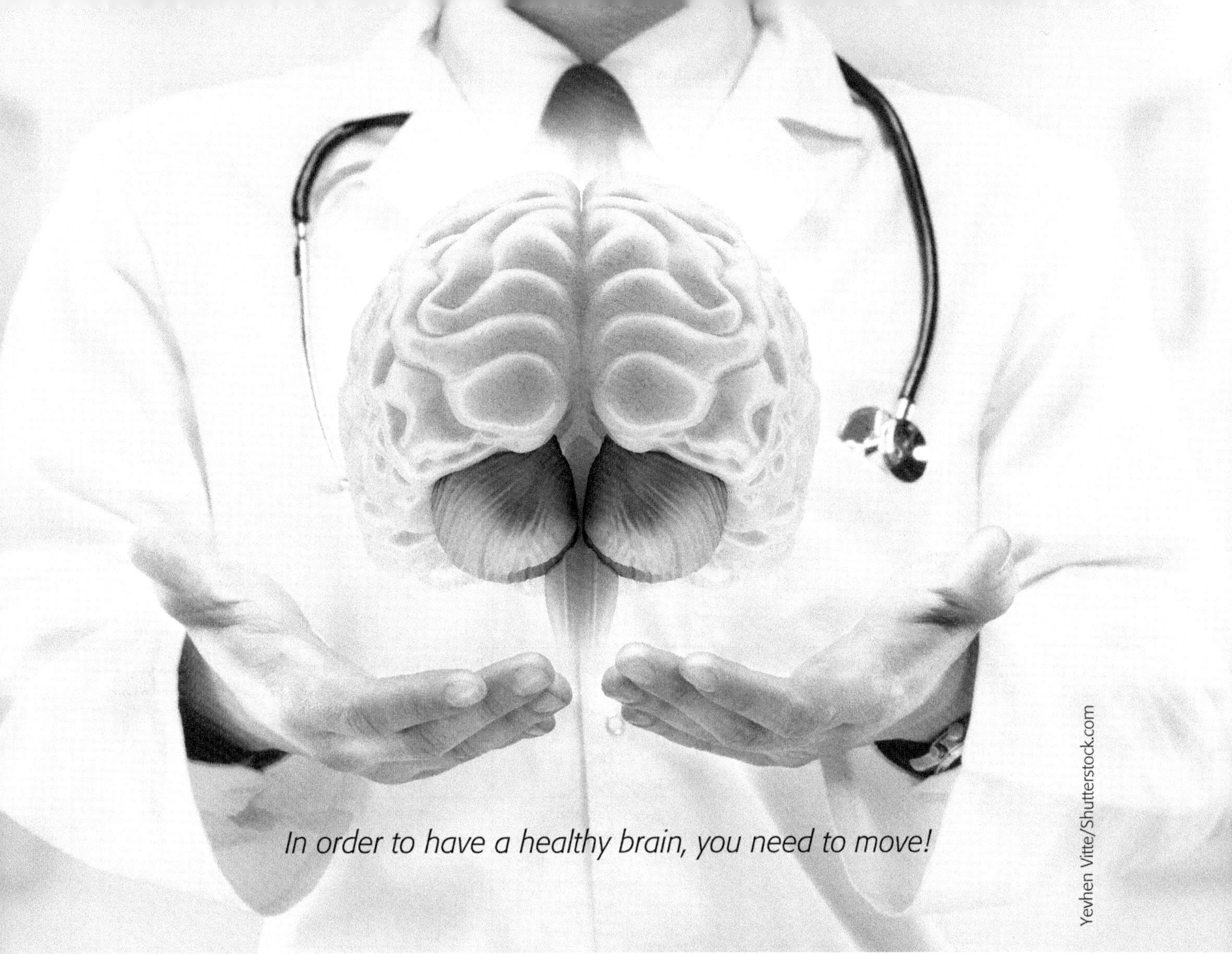

In order to have a healthy brain, you need to move!

❑ Reflection Time:

What role does physical activity play in your physical health? Does knowing that regular physical activity is very important for brain health, change how you view exercise? Explain. Do you notice any changes physically, emotionally, or cognitively when you are more versus less physically active?

___

___

___

___

___

___

___

___

___

Physical Activity Types[2]

Physical activity can be broken down into different "types." Some physical activities may be included in more than one "type" of movement.

Type of Physical Activity	Aerobic Activities	Muscle-strengthening Activities	Bone-strengthening Activities
What is it?	Activities that involve rhythmically moving the large muscles of the body for a sustained period of time	Activities in which the muscles do more work than usual in daily life	Activities that produce a force on the bones and/or involve jumping or rapid change in direction
Activity examples	Hiking, swimming, running, dancing, tennis, roller skating, biking, basketball, etc.	Lifting weights, using weight machines, using resistance bands, some forms of yoga	Running; jumping rope; using stair-climbing machines; hopscotch; playing sports, such as basketball, figure skating, tennis, etc.
How much?	Most of your 150 minutes or more of weekly physical activity should be aerobic activity, in bouts of at least 5 minutes.	At least three days a week as part of your weekly 150 minutes or more of physical activity	At least three days a week as part of your weekly 150 minutes or more of physical activity
Why do it?	Increases the ability of the lungs and the heart to take in, deliver, and utilize oxygen. Important for physical, emotional, and cognitive health.	Increases muscular strength (needed to get up from a seated position) and muscular endurance.	Promotes bone growth and strength.

Figure 4-1. An overview of different types of physical activity (modified and used with permission from *The Teen Lifestyle Medicine Handbook*; Beth Frates, et al.; Monterey, CA: Healthy Learning; 2021)

- *Aerobic activity/cardio activities:* Aerobic fitness is sometimes referred to as cardiorespiratory fitness and involves activities such as shoveling snow, running, riding a bicycle, or carrying something heavy upstairs for example.
  - ✓ Recommended minimum: 150 minutes of moderate-intensity physical activity per week or 75 minutes of vigorous physical activity per week
  - ✓ More extensive health benefits: 300 minutes of moderate intensity physical activity per week or 150 minutes of vigorous physical activity per week. Physical activity intensity (moderate or vigorous) is determined based upon the level of physical challenge for the person doing the activity. Moderate intensity makes the heart beat faster and usually you can still talk to someone but not sing while doing the activity. Vigorous intensity physical activities require a large amount of effort and raise your heart and breathing rate even higher. When engaging in vigorous intensity physical activity you usually cannot carry on a conversation with someone.
- *Strength training:* Strength and resistance training is associated with muscular fitness (strength and endurance). Adults begin to lose muscle mass after their 3rd decade and women often experience an acceleration of muscle mass loss with menopause. In order to continue to do activities of daily living, such as walking up stairs and living independently, it is important to maintain muscle fitness, which

is accomplished through strength and resistance training. The guidelines are to perform strength training exercises twice a week on non-consecutive days. Work all the major muscle groups twice a week. You do not need a gym or weights to do this. You can use your own body weight. Also, bands can be used for increasing strength. In fact, some yoga classes focused on body weight poses like plank, tree pose, and headstands can work your core, arms, and legs.

- *Balance activities:* Along with a loss of muscle mass can come challenges, with balance and falls associated with fractures, which can lead to a loss of independence. Activities such as yoga, Tai-Chi, walking heel to toe, and standing on one foot, for example, can help adults maintain and improve their balance. Consider engaging in balance-enhancing activities three times a week or more to reduce your risk of falls and help with everyday activities.
- *Stretching:* In order to increase and maintain flexibility, the range of motion of joints, and the elasticity of muscles and connective tissues, stretching is important. It can also improve posture, reduce soreness, release tension, and help prevent injury. Consider pre- and post-activity stretching or stretching at least twice a week for 10 minutes at a time. Hold each stretch for a total of 60 seconds. If you can only hold it for 20 seconds initially, that's ok. Try to perform the same stretch again and hold it for another 20 seconds. If you do 20 seconds three times, that will equal the goal of 60 seconds, and with time, you will find it easier and easier to hold the stretch longer and longer, reaching the goal of 60 seconds. Of note, the bouncing technique of stretching that many of us did as a kid is no longer advised. Stretching when the muscles are warm, after exercise, is also recommended.

Consider engaging in balance-enhancing activities three times a week or more to reduce your risk of falls and help with everyday activities.

Robert Kneschke/Shutterstock.com

❏ Reflection Time:

Think about a typical week. Do you engage in aerobic, strength, balance, and stretching physical activity? After reflecting on your typical activity or inactivity in these areas, would you like to make any changes? Explain.

____

____

____

____

____

____

____

____

____

If you are not as active as you would like to be, you are not alone. According to the World Health Organization,[1] five million global deaths could be prevented annually if people were more active, given that three-quarters of the adult world population don't meet the physical-activity minimum guidelines.

It is important to understand your current level of activity or inactivity before making mindful changes.

Monkey Business Images/Shutterstock.com

Initially, it is important to understand your current level of activity or inactivity before making mindful changes. Remember, even if your goal is to significantly increase your level of physical activity, you can start just by walking a little more and some gentle stretching. Significant benefits occur when moving from sedentary to being even minimally active, though greater benefits can be obtained from going further.

Physical Activity and You!

❏ Reflection Time:

Visioning: Consider your current level of physical activity now and imagine how physically active you believe you can be (and hopefully want to be) a year from now. Imagine what your life would be like if you were exercising each day. Picture yourself being physically active decades from now: what do you see, hear, smell, and touch while being physically active? What types of activities do you want to try? What types of physical activities align with your interests, resources, and schedule? What motivates you to be physically active? How would others whom you love, be impacted by you being physically active?

____

____

____

____

____

____

____

Imagine what your life would be like if you were exercising every day.

fizkes/Shutterstock.com

Overcoming Physical Activity Barriers

Common barriers to physical activity include a lack of time, motivation, or not enjoying physical activity. Many people express that the greatest challenge is overcoming the inertia of being sedentary, but once they start moving, they notice that they feel better, and it is easy to continue. You may want to ask your doctor for a referral to a physical therapist to help you create an activity plan that is tailored to you, your current health, and your goals. Insurance often covers these visits and assistance.

❏ Reflection Time:

What barriers and obstacles do you envision may get in the way of you achieving your desired level of physical activity? Brainstorm strategies for overcoming some of these barriers. What resources do you have to help you overcome these barriers?

____

____

____

____

____

____

____

____

Regardless of your current physical activity status, you have the power to be healthier. The following are a few suggestions to support you with PAVING the Path to Wellness through physical activity:

- Start today! Make a commitment to your physical, emotional, and cognitive health!
- Focus on making progress: even small changes can make a big difference over time.
- Find activities that are enjoyable.
- Create healthy habits to last a lifetime.
- Focus on overall health and not your body weight.
- Join a class or exercise with a friend.
- Explore classes offered by your local YMCA or community center.
- Move to music by creating a playlist to listen to while exercising.
- Enlist the help of a professional, such as a physical therapist or a certified personal trainer.
- Focus on your personal improvement rather than on comparing yourself to others.
- Be gentle with yourself; temporary setbacks are normal.
- Investigate what exercise feels best for you by journaling and being mindful.
- Mix it up and add variety to your activity routine.

Ideally, physical activity will bring joy to your life and not be a chore. Regardless of where you are on the physical inactivity-activity spectrum, hopefully you will seek ways to increase your physical activity. Even if increasing physical activity is challenging at first, you, like countless others before you, will likely find that being physically active is one of the best things you've ever done for yourself.

❑ Reflection Time

In this section, you learned about the habits of people who maintain a physically active lifestyle. What habits do you need to change or begin, to have a physically active lifestyle?

____

____

____

____

____

____

____

Exercise Safely

For most people, the risk of physical inactivity (being sedentary) is greater than the risk of engaging in physical activity. However, before beginning a new exercise routine or altering your current routine, you should talk with your physician to ensure that you can safely do so. You can also undertake the following to help minimize the likelihood of injury while exercising:

- Warm up.
- Start low.
- Go slow.
- Cool down.
- Stretch afterwards.

❑ Reflection Time:

What should you do to help ensure that your physical activity plans are safe for you?

____

____

____

____

____

____

____

____

Reducing Inactivity

Over the past century, individuals have become much more sedentary. In other words, too many people sit too much and participate in too little physical activity for optimal health. Even if you engage in aerobic activity daily, think about how you spend the remainder of your day. Sedentary behavior increases your risk of dying prematurely, as well as numerous health problems, even if you are physically active. Accordingly, you need to look for ways to become more active and decrease inactivity. Some examples include the following:

- Reduce the amount of time you spend sitting by taking a break at least once every hour to get up and move.
- If you are pre-diabetic or diabetic, stand and move at least once every 30 minutes.
- Set an alarm or reminder on your phone, watch, or other smart device to prompt you to get moving.

Individuals who commit to a healthy lifestyle have numerous options that can help them "move to improve." In that regard, you should consider the following:

- Get a standing, bicycle, or treadmill desk.
- Sit on a balance ball chair.
- Take walking meetings.
- Stand rather than sit while watching television.
- Stand and stretch during commercials.
- Take the stairs rather than the elevator.
- Choose a parking space farther away from the entrance to your office.
- Go for a walk after meals or during your lunch break.
- Walk your dog.
- Bicycle to work or walk to the bus stop.
- Rake the leaves.
- Vacuum your home or apartment.

❑ Reflection Time:

How many hours in a typical day are you sedentary? What are some ways that you could increase your activity throughout the day to be less sedentary?

____

____

____

____

____

____

____

The MOSS technique can be employed to help you identify the obstacles you face for becoming more physically active, in addition to developing strategies to overcome those obstacles.

Rawpixel.com/Shutterstock.com

Get Rolling Through MOSS: Motivation, Obstacles, Strategies, and Strengths

MOSS™ is an acronym to help you create a plan to increase your level of physical activity, as well as decrease sedentary behavior. In conjunction with the PAVING Wheel, it is a tool that can help you enhance your health.

"A rolling stone gathers no moss, but it gains a certain polish."

—Oliver Herford
English Writer

❑ Reflection Time:

✓ Motivation: Why are you motivated to increase your level of physical activity?

____

____

____

____

✓ Obstacles: What obstacles are you likely to encounter?

____

____

____

____

✓ Strategies: What strategies can you use to overcome these obstacles?

____

____

____

____

✓ Strengths: What strengths can you draw upon as you work toward your goal? Consider strengths that you've used to overcome previous challenges and your support system, including your healthcare team, family, and friends.

____

____

____

____

SMART Goal

In order to take what you have learned about physical activity and put it into action, create a SMART goal for yourself. In that regard:

- My goal is *specific* and easy to understand.
- My goal is *measurable*, and I have a way to track my progress.
- My goal is *action-oriented* with the right amount of challenge. I have the resources I need, and it makes sense for my life.
- My goal is *realistic*, so I am intrinsically motivated to accomplish it, and it is safe.
- My goal is *time-sensitive*.

❑ SMART Goal Time:

What is your SMART goal concerning physical activity?

____

____

____

____

____

____

The SMART acronym is a viable tool you can use to plan and achieve your goal of becoming physically active.

Photoroyalty/Shutterstock.com

References

❑ Cited References:

1. Physical activity. World Health Organization. https://www.who.int/news-room/fact-sheets/detail/physical-activity
2. Piercy KL, Troiano RP, Ballard RM, et al. The physical activity guidelines for Americans. *Jama*. 2018 Nov 20;320(19):2020-8.

❑ Book Resources:

- Atkinson D. *You Still Got It Girl.* Monterey, CA: Healthy Learning; 2016.
- Bean A. *The Runner's Cookbook.* London, England: Bloomsbury Sport; 2018.
- Moran D. *Beating Osteoporosis.* Newnan, GA: Green Tree; 2019.
- Ratey J. *Spark: The Revolutionary New Science of Exercise and the Brain.* New York: Little, Brown Spark; 2008.
- Richmond M. *The Physiology Storybook*, 3rd ed. Monterey, CA: Healthy Learning; 2011.
- Wei M, Groves JE. *The Harvard Medical School Guide to Yoga: 8 Weeks to Strength, Awareness, and Flexibility.* Boston, MA: Da Capo Lifelong Books; 2017.
- Westcott W. *Building Strength and Stamina*, 3rd ed. Monterey, CA: Healthy Learning; 2016.
- Yoke M, Kennedy C. *Functional Exercise Progressions.* Monterey, CA: Healthy Learning; 2004.

❑ Other Resources:

- Active People Healthy Nation—www.cdc.gov/physicalactivity/activepeoplehealthynation/join-active-people-healthy-nation/index.html
- American College of Sports Medicine (ACSM)—www.acsm.org
- American Council on Exercise (ACE)—www.acefitness.org
- Department of Health and Human Services Physical Activity—health.gov/our-work/physical-activity
- Exercise is Medicine—www.exerciseismedicine.org

CHAPTER 5
ATTITUDE

"Attitude is a little thing that makes a big difference."

—Winston Churchill
British Prime Minister

PAVING the Path to Wellness: Questions for Attitude

For each of the following five statements, choose the number on the frequency scale that best relates to you (frequency: 1= never, 2= rarely, 3= sometimes, 4= often, 5= routinely).

- I use mistakes as opportunities to learn and grow.___
- I write thank you notes or express my gratitude verbally.___
- I celebrate success when it happens.___
- I concentrate on the task at hand fully without distraction.___
- I am optimistic about the day.___

Subtotal—attitude: _____

KieferPix/Shutterstock.com

Live and Learn: PAVING Program Participant

I can't remember a time when I was not overweight. When I experienced any negative emotion, such as anger, sadness, anxiety, or frustration, I ate. When I was stressed, I ate. I ate whatever I could find, but I was drawn to foods like doughnuts, ice cream, cake, and cookies. My New Year's resolution was to get healthier and change my relationship with food. I exchanged my sweet processed foods for the natural sweetness of fruit. I focused on being healthier and not just my weight, though I lost about 30 pounds.

After a stressful day at work, when I had not had time to eat lunch due to pressing deadlines, I stopped at the grocery store on my way home. Although I had intended to purchase healthful food, an enticing display of snack cakes was by the entrance. They weren't just any snack cakes, they were my favorite snack cakes, and they were on sale! As I tried to walk by, my gremlin started to speak to me. The gremlin said "you can never stick to a diet. You've had such a hard day. You deserve a treat. One snack cake won't ruin your progress. Don't pass up the sale!"

Subsequently, I purchased a couple snack cakes, since I wanted the discount. I finished both before I pulled into my driveway. My gremlin continued to feed me messages filled with shame, blame, and guilt throughout the night. After reflection, I decided to fire my gremlin. I told it "you have no right to speak to me again. I'm hiring a princess to talk to me moving forward."

The next time I went to the grocery store after a stressful day at work, I brought my princess with me. My princess told me "those sweets will only taste good for a moment. Imagine how good you will feel after you eat a healthy snack or meal. Walk by those snack cakes and go to the produce aisle. You can do this!"

Do you have a gremlin that you need to fire and a prince or princess that you need to hire? If I can do it, you can too! Our self-talk is powerful, and I intend to use it as a force for healthy living moving forward.

Attitude

Attitudes are formed by your values and past experiences, and influenced by your family, friends, community, work, environment, and marketing. Most people rarely consider how their attitudes impact their health-related behaviors. Since attitudes influence your thoughts and behaviors, they are critical to your wellness.

❑ Reflection Time:

Describe your attitude toward one or more of the following health-related behaviors. Consider choosing a behavior that you struggle with or you would like to focus on improving, such as:

- Eating nourishing food
- Engaging in physical activity on a regular basis
- Fostering meaningful relationships

- Prioritizing sleep
- Adopting stress management behaviors
- Avoiding risky substances

❑ Reflection Time:

What do you believe influenced your attitude toward this behavior? Consider societal expectations, the media, your family and friends, academic education, etc.

____

____

____

____

____

____

____

____

Your attitude relates to your ability to engage in health-promoting behaviors (refer to Figure 5-1). Fortunately, health-defeating attitudes can be changed! You may not be able to choose your situation, but you can choose how you react to your circumstances. If you have attitudes toward your situation, your health conditions, or your health behaviors that you want to change, consider using the following techniques to support your well-being journey.

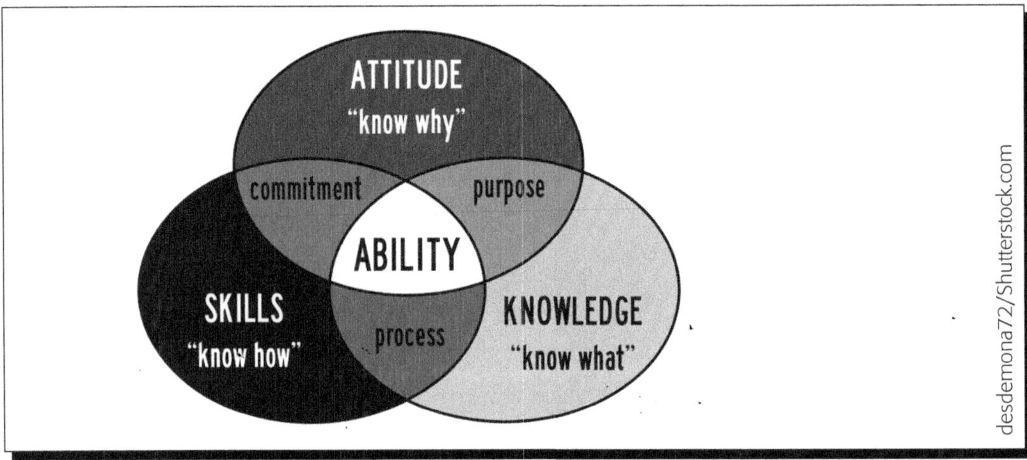

Figure 5-1. The interconnected relationship between a person's attitude and their skills and knowledge

❑ Attitude Adjustment (ATTITUDE)—Developed by Drs. Frates, Comander, and Tollefson:

- A = Acquiring knowledge
- T = Trying new things repeatedly
- T = Trusting yourself
- I = Identifying support systems
- T = Taking time to reflect
- U = Understanding emotions
- D = Developing your new normal
- E = Examining expert advice and assimilating it

Look at the ATTITUDE list and then answer the following reflection prompt. Explore how you can undertake this mnemonic:

- A: Acquire more knowledge by reading books, such as *The Lifestyle Medicine Handbook* or other evidence-based articles, chapters, and blogs.
- T: Try new things repeatedly, given that continued exposure can change taste buds, neural circuitry (brain cells that fire together– wire together), and excitement about new activities.
- T: Trust yourself to be successful by thinking of previous times when you've met a difficult challenge.
- I: Identify support systems by thinking about who has been there for you in the past during tough times, as well as during triumphs.
- T: Take time to reflect by carving out 10-15 minutes to brainstorm empowering self-talk that you would say to a friend if they were going through a difficult time and practice using the same talk for yourself. Reflect upon how this process feels.
- U: Understand that your emotions, like all emotions, are valid and will come and go like waves, both pleasant and unpleasant. Enjoy the pleasant while they last and understand that unpleasant emotions will wash away with time. Nothing is permanent in this world. It is our attitude that can help us rise above the difficulties that drag us down.
- D: Develop a new normal. Just as genes are not your destiny, your attitude is not set in stone. You have the power to adopt a new belief system about yourself and others. By focusing on your own inner wisdom and true beauty, you can let your light shine. This light can guide you and others.
- E: Explore expert advice and assimilate it: There will be times when you need to reach out to certified personal trainers, psychologists, counselors, registered dietitians, physicians, and other health professionals for expert input regarding your symptoms, dietary needs, and exercise risks. Be proactive and reach out, when needed, as reaching out is a sign of strength.

❑ Reflection Time:

Describe a behavior (or lack of a particular behavior) that you would ideally like to change. What types of attitudes would support your change?

self doubt, fear of failure / making mistakes. Recognize I have a lot to offer and be proud of it. Don't let self doubt prevent me from trying.

❑ Reflection Time:

Reflect on the ATTITUDE list above. What, did you learn that you can use to support any attitude adjustments that you would like to make?

____

____

____

____

____

____

Live and Learn: Dr. Michelle Tollefson

Throughout childhood and into young adulthood, I had a negative attitude toward vegetables. I saw them as a food that I "should" eat more of, even though I didn't enjoy them. I did not find them appetizing. I did not put any energy into learning how to prepare them and "made" myself try to eat a serving or two each day.

As I acquired knowledge about the health benefits of vegetables and fiber, I knew I wanted to change my relationship with vegetables for my health. I tried to eat vegetables during lunches, dinners, and snacks (frequent exposure). I engaged in new experiences with vegetables, as I looked for recipes that included vegetables and prepared them with herbs and spices that enhanced their flavor. I made an appointment with a registered dietitian (expert connection) to learn about improving my nutrition through eating a variety of vegetables. I predicted the emotions that I would feel from cooking and eating health-promoting foods with my family. I reflected upon my relationship with health-promoting foods, experimented with mindful eating, and gradually increased my self-efficacy around incorporating vegetables into my daily routine.

As my attitude toward vegetables changed, so did my behavior. Similarly, you can use the techniques discussed in this chapter to modify your attitudes toward healthy behaviors in order to impact your health and well-being. Attitude adjustments are possible!

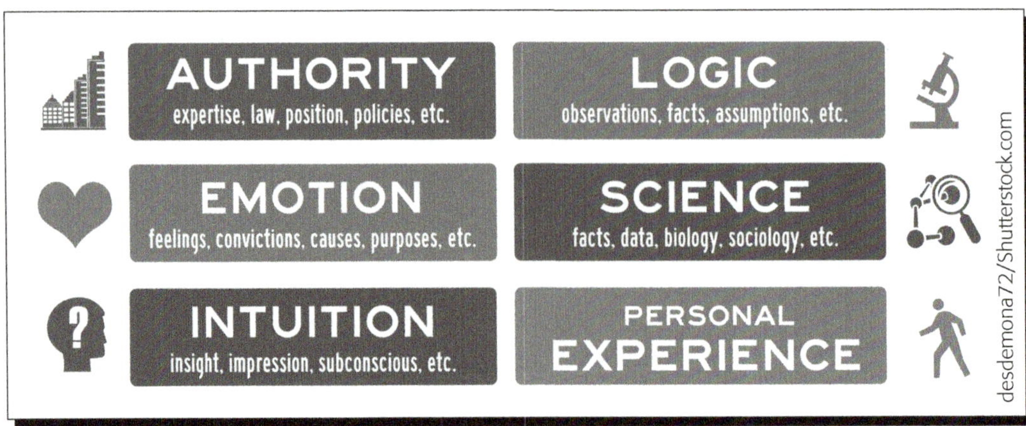

Figure 5-2. Where do a person's beliefs come from?

Components of Attitude—ABC

Attitudes are positive (favorable) or negative (unfavorable). According to a Rosenberg and Hovland's model of attitude structure,[1] attitude has three components: an affective component (feelings and emotions), a cognitive component (beliefs and thoughts), and a behavioral component, as the following ABC listing details:

- Affective—feelings and emotions
- Behavioral—how our attitude impacts behavior
- Cognitive—beliefs and thoughts

Behavior is impacted by your attitude toward the behavior (or behavior change), confidence in your ability to change, and your readiness to change. Before successful change is made, consider addressing any concerns or questions you have about the behavior or changing it. Accordingly, the key is to use this information to identify cues to action, motivating factors, and self-help (self-efficacy) actions.[2]

❑ Reflection Time:

Think about a healthy behavior that you want to implement in your life. What attitudes and beliefs do you have about your ability to successfully change your behavior?

Ability to try new things, experiences with ease.

____

____

____

____

____

____

❑ Reflection Time:

What could increase your certainty that you can accomplish the new behavior? For example, if you want to start exercise and you are a social person, would calling a friend to join you in this new endeavor, increase your chances of accomplishing this goal? Or, if you want to eat healthier, would buying a new knife and cutting board help you incorporate more vegetables into your diet?

____

____

____

____

____

____

____

You can choose to see the good, or you can focus on the bad. You can wallow in your own misery or disappointment and throw a temper tantrum. On the other hand, you can choose to have a positive approach to life.

Positivity

Positivity involves being positive or having an optimistic attitude. Thinking positive thoughts will crowd out the negative thoughts. As stated previously, what you appreciate, appreciates. Being positive doesn't mean ignoring negativity. Everyone experiences a spectrum of emotions daily, which is normal. Your goal is to make the best of any situation that comes your way, day to day, moment to moment. Some people are naturally more positive than others; however, certain practices cultivate positivity and optimism, even in people who have a tendency to be more negative and pessimistic.

❑ Reflection Time:

Think about a situation or stressor that you are dealing with currently. What is working well for you about the situation?

____

____

____

____

____

____

____

❑ Reflection Time:

What is enabling you to handle the stressor?

____

____

____

____

____

____

____

____

____

____

❑ Reflection Time:

What has worked well for you in the past when you have encountered similar struggles?

____

____

____

____

____

____

____

❑ Reflection Time:

Can you think of ways that a more positive mindset may help you with this problem? Explain.

____

____

____

____

____

____

____

Behavior is impacted by your attitude toward the behavior (or behavior change), confidence in your ability to change, and your readiness to change.

Pressmaster/Shutterstock.com

Growth Mindset vs. Fixed Mindset

Figure 5-3. A comparison between a growth mindset and a fixed mindset

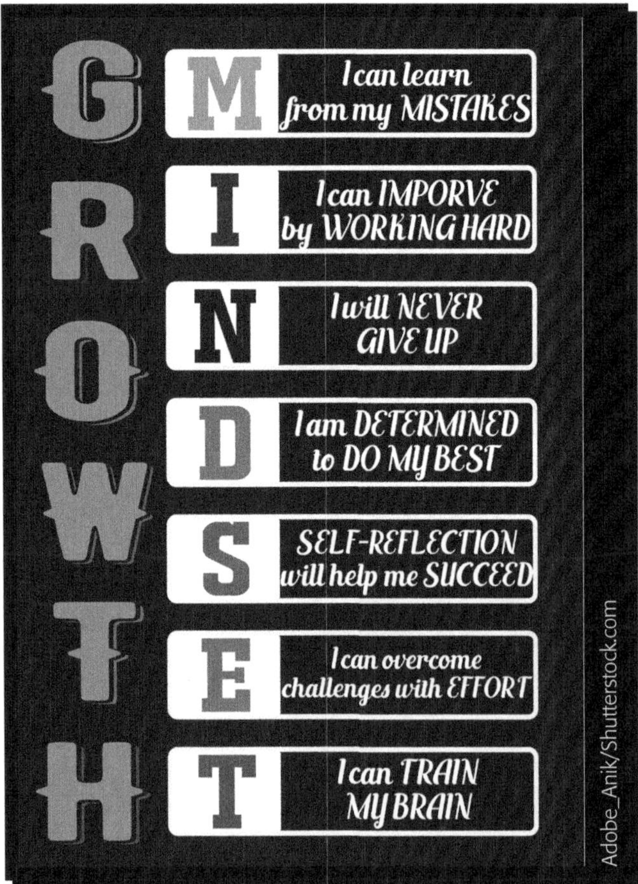

Figure 5-4. Wordplay on the word "mindset"

A growth mindset is associated with increased positivity, success, and well-being, when compared to a fixed mindset. In her book *Mindset: The New Psychology of Success*,[3] American psychologist, Carol Dweck, encourages people to adopt a growth mindset. Embracing this mindset is associated with practicing health-supporting behaviors and thus overall health.

With a growth mindset, your abilities can be obtained and developed through effort, learning, and persistence. Failure is thought to occur due to the lack of having the abilities leading to success, which can be obtained or developed. All factors considered, people with a growth mindset are more likely to persevere, even with setbacks.

❑ Growth Mindset Elements:

- You are constantly learning and growing; you have the potential to grow and learn.
- "Mistakes" are opportunities to learn and grow; you can improve with effort.
- There is no "failure," just lessons to be learned on your path to wellness.

What can I say to myself?

INSTEAD OF:	TRY THINKING:
I'm not good at this	What am I missing?
I'm awesome at this	I'm on the right track
I give up	I'll use some of the strategies we learned
This is too hard	This may take some time and effort
I can't make this any better	I can always improve so I'll keep trying
I just can't do math	I'm going to train my brain in math
I made a mistake	Mistakes help me to learn better
I'll never be that smart	I'm going to figure out how others do it
It's good enough	Is it really my best work?
Plan "A" didn't work	The alphabet has 25 more letters!

desdemona72/Shutterstock.com

Figure 5-5. A comparison of inner thoughts between a fixed mindset and a growth mindset

Someone with a fixed mindset believes that their abilities, intelligence, and talents are permanent. Failure is the result of lack of ability, which is considered unchangeable by a person with a fixed mindset. It's important to realize that awareness and reflection can impact our mindset and change our attitudes, which, in turn, can enhance our overall sense of well-being.

❑ Reflection Time:

Reflect on a challenge that you overcame recently. Did a growth mindset help you overcome the challenge? If so, describe the elements of a growth mindset that you used. If you did not use a growth mindset to overcome the challenge, describe how you could have used a growth mindset to help you deal with this challenge.

❑ Reflection Time:

What can you do to encourage yourself to have a growth mindset attitude the next time you experience a challenge or obstacle?

Curiosity

Curiosity is an essential element of a growth mindset and positivity. When someone experiences a crisis, they enter the learning mode or a protective mode. The learning mode allows you to feel confident, calm, and collaborative, as you view an event with curiosity and non-judgment. In a protecting mode, you feel scared, threatened, and combative. The protecting mode comes from a place of judgment and defensiveness. When the danger of harm is present, engaging in the "flight or fight mode" might be necessary. In many situations at the present time, however, that mechanism gets triggered unnecessarily, which can lead to an undue state of distress.

You can move from the protecting mode to the learning mode by:

- Finding your strengths and sitting with them
- Realizing that you are unique and worthy
- Understanding that there is no need to protect yourself

❑ Reflection Time:

When you encounter a challenge, do you tend to use the learning mode or the protective mode?

❑ Reflection Time:

Give an example of when you used a learning mode to overcome a challenge.

❑ Reflection Time:

How can you increase the likelihood that you will use the learning mode with an obstacle in your future?

Automatic Negative Thoughts (ANTs)

ANTs are thoughts that arise automatically in response to an emotional trigger. A person may not often be consciously aware of these thoughts, but they still cause distress or sub-optimal reactions. There are two self-talk voices in your head. You can decide to which one you will listen.

- Gremlin: The gremlin says that you "should have" and "could have" done things differently. It asks, "why didn't you" and employs the nasty trio of shame, blame, and guilt.
- Prince or princess: The prince or princess points out your strengths, is a cheerleader, is confident in you, proud of you, accepts your faults and mistakes, and finds the positive in situations and your behavior.

Gremlins are loud and like to take control. With some practice, you can learn to recognize automatic negative self-talk and choose to focus on a more positive voice.

❑ Reflection Time:

With what types of behaviors do you struggle with "gremlins," who use shame, blame, and guilt?

____

____

____

____

____

____

____

____

❑ Reflection Time:

How can you replace these ANTs with self-talk that supports your well-being?

____

____

____

____

____

____

____

____

❑ Reflection Time:

What would a "prince or princess" say to you or your gremlin?

Gratitude

An attitude of gratitude and appreciation is another powerful tool to increase positivity and well-being. Gratefulness decreases negative emotions, increases positive emotions, and enhances happiness. Engaging in gratitude activities has also been linked with improved self-esteem, psychological health, and even physical health. Gratitude activities can be as simple as thinking of three good things at the end of each day, as well as reflecting on what caused these "good things." A pioneer in gratitude and happiness, Dr. Martin Seligman and gratitude pioneer, Dr. Robert A. Emmons have conducted research demonstrating the power of gratitude activities to increase positivity.

❑ Reflection Time:

Make a list of everything that you are grateful for including situations, people, and events.

husband, children, dog, family, friends, nice life style,

❑ Reflection Time:

Is there a way that you could incorporate a gratitude practice (e.g., thinking of and possibly writing what you are grateful for and what precipitated the event, every time that you wash your hands, when you gather for dinner, or when journaling before bed)? Explain.

❑ Reflection Time:

Explain how you will incorporate a gratitude practice into your daily routine.

❑ Reflection Time:

If you want to take it a step further, write a letter of gratitude to someone who has not been properly thanked and include what they did for you and how it impacted your life. Consider delivering the letter to them in person, or calling them and reading it, or recording a video of you reading it and send it to them.

PERMA: The Five Building Blocks of Well-Being

According to Dr. Seligman, there are five key elements to well-being that correspond with the mnemonic PERMA:[4]

- P: Positive emotions—can be achieved through gratitude, savoring, mindfulness, hope, and optimism.
- E: Engagement—is experienced while in a state of flow, when a challenging task is addressed through skills and strengths.
- R: Relationships—are high quality social connections with family, friends, and others.
- M: Meaning—involves serving or belonging to something bigger than or beyond yourself.
- A: Achievement—is an accomplishment or success that is pursued.

❑ Reflection Time:

P—Positive Emotions: What types of positive emotions have you experienced recently? Describe what led to these positive emotions.

____

____

____

____

____

____

____

____

❑ Reflection Time:

E—Engagement: When do you typically feel most engaged? Get specific. What are you doing? Who are you with? Where are you? What is the activity like?

____

____

____

____

____

____

____

____

____

❑ Reflection Time:

R—Relationships: Describe your high-quality relationships that support your well-being. What can you do to nurture these relationships this week?

___

___

___

___

___

___

___

❑ Reflection Time:

M—Meaning: What gives you a sense of meaning in your life?

___

___

___

___

___

___

___

❑ Reflection Time:

A—Achievement: What accomplishments make you feel most proud (eg. raising your children, finishing school, volunteering with a non-profit organization regularly for several years)?

___

___

___

___

___

___

___

___

Positivity Ratio

Ideally, you want to have three to five positive thoughts or comments to counteract every negative thought or comment. Furthermore, positive emotions do more than just make you happy. According to noted psychologist Dr. Barbara Fredrickson,[5-8] they also build and broaden your skills, problem-solving, and creativity. Interestingly, there was a question about the statistical method that brought 3:1 to the forefront. She addressed it in the broaden-and-build model, which emphasizes building on the positive, which is something that can be used in any situation. Finding the positive, whether it is three or five or six items in a situation, will help the group reach higher ground and increase a person's creative processes. Research has shown that having more positive emotion and input than negative will help continue drive and motivation for a process or product to reach completion. Examples of positive emotions include joy, pride, gratitude, love, hope, serenity, forgiveness, awe, interest, inspiration, excitement, wonder, and amusement.

Signature Strengths

According to Martin Seligman & Christopher Peterson and their efforts involving character strengths (VIA—Values in Action),[9] people have 24 character strengths that constitute the basis of their personality, as the following classification details:

- Wisdom: creativity, curiosity, judgment, love of learning, and perspective
- Courage: bravery, perseverance, honesty, and zest
- Humanity: love, kindness, and social intelligence
- Justice: teamwork, fairness, and leadership
- Temperance: forgiveness, humility, prudence, and self-regulation
- Transcendence: appreciation of beauty and excellence, gratitude, hope, humor, and spirituality

❏ Reflection Time:

Consider taking the signature strengths survey at https://www.viacharacter.org/ What did you learn from the survey that surprised you?

____

____

____

____

____

____

____

____

____

____

❏ Reflection Time:

What do you believe are your key strengths?

❏ Reflection Time:

How have these strengths helped you with overcoming adversity or getting through difficult times?

❏ Reflection Time:

How can you use these strengths in the future when you encounter obstacles?

Mindfulness

Mindfulness involves being present in the moment without judgment. In order to increase mindfulness, you can focus on your breath without trying to alter your breath and become aware of the air flowing into and out from your lungs. You can also do four-seven-eight breathing (inhale to the count of four, hold your breath to the count of seven, and then exhale to the count of eight).

Meditating is another way to be mindful and more present. There are several different types of meditation, and although some forms of meditation are associated with a particular religion or form of spirituality, not all forms of meditation have a religious/spiritual connection. Accordingly, you need to do some research to find one that is right for you. The relaxation response is another way to be more present and mindful. You can search for "relaxation response" by Dr. Herbert Benson on the internet to learn more about eliciting the relaxation response or refer to the chapter in this book on stress resiliency. A deeper dive into mindfulness will be undertaken in the Stress Resiliency Chapter.

Healthy Mindset

There are several keys to a healthy mindset, including the following:

- Focus on strengths.
- Be curious.
- Live in a learning (not protecting) mode.
- Engage in empowering self-talk (chose to listen to a prince/princess instead of a gremlin).
- Strive for more positivity than negativity.
- Acknowledge the power of positivity to broaden and build, leading to increased creativity.
- Practice mindfulness.
- Develop a growth mindset.
- Celebrate success and good times to strengthen relationships.
- Appreciate the little things.
- Surround yourself with positive people, websites, books, and social media.
- Laugh hard and laugh often, which is good for your body and mind.
- Savor the moment by acknowledging hard work.
- Express your love and gratitude.

SMART Goal

In order to take what you have learned about attitude and put it into action, create a SMART goal concerning your attitude (refer to Chapter 4 page 55 for a detailed overview of what a SMART goal entails).

❑ SMART Goal Time:

What is your SMART goal for attitude? (Specific, Measurable, Action-oriented, Realistic, Time-sensitive)

Perfect Angle Images/Shutterstock.com

References

❑ Cited References:

1. Rosenberg MJ, Hovland CI, McGuire WJ, et al. *Attitude Organization and Change: An Analysis of Consistency Among Attitude Components, Vol. III.* New Haven, CT: Yale University Press; 1960.
2. Becker SJ. Empirical validation of affect, behavior, and cognition as distinct components of behavior. *Journal of Personality and Social Psychology.* 1984;47(6):1191-205.
3. Dweck CS. *Mindset: the New Psychology of Success—How We Can Learn to Fulfill Our Potential.* New York: Ballantine Books; 2007.
4. Seligman ME. *Flourish: A Visionary New Understanding of Happiness and Well-Being.* New York: Simon and Schuster; 2012.
5. Frederickson B. *Love 2.0: Finding Happiness and Health in Moments of Connection.* New York: Plume; 2013.
6. Fredrickson. BL (2004). The broaden-and-build theory of positive emotions. *Philosophical Transactions of the Royal Society of London. Series B: Biological Sciences.* 359(1449), 1367–1377.
7. Fredrickson B. *Positivity.* New York: Harmony; 2009.
8. Fredrickson BL, Joiner T. Reflections on positive emotions and upward spirals. *Perspectives on Psychological Science.* 2018 Mar;13(2):194-9
9. Peterson C, Seligman ME. *Character Strengths and Virtues.* American Psychological Association/Oxford Press; 2004.

❑ Book Resources:

- Ben-Shahar T. *Choose the Life You Want: The Mindful Way to Happiness.* New York: The Experiment; 2014.
- Branden N. *The Six Pillars of Self-Esteem: The Definitive Work on Self-Esteem by the Leading Pioneer in the Field.* New York: Bantam; 1995.
- Cousins N. *Anatomy of an Illness: As Perceived by the Patient.* New York: W.W. Norton & Company; 2005.
- Csikzentmihalyi M. *Flow: The Psychology of Optimal Experience.* New York: Harper Perennial Modern Classics; 2008.
- Dweck CS. *Mindset: the New Psychology of Success—How We Can Learn to Fulfill Our Potential.* New York: Ballantine Books; 2007.
- Frederickson B. *Love 2.0: Finding Happiness and Health in Moments of Connection.* New York: Plume; 2013.
- Hanley K. *How to Be a Better Person: 400+ Simple Ways to Make a Difference in Yourself—And the World.* Avon, MA: Adams Media; 2018.
- Kabat-Zinn J. *Mindfulness for Beginners.* Chicago: Sounds True, Inc.; 2007.
- Lianov L. *Roots of Positive Change.* Middletown, DE: HealthType LLC; 2019.
- Peterson C, Seligman ME. *Character Strengths and Virtues.* American Psychological Association/Oxford Press; 2004.
- Rath T. *Strengths Finder 2.0.* Washington, DC: Gallup Press; 2007.

- Ryan MJ. *The Happiness Makeover: How to Teach Yourself to Be Happy and Enjoy Every Day.* New York: Harmony; 2005.
- Seligman ME. *Authentic Happiness: Using the New Positive Psychology to Realize Your Potential for Lasting Fulfillment.* New York: Atria Books; 2004.
- Seligman ME. *Flourish: A Visionary New Understanding of Happiness and Well-Being.* New York: Simon and Schuster; 2012.
- Sood A. *The Mayo Clinic Handbook for Happiness: A 4-Step Plan for Resilient Living.* Boston, MA: De Capo Lifelong Books; 2015.
- Urban H. *Life's Greatest Lessons.* New York: Fireside; 2003.
- Velasquez L. *Dare to Be Kind: How Extraordinary Compassion Can Transform Our World.* New York: Hachette Books; 2017.
- Zander RS, Zander B. *The Art of Possibility: transforming Professional and Personal Life,* rev. ed. Westminster, London, England: Penguin Books; 2002.

❏ Other Resources:

- Benson-Henry Institute—bensonhenryinstitute.org
- Gratitude Journal—positivepsychology.com
- The Happiness Lab podcast with Yale professor Dr. Laurie Santos—happinesslab.fm

CHAPTER 6
VARIETY

"Variety is the very spice of life. That gives it all its flavor."

—William Cowper
English Poet

PAVING the Path to Wellness: Questions for Variety

For each of the following five statements, choose the number on the frequency scale that best relates to you (frequency: 1= never, 2= rarely, 3= sometimes, 4= often, 5= routinely).

- I do a variety of different exercises___
- I try to have a rainbow of colors on my plate___
- I enjoy a variety of fruits and vegetables___
- I like to try new activities___
- I spend time and connect with a wide range of friends___

Subtotal—variety: _____

Live and Learn: Dr. Beth Frates

During one of my PAVING the Path to Wellness sessions for stroke survivors, I met Will. He came to support his mother, who was recovering from a recent stroke. He was a recent college graduate who just had hip surgery. When he entered the room, you could feel his warmth and compassion. It was clear that he adored his mother and wanted to support her in any way possible. It was also clear that he was bright and enthusiastic about learning how to be healthy. More than likely, Will had no idea what he was getting into when he agreed to accompany his mother to the PAVING the Path to Wellness class. Not shy, Will raised his hand and contributed insightful comments, much to the delight of the other participants, who were at least 20 years older and loved Will's positive energy. Will's readiness to try new things and add variety into his life were two characteristics that allowed him to open the door to the sessions and figuratively and literally walk right in.

As the weekly sessions progressed, Will participated more and more and began interacting with the other participants. His enthusiasm for being an active part of the group, confidence in interacting with others, and interest in the PAVING content were evident. Will tried all the different stress-resiliency techniques, explored his sense of purpose, and kept an open mind about adding variety into his life with his friends and social connections too. Interestingly, Will enjoyed the program so much that he decided to pursue a career in wellness and lifestyle medicine. He had no intention of going back to school but ended up enrolled in a master of psychology program at the Harvard Extension School, where he excelled. He took Dr. Frates' Introduction to Lifestyle Medicine course there, received a solid A, and then became a teaching assistant the following year. Being open to a variety of options and trying new things (which we cover in Investigations) led Will to find his passion and set him off on a new career trajectory. Because both Will and I embraced the concept of variety through becoming friends with someone who was not part of our age group, work environment, nor typical friend circle, we made a meaningful connection that continues to this day.

Basic Definitions and Terms

Variety—"The quality or state of being different or diverse; the absence of uniformity, sameness, or monotony"[1]

Variety is necessary in most aspects of life. It keeps people interested and engaged. Don't be afraid to try something new each day. When you encounter variety, you are more likely to engage. For example, if there is a greater variety of exercise equipment at your gym, you are more likely to exercise than if there are only a few options. If there are a greater variety of foods present, you are more likely to eat the food. The science of variety can be used to support healthy habits.

This book does not need to be read chapter by chapter. You can "vary it up" and read the chapters that resonate with you and your needs. Be flexible with your approach to the book and overall well-being. The key point is that incorporating variety in all 12 steps of PAVING the Path is strongly recommended.

P = PHYSICAL ACTIVITY

Aerobic activity (cardio), strengthening, stretching (flexibility), and balance activities each have a particular purpose. In order to enjoy the full benefits of physical activity, it is important to engage in activities that address each of these categories. Furthermore, participating in a variety of types of physical activities, even within a particular category (such as aerobic activity), decreases the chances of becoming bored with our physical activity regimen. This factor is essential, given that regular physical activity and limiting sedentary behavior are important for a lifetime of health. Figure 6-1 details examples of various types of physical activities.

- Aerobic activity: any movement that places a demand on the body's cardiovascular system, e.g., brisk walking, swimming, cycling, jumping rope, Zumba, ballroom dancing, basketball, elliptical, treadmill, stationary bicycle, jogging, hiking, skiing, vacuuming, pickleball, stairclimbing machine, hula hooping
- Strength training: activities that place a load (force) on the muscles, e.g., push-ups, pull-ups, sit-ups, barbell or dumbbell exercises, certain types of yoga, interval training
- Stretching (flexibility) activity: range of motion-enhancing movements (exercises), e.g., Physio ball, foam rolling, yoga
- Balance activity: Tai-chi, Qi-gong, Bosu ball, balance beam, yoga

Figure 6-1. Examples of various types of physical activities

Among the steps that you can take to add variety to your physical activity regimen are the following:

- Record all the different types of exercise that you complete in a month.
- Work with a certified personal trainer or physical therapist to vary your exercise routine.
- Try physical activity in different locations, with different people, while either listening to different music or undertaken at a different time of day.
- Try a new class, activity, or form of movement.
- Walk or ride your bicycle along a different route.
- Vary the intensity of your physical activity.

❑ Reflection Time:

What are some different types of physical activity that you want to try this month? Consider aerobic (cardio), strengthening, stretching (flexibility), and balance activities.

____

____

____

____

____

____

❏ Reflection Time:

What steps do you need to take to try these different types of physical activity (sign-up for a class, get medical clearance, research how to do the activity, etc.)?

❏ Reflection Time:

What needs to be in place for you to start your desired activity?

❏ Reflection Time:

How can you vary your current physical activity routine (think time of day, frequency, where, when, who you are with, what you do, etc.)?

❏ Reflection Time:

What can you do to add variety to your daily routine in order to decrease sedentary behavior? For example, sitting on an exercise ball as a desk chair, standing desk/ treadmill desk, taking phone calls standing-up, walking while talking on the phone, walking meetings, etc.

A = ATTITUDE

Emotional well-being involves being able to experience and express a spectrum of emotions. Attitudes that align with emotional well-being include having a growth mindset, positivity, gratitude, savoring, celebrating, being mindful, sincere, optimistic, and having a beginner's mind. Appreciating and thoughtfully expressing your emotions and attitudes allows you to connect with others in a more authentic way.

As a human being, you will experience difficult emotions, like fear, anger, and disappointment, which will come and go like waves. If the emotions are overpowering, it's important to reach out to a friend or health/wellness professional, especially if the difficult emotion is a tsunami that is ongoing. Keep in mind that processing and experiencing feelings is an integral part of having a full life. Emotions—pleasant and unpleasant—come and go.

❑ Reflection Time:

Describe the last time you felt like celebrating and why.

____

____

____

____

____

____

____

____

❑ Reflection Time:

Are you able to experience a variety of the attitudes that enable you to be creative, positive, optimistic, and hopeful? Explain.

____

____

____

____

____

____

____

____

____

❏ Reflection Time:

What empowering attitude propels you forward each day and why?

____

____

____

____

____

____

____

____

❏ Reflection Time:

Is there anything that you want to do to add to the empowering attitudes you currently use?

____

____

____

____

____

V = VARIETY

It is easy to become so accustomed to your daily routine that you don't notice the lack of variety in your life. While routine can be beneficial, novelty supports learning and making new connections between areas of your brain. Variety can add joy, excitement, and renewed energy to your life. Although this section focuses on exploring variety as it relates to healthy lifestyle behaviors, variety is also important in other areas of your life. You can experience variety, for example, by learning new things, watching a new show, reading a different type of book, listening to different music, traveling somewhere new, taking a class, joining a club, or meeting new people.

❑ Reflection Time:

How can you increase variety in at least one area of your life?

Dmytro Zinkevych/Shutterstock.com

❑ Reflection Time:

Is there something that you want to learn more about or somewhere that you want to explore? Think outside of your "box" and have fun considering ways to increase variety in your life. Explain.

____

____

____

____

____

____

____

I = INVESTIGATIONS

Think of yourself as a detective. As you try new things by incorporating variety in your life, you can investigate how these new experiences make you feel. Consider getting a journal that you use to record how your body and mind feel, when you try new things or engage in new behaviors. Keep track of what you try, your energy level, and note whether you want to try it again. Try new things in all areas of life. Try new monitoring techniques.

❑ Reflection Time:

How will you monitor and record the effects of your investigations (journal, discussion with a friend, etc.)?

____

____

____

____

____

____

____

❑ Reflection Time:

What do you want to investigate or learn more about?

____

____

____

____

❏ Reflection Time:

How are you going to start your investigation? What questions do you want to answer?

N = NUTRITION

The more variety you have with food choices, the more likely you are to eat more of the food. You can use this to your advantage with foods that you are trying to eat more of, such as whole foods. Most people can benefit from increasing their intake of vegetables. Consider exploring the produce section of your grocery store and choosing a variety of vegetables, some that are favorites and others that you have never tried. Expand your food repertoire by trying herbs, spices, grains, fruits, and vegetables. Try different food combinations, ways of food preparation, new recipes, meal delivery services, and restaurants.

You can also utilize food research to decrease your intake of highly processed, less-healthful foods by exposing yourself to less variety. Just as an increased variety of vegetables is associated with increased vegetable intake and a lower weight, an increased variety of readily available ultra-processed foods is associated with weight gain.

Among the options that exist for you to add variety to what you eat include the following:

- Try a different herb, spice, grain, or vegetable each week.
- Cook new meals—check websites or cookbooks, or ask friends and family for recipe suggestions.
- Try new restaurants that fit your overall healthy eating plan.
- Try whole-food, plant-based meals.
- Read the *China Study* book by Colin T. Campbell.
- Read the *Mayo Clinic Diet* book by Donald D. Henstrud.
- Read the chapter in the *Lifestyle Medicine Handbook* by Beth Frates, et al. on nutrition.
- Post the Harvard Healthy Eating Plate on your refrigerator.
- Label items with red stickers, yellow stickers, and green stickers to remind yourself which foods you want to limit or increase.
- Involve your family.

Tatjana Baibakova/Shutterstock.com

❑ Reflection Time:

Draw (or take a photo) of what a healthy plate is/would be for you.

❑ Reflection Time:

How can you use variety to increase your intake of healthful, nourishing foods?

❑ Reflection Time:

It's easy to get stuck in a boring food routine. What parts of your food routine would you like to make more varied?

❏ Reflection Time:

What are your next steps to make this part of your food plan more exciting?

G = GOALS

Many people set New Year's resolutions, but rarely do they follow through with their goals beyond a few weeks or months. Goal-setting is a powerful way to increase the chances that you will be successful with a desired behavior change. In addition, there are several tools that can be used to support your goals, such as using a paper journal, tracking your progress with a phone or computer application, or discussing your goals with a friend. Of course, following the SMART goal plan (Specific, Measurable, Action-oriented, Realistic, Time-sensitive) will also increase your chances of success.

❏ Reflection Time:

What types of goals do you commonly set?

❏ Reflection Time:

Can you increase variety in your goal setting by choosing a goal that is of a shorter or longer duration (daily versus one month, three months, one year, five years, or 10-year goals) than you typically set? Explain.

____

____

____

____

____

S = STRESS MANAGEMENT

Think about how you commonly deal with stress. Most people know what helps them deal with stress, based on what has worked well for them in the past. Maybe, you are someone who listens to relaxing music or calls a best friend when you are really stressed, because you know that this will help you to relax. Other people may go for a run or take a few deep breaths to feel calmer.

It's great to have a toolbox of stress management techniques that you can use when you are stressed, but how many tools do you have in your toolbox? Most people could benefit from having some new stress management tools to employ. Some tools work better in certain circumstances or at various times in your life, than others. There are many stress management techniques to choose from, so have fun experimenting with fun and healthy ways to manage stress, including the following possible options:

- Practice breath focus: 4-7-8.
- Exercise, e.g., walk, yoga, Tai Chi, stretch, etc.
- Read or listen to a book/podcast.
- Try a hot bath or massage.

- Engage in gratitude practices.
- Use fidget items or distraction techniques.
- Elicit the relaxation response.
- Spend time in nature.
- Practice meditation, e.g., mantra, loving kindness, etc.
- Practice mindfulness.
- Foster supportive relationships.
- Practice acceptance and forgiveness.
- Eat nourishing foods.
- Make sleep a priority.
- Avoid excessive caffeine.
- Get professional mental health support, if needed.
- Manage expectations.
- Play and laugh.
- Serve others.
- Volunteer your time and energy.

❑ Reflection Time:

What unhealthy ways have you used to cope with stress (e.g., binge eating, biting your nails, yelling, drinking alcohol, smoking, using addictive substances)? What strategies, organizations, or healthcare providers can help you manage these (e.g., Alcoholics Anonymous www.aa.org, Overeaters Anonymous www.oa.org)?

____

____

____

____

____

____

____

____

❑ Reflection Time:

What healthy stress management techniques have you used in the past but not recently, that you would like to try again? Consider relaxing hobbies, spending time in nature, visiting a favorite place, listening to relaxing music, breathing techniques, meditation, massage, warm baths, mindful movement, or other calming activities.

____

____

____

❑ Reflection Time:

What is a stress resiliency technique or tool that you have never used but would like to try?

❑ Reflection Time:

What do you need to learn, purchase, or do to move forward with incorporating this into your stress resiliency practices?

Most people could benefit from having some new stress management tools to employ.

Halfpoint/Shutterstock.com

T = TIME-OUTS

Most people do not take enough time away from their daily routine to really recharge and refresh. When individuals do take time-outs, they often look very similar. In that regard, there are several ways that you can add variety to your time-outs that you take for yourself, for example, stand-up breaks, walking breaks, breathing breaks, counting breaks, mini-vacations, time-outs from email and electronics for a day or weekend, or just about any activity that you can think of that gets you away from your normal routine. Taking a break every hour helps you increase your productivity. To avoid unhealthy physiologic health consequences of sedentary behavior, it's beneficial to stand every half-hour if you have diabetes or pre-diabetes, or at least hourly if you do not have these conditions.

❑ Reflection Time:

What do you usually do when you take a time-out from your regular routine?

❑ Reflection Time:

Brainstorm some new ways of taking time-outs for yourself that you can implement in the near future, as well as others that may require more planning (e.g., stand up, walk in place, call a friend, look at pictures of nature, listen to music, sing, dance, meditate, drink a glass of ice water, take a 20-minute nap in the afternoon, pet your dog, find some flowers to smell or look at, water a plant, write a thank-you note, etc.).

❑ Reflection Time:

What are your next steps for making at least one of these new time-outs a reality?

E = ENERGY

Think of times in your past that you felt most energetic. You need to appreciate that energy is a finite resource. Managing time is important, and managing energy throughout your day is equally important. Identify those things that give you energy and identify things that drain your energy.

There are unnatural sources of energy that many people use including excessive caffeine, drugs, processed food and candy. Now is the time to acknowledge these and work on finding natural healthy sources of energy. Having a variety of natural sources of energy is key. A main source of energy will be nourishing foods, like nuts, that contain magnesium, which is often lacking in people's diet and may be a cause for feeling fatigued. Sunlight is a natural source of energy, as well as vitamin D, which helps to stabilize mood. Working to get enough vitamin D from sunlight but also protecting your skin from cancer is important. Other sources of energy could be friendships. Your partner and/or close friends are often huge sources of natural energy in a variety of ways. Most people have a "happy place" and thinking about this location or viewing photographs of this place can bring a sense of calm and quiet energy. It's not healthy to rely on one source of natural energy. Having a variety of sources and continuing to find new sources is key!

❑ Reflection Time:

Make a list of all the things that bring you energy (people, places, things, and activities).

____

____

____

____

____

____

____

❑ Reflection Time:

Make a list of all the things that drain your energy.

____

____

____

____

____

____

____

____

❑ Reflection Time:

Describe a time when you were full of energy. Was it because you were around friends you enjoy, because you had gotten a restful night's sleep, or because you had engaged in physical activity that led to your increased energy? Maybe you were on a vacation or were engaged in your favorite hobby.

❑ Reflection Time:

What can you do to add variety to the ways that you increase your energy? Some ideas include green tea, veggies as snacks, fun activities, favorite hobbies, travel, spending time in nature or with fun friends, and getting more restful sleep.

P = PURPOSE

If you think about your life's mission, often a primary purpose will come to mind. However, if you spend more time reflecting, you can usually think of other purposes that you have. As you explore variety, you are encouraged to reflect upon your priorities, strengths, and mission in life. The world needs the strengths and gifts that only you have.

Your purpose in life can change with age, circumstances, health conditions, employment, and world events. Not surprisingly, your purpose at age 25 can be different from your purpose at age 85. You may not be able to identify your purpose right away. In that case, start with your strengths.

Variety is used to help you elicit your mission, your purpose, and how you see the meaning in your own life. For some, sitting down with pen and paper and writing out a mission statement for your own life can work wonders. For others, listing strengths and how to use those strengths day in and day out will help to identify purpose in life. Others will enjoy engaging in conversations with friends about how to use this one precious life to help others and help this planet be a better place.

❑ Reflection Time:

What are your strengths at work, at home, in groups, and on solo projects?

❑ Reflection Time:

What are your priorities now?

❑ Reflection Time:

What do you view as your personal mission in life, currently?

❑ Reflection Time:

What can you do to move that mission forward?

❑ Reflection Time:

How can you add variety to the ways you address your purpose, priorities, and mission, while engaging your strengths?

S = SLEEP

Routinely, you should keep your bedroom like a cave—cool, dark, and quiet. There are a variety of ways in which you can achieve this outcome, for example, blackout shades, white noise, and experimenting with different temperatures 60-70 degrees (ideally 67 degrees Fahrenheit).

Routines are beneficial for restorative sleep. Keeping your sleep routine consistent, seven days a week, is the way to achieve sustainable, sound sleep. Maybe your pre-bed or daily routine could be altered for improved sleep. You can try a variety of relaxing bedtime routines. If you already sleep seven to nine hours per night and wake feeling refreshed every morning, you might want to skip this section. However, if you struggle with falling asleep, maintaining sleep, or experience fatigue during the day, you may want to add some variety to your sleep routine to hopefully improve your sleep experience. If you are struggling with sleep, please refer to the sleep chapter.

Variety with sleep is important if you are seeking sound sleep. Try a variety of relaxing routines before bed. Try a variety of mental imagery that can soothe your heart, mind, and soul before bedtime. If you enjoy chamomile tea before bed, you can shake things up and experiment with a different herbal tea and see how that works. In some cases, routines that work are not meant to be altered. So, if you try something new with a sleep routine, and it does not work, then go back to the old, tried and true method.

Sleep is a step where consistency each night is key. That is—sleeping seven to nine hours a night (weekdays and weekends) is the goal.

❑ Reflection Time:

Think about behaviors that help you prioritize sleep, such as exercising during the day, not eating spicy foods late at night, avoiding late night stressful conversations, getting outdoor light during the day, keeping your bedroom very dark at night, and going to bed at about the same time every evening. What can you do (that you are not already doing) or improve upon, that would help you prioritize sleep?

____

____

____

____

____

____

____

S = SOCIAL SUPPORT

The quality of your relationships is more important than the number of people who you know. In the fast-paced society that most people encounter, it is often challenging to make meaningful social connections where they can express who they are and what they are thinking openly. Social media can leave individuals feeling like they have more superficial connections but are, on occasion, lonely and longing for deep connection. Finding and maintaining meaningful connections with others takes time and effort but is central to happiness and the human experience.

A variety of social connections help you to stay nourished, mind and soul. Having friends from your childhood, work, family, neighborhood, volunteering, and other areas of your life is key. For example, if you are a physician and you only have physician friends, you are missing out on the wide range of experiences that many people have—the joys, the struggles, the complexities and the wisdom. Friends from different walks of life, different ages, and different countries can help bring new perspectives into your life.

❑ Reflection Time:

List relationships that have been empowering for you during your lifetime.

❑ Reflection Time:

List friends and family members who have been important to you and identify why.

❑ Reflection Time:

How many times are you connecting with these important people in your life each month? Is there anything that you want to do to change this frequency?

❑ Reflection Time:

When was the last time you made a new connection with someone?

❑ Reflection Time:

List friends you have from growing-up, high school, college, post-graduate studies, your jobs, your summer experiences, your religious affiliations, your neighborhood, social media–Facebook, Instagram, Twitter, etc.

❑ Reflection Time:

What can you do to find or connect with friends from different places who encourage you, make you feel good, give you energy, and honor you for the person you are today?

❑ Reflection Time:

How can you connect with neighbors, high-school friends, college friends, religious organization friends, volunteer organization friends, and people you might meet when you are out and about?

❑ Reflection Time:

What do you want to do to increase variety in your social connections?

SMART Goal

In order to take what you have learned about variety and put it into action, create a SMART goal for yourself (refer to Chapter 4 page 55 for a detailed overview of what a SMART goal entails).

❑ SMART Goal Time:

What is your SMART goal for variety? (Specific, Measurable, Action-oriented, Realistic, Time-sensitive)

____

____

____

____

____

____

____

____

Variety is necessary in most aspects of life.

References

❑ Cited Reference:

1. Hobson A, editor. *The Oxford Dictionary of Difficult Words.* Cary, NC: Oxford University Press, USA; 2004.

❑ Book Resource:

- Sortun A *Spice: Flavors of the Eastern Mediterranean*. New York: William Morrow; 2006.

CHAPTER 7
INVESTIGATIONS

"We learn more by looking for the answer to a question and not finding it than we do from learning the answer itself."

—Lloyd Alexander
American Author

PAVING the Path to Wellness: Questions for Investigations

For each of the following five statements, choose the number on the frequency scale that best relates to you (frequency: 1= never, 2= rarely, 3= sometimes, 4= often, 5= routinely).

- I perform mini-experiments on myself regularly._____
- I am curious as to what foods are good for my body._____
- I am curious as to what effect physical activity has on my body._____
- I read about the latest research findings in medicine, nutrition, sleep, stress management, and/or exercise._____
- I talk about health with family and friends. _____

Subtotal–investigations: _____

Andrey_Popov/Shutterstock.com

Live and Learn—From a Garden: Lynn Hewes (PAVING Program Participant)

Someone gave me a stone inscribed with words by educator Amos Bronson Alcott: "Who loves a garden still his Eden keeps." I put this stone in my garden and thought, this small plot of living soil, replete with worms, compost, roots, and leaves, is in fact my Eden! It's not a show-stopper fancy garden but a practical place where perennials, vegetables, and herbs grow. To me, it's a drawing board for my state of being.

First, the garden teaches me about work. There is labor, yes, but it is glorious. It has purpose. My muscles toil, pull weeds, haul hoses, push soil, but the reward in beauty and deliciousness gives great satisfaction. By growing some of the foods I eat, I also learn to pay attention—to follow the sun, listen for rain, and track the startling wilt of leaves on a blistering day that reverts to perkiness with the sun's decline. This, being in the moment, has its own magic.

I didn't know until I researched it that most vegetable seeds are propagated for the yield and shelf life of their progeny, not for flavor or nutrition! I thought this outrageous, as did a group of chefs, regenerative farmers, and plant breeders. They got together and started Row Seven, a seed company that selects vegetables through cross-breeding for flavor, resistance to disease, and high phytonutrient content.

When I started growing Row Seven seeds, I fell even more in love with my garden. Their vegetables are BIG on flavor and make it easy to eat, like I am supposed to. The beets, cucumbers, and purple snow peas, which are anthocyanin rich, have been winners. Their amazing Tromboncino, a zucchini heirloom, has a sweet nutty flavor and meaty texture that is superior in all renditions, whether in salads, breads, sautéed, or stuffed. From this garden, vegetables are the centerpiece of dinner, because they're the part of the meal that tastes the best!

As a gardener, I've also been learning that preparation is key. Plants grow better, resist insects, and do not need high fertilizer application, when they're nourished with organic matter that supports the life of soil microbes. The microbes convert and hold nutrients in soil for plant use. In other words, preparing good dirt is important. We're not so different from plants and eating to support my own healthy microbes has become a mantra. I love that one of the best sources of prebiotic fiber comes from an easy to grow plant, the sun choke or Jerusalem artichoke that literally grows like a weed. Another great fiber source is found in Shiitake mushrooms, which, to my surprise, need little care to grow. The hardwood mushroom logs, once inoculated, require only shade and moisture to sprout their bounty, and my family has been thrilled with our Shiitake harvests three to four times a year. Once spent, the log easily breaks down in the compost pile where, once again, it becomes food for microbes.

I have learned so much from my little patch. What started as a way to save money has become entwined so purposefully with my own inner destiny. There is always more to learn, as well as receiving a great reward. Life is better with a garden.

Basic Definition

Investigation = carry out a systematic or formal inquiry to discover and examine the facts of (an incident, allegation, etc.) in order to establish the truth.[1] A formal definition of the word "investigation" entails the following two aspects:

- Carry out research or study into (a subject, typically one in a scientific or academic field) in order to discover facts or information.
- Make inquiries as to the character, activities, or background of (someone).

Now that you've looked at variety for each of your PAVING the Path to Wellness Steps, it is time to INVESTIGATE!

Investigations

In a research study, the letter "n" indicates the number of individuals that are being studied. Typically, researchers like to see a large number of people involved in studies, as the results are more meaningful. However, in this instance, you need to consider experimenting on yourself. YOU are the only person who knows, for example, how a particular stress management technique makes you feel, how much energy you gain from walking before work, or what type of foods you most enjoy. Therefore, you are the subject of the experiment where n = 1. You are the one. In addition, you are the experimenter. You are controlling the experiment.

The field of Lifestyle Medicine is built upon evidence.

The field of Lifestyle Medicine is built upon evidence. That means that the field is changing, as research continues to be conducted and new things continue to be learned. An appropriate starting point is to determine your current situation (jumping off point), if you haven't already done so. Now is the time to complete the PAVING the Path to Wellness wheel (pages 27-28), if you haven't yet completed it. You may also complete it again at this time, if you think it would be useful. Plot yourself on the wheel. Many people use the wheel two to three times per year to keep them on track. The wheel provides data about you and your current status to guide your personal investigation.

Elements of Investigation:

- Choose the subject of investigation.
- Make a hypothesis.
- Experiment and test the hypothesis.
- Analyze your data and make conclusions.
- Define what the limitations of your study were.
- Make plans for future studies and steps.

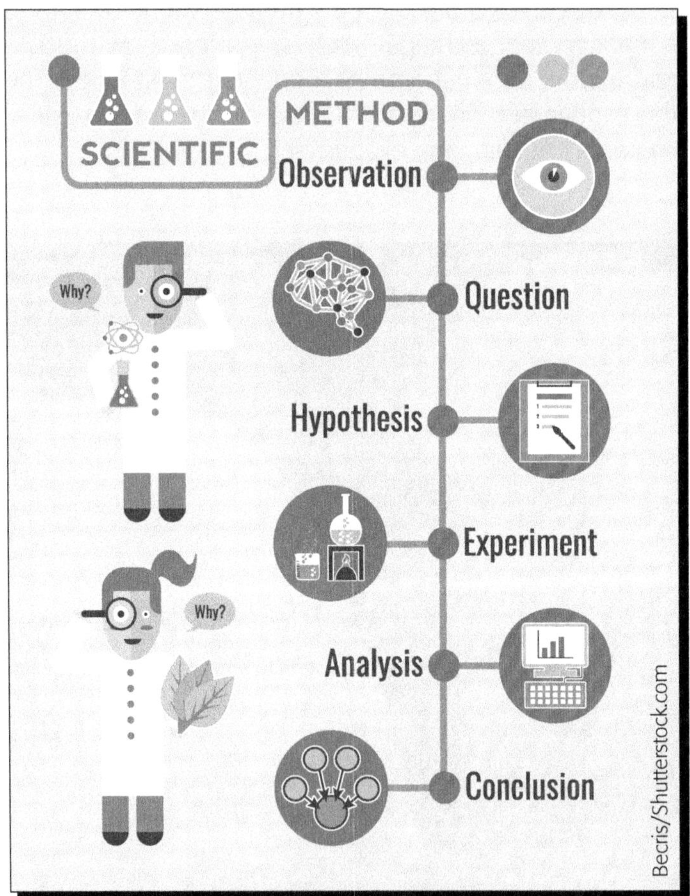

Figure 7-1. The steps involved in the scientific method

Figure 7-1 illustrates the steps involved in the scientific method. These are the steps that scientists follow when conducting experiments.

After you choose the subject of your investigation, the next step is to make a hypothesis. A hypothesis is an educated guess. It is what you think will happen, if you undertake a certain action. For example, I think that I will feel joy, if I reconnect with my friends from childhood.

The experiment to test this hypothesis may involve tracking down your childhood friends. You may need to search for them on social media, look through your old contacts, or use other ways of locating their information. Then, you reach out and connect. After connecting with your friends, you can evaluate whether your hypothesis was correct. Did reconnecting bring you joy? If so, do you want to stay connected with them? Or, was your hypothesis incorrect? Maybe the connection was not beneficial to your overall well-being and did not bring you joy. You may decide that you don't want to put effort into staying connected with them moving forward. That is all right too. You made a hypothesis, tested it, and learned from it.

In traditional research, investigators discuss the limitations of the study. For example, a limitation of connecting with an old friend may be that just because this reconnection did not increase your joy and well-being, does not mean that this is generalizable to all reconnections with old friends. This study had limitations. This is all right as well and helps you to decide how best to move forward. You can try the same experiment with a different set of friends.

The next part of the research process is to decide how you want to proceed. For example, you can consider reaching out to another old friend. Or, you may decide to focus on something completely different, such as physical activity. Another option might be to invite a friend on a walk and see how that goes. It's up to you. You are the subject of your wellness investigations!

Going through the PAVING wheel questionnaire can help guide you. Your results may change month to month or even week to week. Review your assessment. Just because you scored low in an area does not indicate you need to focus on that area. It is just information that you obtain while investigating. Conversely, just because you scored high in an area doesn't mean that you shouldn't focus on it.

❑ Reflection Time:

What surprised you when reviewing your results of the wellness wheel?

____

____

____

____

____

____

____

____

❑ Reflection Time:

What area of the wheel calls to you? Why?

____

____

____

____

____

____

____

____

❑ Reflection Time:

What you monitor ends up mattering to you. How can you monitor your progress or measure this aspect of your life this week?

____

____

____

____

____

____

____

____

❑ Reflection Time:

You may want to refer to the previous chapter on variety throughout this chapter's focus on investigations. Furthermore, a number of resources can be utilized to help you, as you undertake your investigation, including the following:

- American Cancer Society
- American College of Lifestyle Medicine
- American Heart Association
- American Institute of Cancer Research
- American Stroke Association
- Centers for Disease Control
- Harvard T. Chan School of Public Health
- Local library
- Minder by ObVus Solutions
- PubMed—search medical articles
- Science Direct
- Spark people
- US Health and Preventive Services
- WebMD
- Other phone, smart watch, or web-based applications

____

P = PHYSICAL ACTIVITY

Think of something related to physical activity that you would like to explore. Perhaps, it is a certain type of exercise or an activity class you have heard of that you would like to try. Maybe, you want to learn more about how physical activity impacts an aspect of wellness. Do you want to investigate what classes are offered at your local community center? Remember, this is about experimenting with something that matters to you. Think about aerobic exercise, strength training, balance, and flexibility. There are several directions you can go. There are numerous tools, resources, and strategies that you can employ as part of your effort to investigate, including:

- Smart watch
- Days you are active each week
- Fitness band
- Miles walked
- Minutes of physical activity
- Minutes of sitting (trying to diminish the number each day)
- My Fitness Pal
- Number of sit-ups or push-ups
- Pedometer
- Spark people
- Traditional paper log

❑ Reflection Time:

What physical activity related investigation do you want to do?

____

____

____

____

____

____

____

❑ Reflection Time:

What are the next steps in your investigation?

____

____

____

____

____

____

____

____

❑ Reflection Time:

What did you learn? What do you want to do for follow-up?

____

____

____

____

____

____

____

A = ATTITUDE

Consider investigating what attitudes you feel throughout the day. Do certain physical activities, foods, being around particular people, or stress management practices impact your attitude?

Although everyone experiences various attitudes, many times you are not mindful of your attitudes. Some examples of attitudes that you may want to explore include having a growth mindset, positivity, gratitude, savoring, celebrating, being mindful, sincere, optimistic, and having a beginner's mind.

Krakenimages.com/Shutterstock.com

You can experience variety in a number of ways.

❑ Reflection Time:

How can you use investigation to better appreciate, experience, or express your attitudes?

____

____

____

____

____

____

❑ Reflection Time:

Is there a particular attitude that you would like to learn more about? Explain.

____

____

____

____

____

____

____

V = VARIETY

You can experience variety by learning new things, watching a new show, reading a different type of book, listening to different music, traveling somewhere new, taking a class, joining a club, or meeting new people. In the last chapter, you wrote about a way that you could increase variety in your life and an area that you want to explore. Now take it a step further through investigations.

❑ Reflection Time:

What do you want to investigate to help you increase variety in your life?

____

____

____

____

____

____

____

____

❑ Reflection Time:

What are the next steps you need to take to do this investigation?

____

____

____

____

____

____

____

____

❑ Reflection Time:

What did you learn from your investigation and what are your next steps?

____

____

____

I = INVESTIGATIONS

There are numerous ways to investigate something. For example, you can ask a friend or a trusted colleague, make an appointment to talk to an expert, or do an internet search.

❑ Reflection Time:

What are the typical ways that you investigate when you have a question?

❑ Reflection Time:

Are there other ways to investigate questions that you would like to try, and if so, what are they?

❏ Reflection Time:

What are some new ways of monitoring and recording the findings from your investigation that you would like to use (e.g., journal, discussion with a friend, tracking application)?

N = NUTRITION

There are many topics surrounding nutrition to investigate, such as different types of cuisine, cooking styles, recipes to explore, restaurants to visit, number of vegetables you eat, number of ways you can reduce your sugar intake, substitutes for sweets and candy bars, limiting or eliminating alcohol intake, and new types of food to try. The possibilities are truly endless.

As discussed in the previous chapter on variety, a key factor for health is incorporating different types of fruits and vegetables in your diet. Investigate how you can include a rainbow on your plate with having at least five servings of vegetables per day and two to three servings of fruit per day. In that regard, you can select from a number of vegetables, including peas, onions, bell peppers, zucchini, acorn squash, celery, broccoli, kale, spinach, carrots, turnips, beets, asparagus, green beans, cauliflower, eggplant, Brussels sprouts, and Swiss chard, as well as an extensive variety of fruits, including apples, bananas, pomegranates, passion fruit, pears, kiwi, tangerines, black grapes, pineapple, honeydew, mangoes, strawberries, grapefruit, watermelon, figs, blueberries, blackberries, raspberries, gooseberries, oranges, and nectarines.

❏ Reflection Time:

What other fruits that were not listed above, have you tried? What are some fruits that you would like to learn more about and possibly try eating this week? Search the internet for information about these fruits, such as health benefits or recipes to try that include the fruits. Summarize what you find.

❑ Reflection Time:

What are some vegetables that you would like to learn more about and possibly try eating this week? Search the internet for information about these vegetables, such as health benefits or recipes to try that include the vegetables. Summarize what you find.

Investigate ways to cook your vegetables with a variety of spices. Spices contain flavonoids, phytonutrients, and other chemicals that support mood and overall health. In addition, they make our food taste delicious. Heidi Godman, the executive editor of the *Harvard Health Letter*, detailed the following spices for healthy foods in a 2020 blog:[2]

- Allspice: Use in breads, desserts, and cereals; pairs well with savory dishes, such as soups, sauces, grains, and vegetables.
- Basil: Slice into salads, appetizers, and side dishes; enjoy in pesto over pasta and in sandwiches.
- Cardamom: Good in breads and baked goods, as well as in Indian dishes, such as curry.
- Cilantro: Use to season Mexican, Southwestern, Thai, and Indian foods.
- Cinnamon: Stir into fruit compotes, baked desserts, and breads, as well as Middle Eastern savory dishes.
- Clove: Good in baked goods and breads, but also pairs with vegetable and bean dishes.
- Cumin: Accents Mexican, Indian, and Middle Eastern dishes, as well as stews and chili.
- Dill weed: Include in potato dishes, salads, eggs, appetizers, and dips.
- Garlic: Add to soups, pastas, marinades, dressings, grains, and vegetables.
- Ginger: Great in Asian and Indian sauces, stews, and stir-fries, as well as beverages and baked goods.
- Marjoram: Add to stews, soups, potatoes, beans, grains, salads, and sauces.
- Mint: Flavors savory dishes, beverages, salads, marinades, and fruits.

- Nutmeg: Stir into fruits, baked goods, and vegetable dishes.
- Oregano: Delicious in Italian and Mediterranean dishes; it works well with tomato, pasta, grain dishes, and salads.
- Parsley: Enjoy in soups, pasta dishes, salads, and sauces.
- Pepper (black, white, red): Seasons soups, stews, vegetable dishes, grains, pastas, beans, sauces, and salads.
- Rosemary: Try it in vegetables, salads, vinaigrettes, and pasta dishes.
- Sage: Enhances grains, breads, dressings, soups, and pastas.
- Tarragon: Add to sauces, marinades, salads, and bean dishes.
- Thyme: Excellent in soups, tomato dishes, salads, and vegetables.
- Turmeric: Essential in Indian foods; pairs well with soups, beans, and vegetables.

Investigate ways to cook your vegetables with a variety of spices.

MaraZe/Shutterstock.com

❑ Reflection Time:

Describe your current eating pattern.

❑ Reflection Time:

Which of the aforementioned herbs and spices do you want to try?

❑ Reflection Time:

What would you like to investigate related to nutrition? Consider identifying sources of sugar in your diet or sources of caffeine as it can impact your sleep (see the chapter on sleep for details). Maybe, you could investigate your kitchen and take inventory of the spices and cooking ingredients in your cupboards and pantry. Or you could think about a rainbow and see how many vegetables you could consume in each color group.

❏ Reflection Time:

How will you begin your investigation?

____

____

____

____

____

____

____

____

❏ Reflection Time:

What did you learn from your above investigations? What are your next steps?

____

____

____

____

____

____

____

____

G = GOALS

Setting goals keeps you on track. Goals are like guideposts. They can be beacons of light to guide you on your path. The journey of change is often long, and it is meant to be joyful. So, it's important to work to find ways to add excitement into your goal-setting.

Making SMART goals is key. This mnemonic guide is reviewed in detail in the chapter on goal-setting. Having a vision of yourself in 20 years, 10 years, or even five years can also help guide you in goal-setting. Your vision and your values will help you stay grounded and focused.

❏ Reflection Time:

What would put a spring in your step?

____

❏ Reflection Time:

What goal would help you feel motivated to keep going?

❏ Reflection Time:

Write a goal that sounds fun?

❏ Reflection Time:

How can the fun goal above add to your happiness?

❑ Reflection Time:

Do you have five-year, two-year, one-year, six-month, three-month, one-month, one-week, and daily goals? Describe the goals.

❑ Reflection Time:

Are there any types of goals that you've considered setting but need more information before setting the goal? What type of investigation do you need to do before setting the goal?

❑ Reflection Time:

Do the investigation described above. What did you learn?

❑ Reflection Time:

Based upon your investigation, what is your new goal?

Your sense of purpose and your priorities will also provide strength and help guide your goal-setting. Later in this chapter, purpose is explored in greater detail.

S = STRESS MANAGEMENT

There are numerous stress management techniques you can learn, try, and explore. The internet provides videos and websites devoted to stress management practices. Imagine your stress management techniques as tools in a toolbox. Some techniques may help you more in certain situations compared to others. Some techniques, like deep breathing, can be used in the moment, for example, when you are in traffic or if someone says something alarming to you in a meeting. You may find that you derive benefit from specific techniques when faced with certain challenges and stressors.

The only way that you will know what works best for you is through investigating various stress management techniques. Some techniques and actions, like routine exercise and regular sound sleep, will help manage stress throughout the day. A positive mindset and healthy self-talk can also add to your stress resiliency. The following are examples of stress management ideas you can investigate:

- Nurture a positive view of yourself.
- Treat problematic circumstances as a learning process.
- Develop a healthy sense of self confidence.
- Embrace change.
- Form and maintain relationships.
- Learn to unwind.
- Find time to move.
- Make an effort to find joy.
- Don't sweat the "small stuff."
- Accept the fact that some things are beyond being controlled.
- Make sure to sleep seven to eight hours per night.
- Eat a healthy diet.
- Help others.
- Explore your purpose.
- Foster wonder and delight.
- Practice breath focus: 4-7-8.
- Exercise; walk, yoga, Tai Chi, stretch.
- Read or listen to a book/podcast.
- Try a hot bath or massage.
- Engage in gratitude practices.
- Use fidget items or distraction techniques.
- Elicit the relaxation response.
- Practice mindfulness.
- Practice meditation, e.g., mantra, loving kindness, etc.
- Try progressive muscle relaxation.
- Perform guided imagery.
- Perform a body scan.
- Practice mindfulness-based stress reduction.
- Foster supportive relationships.
- Practice acceptance and forgiveness.
- Make sleep a priority.
- Avoid excessive caffeine.
- Get professional mental health support, if needed.
- Manage expectations.
- Play and laugh.
- Serve others.
- Volunteer.
- Spend time in nature, forest bathing.

❑ Reflection Time:

Describe your current sources of stress.

❑ Reflection Time:

What stress reduction techniques have you tried in the past and which ones were successful?

❑ Reflection Time:

What is a stress-resiliency technique or tool that you would like to investigate (learn more about or try and reflect upon)?

❑ Reflection Time:

How will you begin your investigation?

❑ Reflection Time:

What did you learn from the above investigation? What are your next steps? Be specific.

❑ Reflection Time:

What is your vision of yourself with regards to managing stressful events in the future?

T = TIME-OUTS

In the previous chapter, a variety of ways to take time-outs and the importance of doing this to help manage stress and improve productivity was explored. Time-outs can be viewed as empowerment moments. A time-out can help you focus and recharge your battery. Everyone needs time-outs. They are not just for toddlers or teenagers. Parents often need time-outs, too. Sports teams use time-outs in most games, typically when the game gets out of control or there is a key play that needs to be discussed and executed. Like blowing the whistle and huddling with your team (family, co-workers, loved ones), we can take a pause and regroup. Regrouping entails evaluating the situation and working to make things better together.

In addition to these mental time-outs or empowerment moments, you need time-outs from sitting. It's best to get up every hour to move around and get your blood flowing. You also need time-outs from using your muscles extensively, in order to give them an opportunity to recover from the demands placed on them. This factor is why the standard recommendation for exercisers is to engage in strength training on an every-other-day basis.

On occasion, naps are used as time-outs. If taking a nap, it's best to do so before 3 p.m. and for no longer than 20-30 minutes, in order to not disrupt night-time sleep. Taking a time-out from electronics is also key for mental health. Working on purposefully putting your phone, iPad, computer or other device away for hours at a time during the weekend is important for your mental health, as well as for building relationships with your family and friends.

There are a variety of time-out options that you can consider and investigate, including the following:

- Stand up.
- Walk.
- Breathe.
- Count.
- Go on mini-vacations.
- Take time-outs from email and electronics.
- Engage in any activity that gets you away from your normal routine.
- Take a break every hour.
- Run in place.
- Call a friend.
- Look at pictures of nature.
- Get out in nature.
- Listen to music.
- Sing.
- Dance.
- Meditate.
- Drink a glass of ice water.
- Take a 20-minute nap before 3 p.m.
- Pet your dog.
- Find some flowers to smell or look at.
- Water a plant.
- Play a game.
- Write a thank-you note.

❑ Reflection Time:

What time-outs do you currently use day-to-day?

____

____

____

❑ Reflection Time:

What time-outs did you learn about that you had not considered prior to reading this book?

❑ Reflection Time:

Is there a type of time-out that you would like to learn more about, such as napping or planning a vacation? Explain.

There are numerous ways to investigate time-outs. For example, you could reach out to a friend or relative and get their input. Another option would be doing an internet search for trustworthy sources of information. Often, an investigation involves experiencing the time-out to know how it impacts you. Keep in mind that what works best for one person may not work well for another person.

❏ Reflection Time:

Consider trying a time-out that you don't usually experience. How do you hypothesize (believe) it will make you feel?

____

____

____

____

____

____

____

____

❏ Reflection Time:

How will you specifically investigate this time-out in the next week?

____

____

____

____

____

____

____

____

E = ENERGY

As was discussed in the previous chapter, energy is a finite resource. Accordingly, it is important for everyone to think about which activities boost their energy and which ones deplete their energy stores. A useful way to think about this is what activities or interactions allow you to recharge your own battery and which factors or interactions deplete the stores of your battery?

____

Many people focus on time management. It's also important to consider focusing on energy management. Notice when you are most energized in the day. You may want to create a log of your energy levels in the morning, at noon, and in the evening. Projects can also energize or drain us of energy. In fact, people can do this too.

In the previous chapter, you were asked to make a list of things that gave you energy and things that drained your energy. As such, it can be useful to investigate new strategies to help you improve your energy level. Among the healthy ideas for recharging your battery are the following:

- Connecting with supportive friends
- Eating healthy snacks
- Drinking green tea
- Engaging in your favorite hobby
- Spending time in nature
- Getting more sleep
- Engaging in enjoyable exercise
- Planning travel or traveling

❑ Reflection Time:

What increases your energy?

____

____

____

____

____

____

____

____

❑ Reflection Time:

What drains your energy?

____

____

____

____

____

____

____

____

____

❑ Reflection Time:

Most people think they know when they are most energetic but have never tracked their energy. For at least a day, track your energy, upon waking, throughout the morning, afternoon, evening, and before bed. You can use a journal or the space below to track your findings.

❑ Reflection Time:

What activities increase your energy?

❑ Reflection Time:

What did you learn and how can you use this to support your health moving forward?

If you enjoy doing this or find it useful, you may want to consider doing this for more than a day as it may take several days in order to fully understand your energy patterns.

P = PURPOSE

Your purpose is related to your values, goals, and mission. As noted in the previous chapter, your purpose in life at age 25 is likely different than your purpose at age 85. It's easy to neglect thinking about your purpose until a major life event occurs. However, taking time to investigate your purpose can benefit your health at any time. Your purpose can change with life experiences and as you age.

When you think about ways you can make the world a better place day-to-day or even in a larger way over time, you can start to craft a sense of purpose that is bigger than yourself. For many people, their purpose is to care for others, like their children, aging parents, sick relatives, pets, or their spouse/partner.

During certain periods of a person's life, the individual's purpose can be focused. In some instances, for example, their purpose is to recover their health, protect their health, or gain a sense of well-being. Without their health, they can't really create larger goals or take on a world-changing purpose. That said, not everyone embraces a world-changing purpose, which is okay. For some, doing small acts of kindness each day in some way and expressing compassion is their life purpose. There are so many ways to think about purpose, as well as countless ways to meet your purpose.

❏ Reflection Time:

What are your current priorities and values? Take some time to list your core values and investigate in this way.

❏ Reflection Time:

What are your ideas about your purpose in life at this time?

❏ Reflection Time:

What can you investigate that is related to how you address your purpose, priorities, and mission while engaging your strengths? Refer to the previous chapter for your response to a similar question about adding variety.

❏ Reflection Time:

What did you learn?

S = SLEEP

You can use investigation to learn more about what helps you get a restful night's sleep. The goal is to sleep a solid seven to nine hours every night—weeknights and weekends. Keeping the bedroom like a cave (quiet, cool, and dark) can help. Experimenting with ways to make your room cave-like can be helpful for your overall well-being.

Many people benefit from keeping a sleep diary or wearing a device that enables them to track the time they go to bed, along with any pre-bedtime activities. They also record any night awakenings, difficulties with falling asleep or maintaining sleep, and what time they wake in the morning. You may also consider tracking your caffeine intake, if you woke to use the bathroom during the night, if you woke without or with the aid of an alarm, or if you experienced other things that disrupted your sleep.

One simple investigation is to log the time you go to sleep and the time you wake up. Then, log how energized you feel when you wake up.

❑ Reflection Time:

Describe your current sleep pattern taking into account the variables listed in the paragraphs above.

❑ Reflection Time:

What did you learn from your sleep reflection?

❏ Reflection Time:

Based on your reflection/investigation, is there anything that you want to change in order to improve your sleep? Explain.

❏ Reflection Time:

Have you ever used a wearable device, such as a smart watch, to track your sleep? What did you learn? What do you want to change to improve your sleep habits now that you have this information?

S = SOCIAL SUPPORT

Social connections are important for your overall health, though they are often taken for granted. It is important for everyone to have meaningful connections with friends and family members. Technology affords individuals more opportunities to connect with people who do not live nearby. According to Maslow's hierarchy of needs, a sense of belonging is so important that it comes right after physiologic (food and water) and shelter needs.

Many people ignore this part of their lives, especially if they are focused on work and family obligations. However, cultivating high quality connections can add life to your years and even years to your life. At different times of your life, you can focus on your friends and families to varying degrees, but you never want to entirely ignore your social connections to the point that you feel lonely and disconnected. If you are feeling lonely, it's important to reach out now to someone you know.

There are a variety of ways to connect with others, such as phone calls, online meetings like Zoom, FaceTime, texting, writing notes, connecting on social media with likes, replies and direct messages, and meeting face to face. You need to experiment and investigate what works well for you and determine which methods of connecting feel best to you. For certain family and friends, you might choose FaceTime, while writing notes or phone calls might work well for others.

❑ Reflection Time:

What would you like to investigate that is related to your social connections?

____

____

____

____

❑ Reflection Time:

Do you want to investigate a way for you to be more connected with a certain person or group? Explain.

❑ Reflection Time:

Do you want to join a club or organization? If so, which one and how can you learn more about the club or organization? Consider doing the research now and writing about what you learn.

❑ Reflection Time:

Is there a class that you want to learn more about? Could you join a class with a friend or meet new people while taking the class? Research the class and describe what you learn.

❑ Reflection Time:

What did you learn about your level of social connection, based on your investigation? Is there anything that you would like to change based upon this knowledge?

❑ Reflection Time:

What are your next steps?

SMART Goal

In order to take what you have learned about investigations and put it into action, create a SMART goal for yourself involving investigations (see Chapter 4 page 55 for a discussion of what constitutes a SMART goal).

❏ SMART Goal Time:

What is your SMART goal for investigations? (Specific, Measurable, Action-oriented, Realistic, Time-sensitive)

Rob Marmion/Shutterstock.com

References

❑ Cited References:

1. Simpson JA, Weiner ESC, editors. *The Oxford English Dictionary,* 2nd ed, Vol 9. London, England: Clarendon Press; 2001.
2. Godman H. 21 spices for healthy holiday foods. Harvard Health Blog. https://www.health.harvard.edu/blog/21-spices-for-healthy-holiday-foods-2020120421550?utm_content=buffer9d01b&%3Butm_medium=social&%3Butm_source=twitter&%3Butm_campaign=buffer. Published December 4, 2020. Accessed July 14, 2021.

CHAPTER 8
NUTRITION

"We should all be eating fruits and vegetables as if our lives depend on it—because they do."

—Michael Greger
Author, Physician, and
Nutrition Expert

PAVING the Path to Wellness: Questions for Nutrition

For each of the following five statements, choose the number on the frequency scale that best relates to you (frequency: 1= never, 2= rarely, 3= sometimes, 4= often, 5= routinely).

- I eat four fruits a day.___
- I eat five or more vegetables a day.___
- I know proper portions for protein, carbohydrates, and fats, and I eat those portions.___
- I think about the food that I eat and ask myself if it is good for my body.___
- I view food as fuel and medicine, as well as enjoyment. ___

Subtotal—nutrition _____

Daisy Daisy/Shutterstock.com

Live and Learn: Wendy (PAVING Program Participant)

Because Wendy has a family history of obesity, type 2 diabetes, and heart disease, she has learned about the importance of adopting a healthy diet to prevent these conditions. Wendy has decided that she wants to improve her eating habits. She knows it is important to incorporate at least five servings of fruits and vegetables into her diet each day. She also made an effort to eat more whole grains and legumes, as well as cut back on processed foods.

For breakfast, Wendy often eats at home, before she leaves for work. She has a bowl of oatmeal, which she enjoys with blueberries. At lunch time, Wendy tries to avoid the cafeteria, since she often finds herself tempted to indulge in the "fast food" options. She notes she recently started bringing a healthy salad to work each day, and she has managed to steer clear of the cafeteria.

Because of her demanding work schedule, Wendy's biggest challenge with healthy eating comes at dinnertime. Wendy often stays late at the office, and by the time she leaves work and gets home, it is often 8 p.m. By that time, she is exhausted and hungry, and the last thing she wants to do is cook a healthy meal. Instead, she often rewards herself after a long day at work with a take-out dinner from a nearby restaurant. She has been asking her friends for advice on how she can prepare healthy dinners in advance.

Wendy decides to sign up for a cooking class focused on "Meal Prep Strategies." During the class, she learns that it is preferable to cook meals at home, rather than eating out. The instructor reviews the many advantages to eating at home, including saving money, reducing portion sizes, controlling the ingredients, and avoiding processed foods. Wendy learns about how she can stock her freezer with healthy options, such as frozen fruits and vegetables. She also learns to stock her pantry with nuts, seeds, and legumes, as well as a variety of spices. Most importantly, she realizes she can use a few hours on an afternoon during her weekend to prepare meals for later in the week.

Irina Meliukh/Shutterstock.com

The American College of Lifestyle Medicine (ACLM) strongly advocates a whole food, plant-predominant way of eating.

Wendy gets in the habit of making a large batch of roasted vegetables, a grain (such as brown rice), and a protein (such as beans) on her Sunday afternoons, so she can easily make a stir fry or salad when she gets home from work on weeknights.

In addition, Wendy invests in a few new cookbooks, since she finds that she enjoys exploring new recipes. One of her favorites is "The How Not to Die Cookbook" by Michael Greger, MD, FACLM. She makes a goal to cook at home at least three weeknights per week, and after a few months, she finds that she is able to eat at home almost every night.

Nutrition Timeline

❑ Reflection Time:

Write out or draw what you liked to eat during each of these phases of your life (childhood, adolescence, young adulthood, middle adulthood, older adulthood).

❑ Reflection Time:

Reflect on your relationship with food throughout your life, including what influenced your views on nutrition.

❑ Reflection Time:

Describe what type of relationship you have or would LIKE to have with food.

❑ Reflection Time:

How does your current health and lifestyle impact your food choices?

❑ Reflection Time:

What, where, and how would you like to eat, if all barriers were removed, including food availability, physical condition, financial resources, and time?

❑ Reflection Time:

What types of food or eating do you wish that you could try? We will return to this concept later in this chapter, using the MOSS framework.

Definitions and Terms

❑ Nutrition

"The act or process of nourishing or being nourished; specifically, the sum of the processes by which an animal or plant takes in and utilizes food substances" *Merriam Webster Dictionary*[1]

❑ Calories:

- unit of heat used to indicate the amount of energy that foods will produce in the human body
- the amount of heat required to raise the temperature of one kilogram of water one degree Celsius

  –Protein 1 gram = 4 calories; carbohydrates 1 gram = 4 calories; fat 1 gram = 9 calories; alcohol 1 gram = 7 calories

❑ Diet:

"Diet (noun) from the Greek word *Diaita* meaning a way of life:

- Food and drink regularly provided or consumed
- Habitual nourishment
- The kind and amount of food prescribed for a person or animal for a special reason
- A regimen of eating and drinking sparingly so as to reduce a person's weight

  Diet (verb)–to eat less food or to eat only particular kinds of food in order to lose weight; to be on a diet" *Merriam Webster Dictionary*[1]

❑ Basic Metabolic Rate (BMR):

The amount of energy your body uses at rest for bodily functions such as breathing, your heart beating, your kidneys filtering sodium, your hair growing and other functions of vital organs. Also called the resting energy expenditure (REE).

❑ Calculating BMR:

- For men: BMR = 66.6 + (13.7 X wt in kg) + (5 X ht in cm) – (6.7 X age in years)
- For women: BMR = 655.1 + (9.6 X wt in kg) + (1.8 X ht in cm) – (4.7 X age in years)

–1 kg = 2.2 pounds and 1 inch = 2.54 cm

❑ Thermic Effect of Food (TEE):

The amount of energy required to digest food. As a rule, it is 10 percent of the total calories consumed (e.g., 500 calories will use about 50 calories to digest).

- Energy balance—energy in = energy out
- Calories per-day = BMR + physical activity spent + TEE

❑ Body Mass Index (BMI):

Weight-in-pounds/(height-in-inches)^2 x 703 or weight-in-kg/(height-in-meters)^2

❑ Glycemic Index (GI):

Measures how a carbohydrate-containing food raises blood glucose. Foods are ranked based on how they compare to a reference food—either glucose or white bread.

- Low GI < 55: 100 percent stone-ground whole wheat or pumpernickel bread, oatmeal, whole wheat pasta, barley, bulgur, sweet potato, corn, yam, lima/butter beans, peas, legumes, lentils, most fruits, non-starchy vegetables
- Medium GI (55-69): whole wheat, rye and pita bread, quick oats, brown, wild or basmati rice, couscous
- High GI > 70: white bread or bagel, corn flakes, puffed rice, bran flakes, instant oatmeal, white rice, rice pasta, macaroni and cheese from mix, russet potato, pumpkin, pretzels, rice cakes, popcorn, saltine crackers, melons, pineapple

Relationship With Food

A person's family, culture, and society influence their relationship with food. Many people have a complex relationship with food, as it intersects with their weight and body image. Individuals receive messages, often conflicting, about what they should and should not eat from the media, food marketers, social media, and, on occasion, even their physicians. It's easy to understand why confusion around what to eat is relatively common.

Emotional factors also impact a person's food choices, as physical hunger is often not the only reason that individuals eat. Society encourages the use of food for stress relief, as well as for reward. These types of cues happen at an early age. For example, when a child does well at an athletic competition, they may be rewarded with food to celebrate. Social events are often centered on a shared meal, from Thanksgiving gatherings to birthday celebrations. Emotions, such as anxiety, loneliness, sadness, anger, or boredom, may lead a person to overeat or choose less healthy food options. Awareness of these emotional factors and behavioral patterns can allow an individual to identify these challenges, so they can be mindfully addressed.

Although ideally everyone has a positive health-enhancing view of food and its ability to nourish their body and minds, it is understandable that discussing food makes some people feel shame, guilt, and causes them to remember past dieting and weight-loss attempts. The goal is to support your current health journey, wherever you are at with your relationship with food. One suggestion is that if you've struggled with "diets" in the past, you may want to use the words "nutrition" or "healthy foods" instead.

Nutrition Assessment

Now that you've reflected upon your relationship with food in the past, it would be helpful if you gained a better understanding of your recent food intake. Remember, there's no shame, blame, nor guilt. You need to understand where you are starting, so that you have a better sense of where you want to go moving forward. As an initial step, fill out the following nutrition assessment, using a checkmark (✓) to note your answer for each type of food.

❏ Reflection Time:

How many home-cooked meals are you eating each week? How does this impact your food choices?

____

____

____

____

____

____

____

____

____

Food	Daily	4-6 Times Per Week	1-3 Times Per Week	0 Times Per Week
Vegetables				
Fruits				
Whole grains				
Legumes (beans, peas, lentils, chickpeas)				
Water				
Nuts				
Dairy products				
Beef				
Pork				
Chicken				
Processed meats—hot dogs, bacon, cold cuts/ lunchmeat				
Fish & seafood				
Chips				
Sugar-sweetened beverages				
Fast food				
Pizza				
Fried foods				
Candy				
Cookies, cakes, & donuts				
Ice cream				
Smoothies				
White bagels, bread, pasta, & rice				
Milk				
Cheese				
Whole grain pasta				
Alcoholic beverages				

Figure 8-1. A sample nutritional assessment tool (used with permission from *The Teen Lifestyle Medicine Handbook*; B. Frates, et al; Monterey, CA: Healthy Learning; 2021)

Evidence-Based Nutrition

Eating patterns exist along a spectrum from health-depleting to health-promoting. At one end of the spectrum is the standard American diet (SAD), which focuses on ultra-processed, fast-and-fried foods, sweets, snacks, refined grains, high-sodium foods, processed meat, and high cholesterol foods. This standard American diet (SAD) eating style is associated with an increased risk of type 2 diabetes, heart disease, and obesity, as well as other lifestyle-related chronic diseases.

On the other end of the spectrum are health-promoting eating patterns, such as a whole food, plant-predominant one. It consists of whole foods (nothing is highly processed), mostly plants, like vegetables, whole grains, fruits, beans, legumes, nuts, seeds, herbs, and spices. The beverage of choice for a healthy eating pattern is water. This type of eating pattern has been associated with a decreased risk of heart disease, stroke, obesity, and type 2 diabetes.

Most people follow an eating pattern that is somewhere between these two ends of the spectrum, though any movement toward the healthier end of the spectrum is beneficial for health. The American College of Lifestyle Medicine (ACLM) actively promotes a whole food, plant-predominant way of eating. They have several resources available online, such as the graphic shown in Figure 8-2.

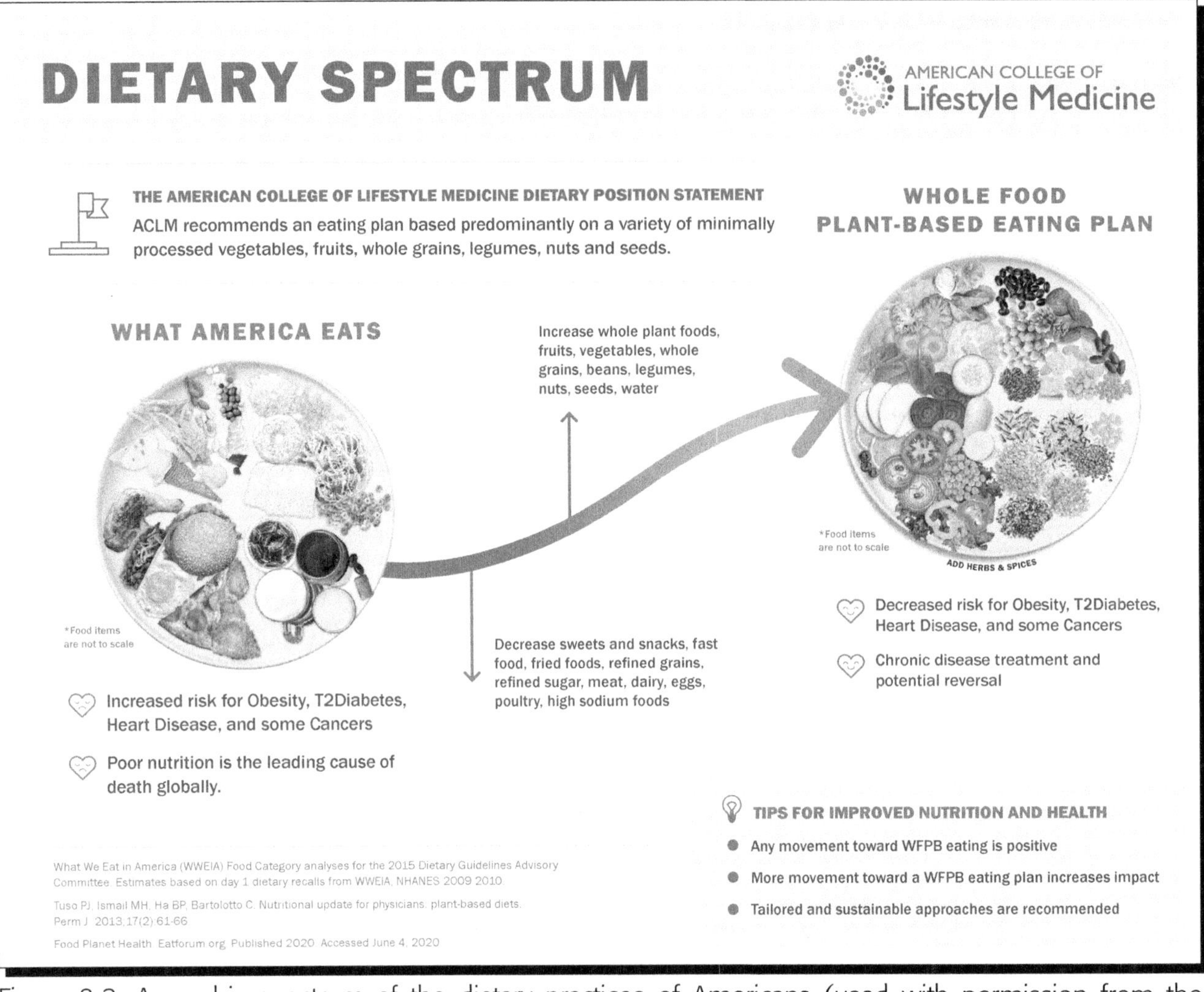

Figure 8-2. A graphic spectrum of the dietary practices of Americans (used with permission from the American College of Lifestyle Medicine)

❑ Reflection Time:

After reviewing the dietary spectrum, how would you describe your pattern of eating?

____

____

____

____

____

____

____

____

____

Healthful Eating Commonalities

Although media headlines tend to highlight the differences between dietary styles, there are many commonalities between healthful styles of eating, for example:

- Eat plenty of fruits and vegetables.
- Consume lots of whole grains, legumes, and nuts.
- Eliminate or limit milk and dairy.
- Focus on plant protein—nuts, seeds, legumes, soy, and may include seafood twice a week, as is included in the Mediterranean diet.
- Eliminate or limit alcohol (no more than one drink per day for women and two for men).
- Eliminate or limit red meat.
- Eliminate processed foods of all types especially meats (bacon, hot dogs, sausages).

Drs. Dean Ornish, Hans Diehl and David Katz are all pioneers in the field of lifestyle medicine nutrition who endorse many of the aforementioned listed healthy eating commonalities:

- Dr. Dean Ornish's landmark studies demonstrated the ability of diet and other healthy lifestyle behaviors to reverse cardiovascular disease, help early stage prostate cancer, alter gene expression, and lengthen telomeres (associated with a longer lifespan). He has authored several books, with his most recent being *Undo It: How Simple Lifestyle Changes Can Reverse Most Chronic Diseases*. His outpatient lifestyle program is reimbursed by insurance agencies for cardiac rehabilitation.
- Dr. David Katz, a well-respected author and founder of the True Health Initiative, also founded DietID, a digital diet assessment and behavior change platform that is working to improve health outcomes through his dietary assessment tool.
- Dr. Hans Diehl is the founder of the Complete Health Improvement Program (CHIP), a lifestyle medicine intervention program completed by over 85,000 participants. He is a clinical professor of Preventive Medicine at Loma Linda University and advocates for a whole-food, plant-based dietary pattern.

Cardiovascular Disease Prevention Diet—American Heart Association

The American Heart Association recommends increasing your intake of high-quality foods and decreasing your intake of nutrient-poor foods. The DASH (Dietary Approaches to Stop Hypertension) eating plan is one way to adhere to this eating style, though you can also adapt their recommendations to your personal preferences and needs. Among the features of the DASH dietary approach are the following:

- Eat a variety of vegetables and fruits.
- Eat unrefined fiber-rich, whole-grain foods.
- Eat a variety of fish at least twice a week.
- Choose fish and poultry without skin.
- Select fat-free & low-fat (1 percent) dairy products.
- Eat nuts and legumes (beans, peas, lentils, chickpeas).

The DASH diet also recommended that you cut back on the following:

- Saturated fats–< 7 percent of calories = 16 grams for a 2,000 calorie diet
- Trans fats–avoid < 1 percent of calories = 2 grams for a 2,000 calorie diet
- Cholesterol–< 300 mg a day
- Red meat and sweets
- Added sugars–women < 100 calories per day (6 tsp); men < 150 calories per day (9 tsp)
- Salt–< 1,500 mg sodium per day
- Beverages with added sugars
- Alcohol–if you drink, drink in moderation (one drink women and two drinks men) (a drink is one 12 oz. bear, five oz. wine, 1.5 oz. of 80-proof spirits, or one oz. of 100-proof spirits)

United States Dietary Guidelines: "Make Every Bite Count"[2]

The *Dietary Guidelines for Americans* is the cornerstone for federal nutrition programs and a consequential resource for health/wellness professionals nationwide. They are updated every five years. Providing food-based recommendations to promote health, help prevent diet-related chronic diseases, and meet a person's nutrient needs, the *Dietary Guidelines for Americans 2020-25* detail the following overarching guidelines, which are available for review at https://dietaryguidelines.gov/:

- Follow a healthy dietary pattern at every life stage.
- Customize and enjoy nutrient-dense food and beverage choices to reflect personal preferences, cultural traditions, and budgetary considerations.
- Focus on meeting food group needs with nutrient-dense foods and beverages and stay within calorie limits.
- Limit foods and beverages that are higher in added sugars, saturated fat, and sodium, as well as limit alcoholic beverages.

Among the features of a dietary approach adhering to the U.S. Dietary Guidelines are the following:

- Eat a variety of fruits and vegetables–eat different colors.
- Ensure that at least half of grains are whole grains.
- Consume fat-free and low-fat milk products, if you consume dairy products.
- Eat a variety of lean protein–seafood, lean meat, beans, peas, soy, eggs, unsalted nuts, and seeds.
- Use oils to replace solid fats.
- Eat foods with more potassium, fiber, calcium, and vitamin D.
- Consume a limited amount of sodium–i.e., < 2,300mg/day. (Note: to avoid a high risk of sodium, eat < 1,500mg/day.)
- Reduce calories from SoFAS (solid fats and added sugars).
- Consume < 10 percent of calories from saturated fats.
- Keep trans-fat consumption as low as possible.
- Limit consumption of refined grains.
- If alcohol is consumed, do so in moderation.

Mediterranean Diet

The Mediterranean diet is an approach to eating based on the traditional cuisines of those countries that border the Mediterranean Sea. It doesn't entail calorie counting or portion measurements. Instead, it focuses on the importance of consuming fresh vegetables, fruits, nuts, legumes, and whole grains, as well as extra-virgin olive oil, lean meats, fish, and red wine in moderation. Furthermore, no single strict version of this diet exists.

The Mediterranean diet is a relatively popular way of eating, not only because it's easy to follow, but also because it's been found to have a positive impact on health. In that regard, research has found that it promotes heart health; helps prevent and manage diabetes; enhances mental health; aids weight management; reduces the risk of cancer; and is environmentally friendly.

Among the features of an eating pattern adhering to the Mediterranean diet are the following:

- High intake of vegetables, fruits, legumes, cereals, fish, nuts, and seeds
- Moderate intake of red wine during meals (limit to one drink per day for a woman and two for a man)
- Low intake of meat and meat products, milk, and dairy products
- Typically consume fish and seafood a couple times per week
- A focus on eating plant-based foods that are primarily fresh and unprocessed

Harvard Healthy Eating Plate

Created by Dr. Walter Willet and nutrition experts at the Harvard University T.H. Chan School of Public Health, the Harvard Healthy Eating Plate is an eating pattern that is primarily plant-based, rich in vegetables, whole grains, healthy fats, and healthy proteins. Based exclusively upon science, with an emphasis on diet quality, this diet has been found to lower the risk of both weight gain and chronic diseases.

Marian Weyo/Shutterstock.com

❑ Reflection Time:

Complete Figure 8-3.

Harvard Healthy Eating Plate Recommendations	**How do my behaviors align or stray from the recommendations?**	**Is there anything that I want to change moving forward?**
Eat lots of veggies; strive for variety (potatoes don't count).		
Eat plenty of fruit of varied colors.		
Drink water, tea, or coffee (limit sugar).		
Limit milk, dairy, and juice.		
Avoid sugar-sweetened beverages.		
Eat a variety of whole grains.		
Limit refined grains (white bread, rice, pasta).		
Use healthy oils, like olive oil and canola oil.		
Choose beans, nuts, fish, and poultry as high quality protein sources.		
Avoid processed meat; limit red meat and cheese.		

Figure 8-3. A sample Harvard Eating Plate self-assessment tool

❑ Reflection Time:

Think about your lunch and dinner plates from the past week. How do they compare with the Harvard Healthy Eating Plate recommendations?

❏ Reflection Time:

Was half of your plate filled with a variety of fruits and vegetables (not counting potatoes)?

❏ Reflection Time:

Do whole grains fill a quarter of your plate?

❏ Reflection Time:

Is there anything that you would like to change moving forward? Explain.

Whole Food, Plant-Based Eating

The American College of Lifestyle Medicine embraces a whole-food, plant-based (WFPB) way of eating that recommends an eating plan focused on a variety of minimally processed vegetables, fruits, whole grains, and legumes, with nuts and seeds in moderation. It minimizes or excludes meat (including poultry and fish), dairy, eggs, added sugar, and processed oils.

Eat the Rainbow

Eating a rainbow of fruits and vegetables is important, as they contain a variety of phytonutrients. Phytonutrients are specific nutrients that come from plant foods that keep the body healthy and fight disease. Variety and quality are important, in addition to the quantity of fruits and vegetables. In addition to phytonutrients, plants have fiber that you need to keep you healthy. Fiber is the indigestible part of plant foods that is beneficial for your health to eat.

❑ Reflection Time:

Considering your typical fruit and vegetable choices throughout a week, do your fruits and vegetables reflect a rainbow? Explain.

____

____

____

____

____

____

____

____

❑ Reflection Time:

Complete Figure 8-4.

Color	**Foods I Already Enjoy and Include From This Color**	**Foods I Want to Try or Increase From This Color**
Green		
Red		
White		
Yellow		
Purple & Blue		

Figure 8-4. A rainbow-eating pattern self-assessment tool

A WHOLE FOOD, PLANT-BASED PLATE

Nutrition Prescription for Treating & Reversing Chronic Disease

The American College of Lifestyle Medicine Dietary Lifestyle Position Statement for Treatment and Potential Reversal of Disease: ACLM recommends an eating plan based predominantly on a variety of minimally processed vegetables, fruits, whole grains, legumes, nuts and seeds.

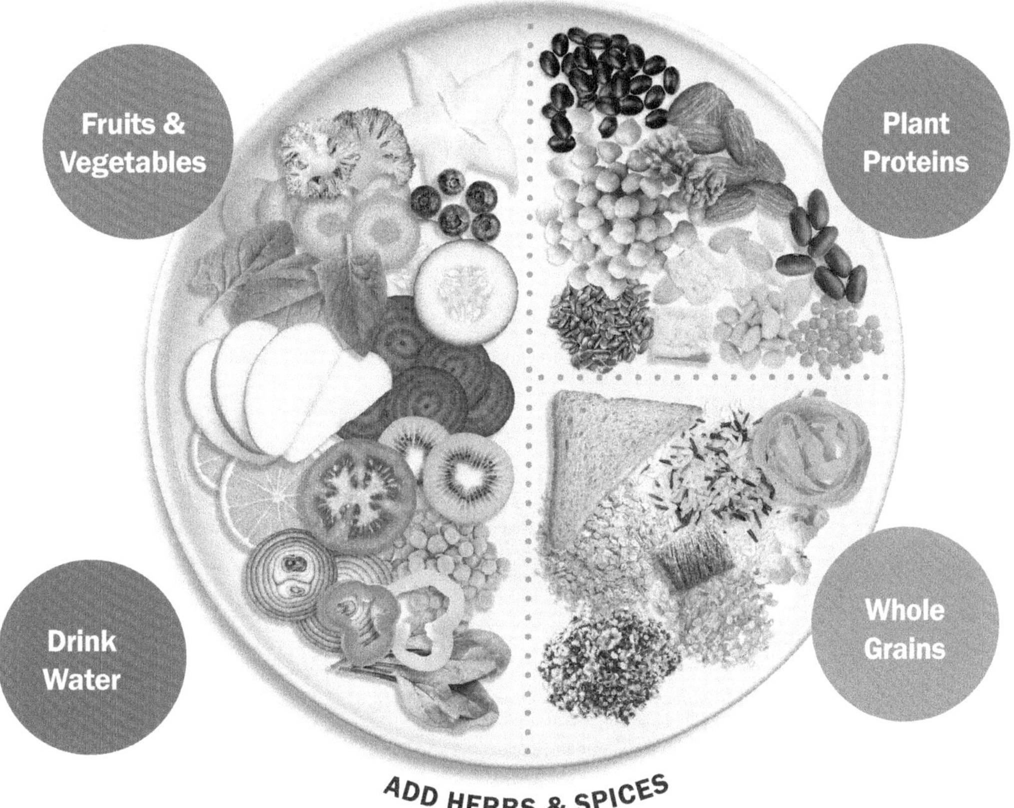

Include a wide array of fiber-filled, nutrient-dense, and antioxidant-rich whole plant foods at every meal. Use a variety of herbs and spices to enhance flavors.

lifestylemedicine.org

- **Focus on whole fruits and vegetables and eat a rainbow of color.**

Vegetables: Dark leafy greens (spinach, kale, arugula, etc.), broccoli, squash, zucchini, carrots, tomatoes, beets, peppers, mushrooms, onions, celery, cauliflower, cucumbers, white & sweet potatoes, green peas, cabbage, whole plant fats (avocados, olives), and more.
Fruits: Apples, bananas, grapes, citrus fruit, berries, peaches, pears, pineapple, kiwi, plums, watermelon, starfruit, mangoes, just to name a few.

- **Drink water for hydration.**

- **Eat a variety of plant protein.**

Legumes: Peas and beans, including kidney beans, pinto beans, white beans, black beans, lima beans, black-eyed peas, garbanzo beans (chickpeas), split peas and lentils, edamame, tofu.

Nuts and seeds: Almonds, pistachios, walnuts, pecans, nut butters, pumpkin/sunflower/chia/flax seeds, and more.

- **Choose whole grains.**

Amaranth, barley, brown rice, buckwheat, bulgur, millet, popcorn, rye, quinoa, whole oats, whole grain bread/ tortillas/cereals/flours, to name a few.

Figure 8-5. An illustration of ACLM's whole-food, plant-based plate (used with permission of the American College of Lifestyle Medicine)

AMERICAN COLLEGE OF Lifestyle Medicine

TIPS TO GET YOU STARTED ON A WHOLE FOOD, PLANT-BASED DIET

Take your journey to a healthy lifestyle step-by-step.

- **STEP 1: Enjoy** - Keep plant-based meals you already enjoy in your meal rotation.
- **STEP 2: Adapt** - Give your favorite recipes a plant-based makeover.
- **STEP 3: Explore** - Begin incorporating new plant-based foods into each week.

Plan ahead.

- Use meal planning apps or a simple calendar to plan meals in advance.
- Set aside time to batch prepare ingredients so meals can be thrown together quickly on busy weeknights. Pre-chop vegetables and cook large portions of grains and beans.

Make the 'healthy choice' the easy choice.

- Keep fresh produce in a bowl on the counter and at eye-level in the fridge so it is the first thing you reach for when wanting a snack.
- Stock your pantry with staple ingredients that can be assembled into a quick meal.

Work with a Registered Dietitian to assist in transitioning to a 100% plant-based dietary lifestyle, the health-protecting, disease-fighting prescription.

Game plan for eating away from home and traveling.

- Check menus ahead of time. Pair side dishes together to create a hearty meal.
- Ask if the kitchen is willing to make a dish with vegetables, beans and whole grains.
- When traveling, pack your own meals or stop at grocery stores instead of fast food.

Include the entire family.

- Allow children to pick a new fruit or vegetable to try each week.
- Start a tomato plant on the porch and have children water and take care of it.
- Assign age-appropriate kitchen tasks to everyone in the family.

Set goals each week on your journey to improved nutrition.

- Identify specific, measurable and attainable steps you can take each week. Instead of "eat more vegetables," set a SMART goal to "make half your dinner plate vegetables five nights this week."
- Celebrate success each and every step of the way!

lifestylemedicine.org

Figure 8-6. Tips for getting started on a whole-food, plant-based diet (used with Permission of the American College of Lifestyle Medicine)

Environmental Working Group

The Environmental Working Group (EWG) releases a shopper's guide each year that includes the "Dirty Dozen" and the "Clean Fifteen." This guide features a review of produce, based upon the level of pesticide contamination. Subsequently, some people decide when to purchase organic produce, based upon their recommendations.

❑ Environmental Working Group—Dirty Dozen:

- apples
- bell and hot peppers
- celery
- cherries
- grapes
- kale
- nectarines
- peaches
- pears
- spinach
- strawberries
- tomatoes

❑ Environmental Working Group—Clean Fifteen:

- asparagus
- avocados
- broccoli
- cabbage
- cantaloupe
- cauliflower
- eggplant
- honeydew melon
- kiwi
- mushrooms
- onions
- papaya
- pineapple
- sweet corn
- sweet peas (frozen)

Spinach is one of the Environmental Working Group's "dirty dozen."

djero.adlibeshe yahoo.com/Shutterstock.com

Plant Sources of Micronutrients

Micronutrients are vitamins and minerals that your body needs in smaller amounts, but are very important to growth and development.

Nutrient	Primary Role in Your Body	Outcome of Deficiency	Good Plant Sources	
Vitamin A	Eyesight	Blindness	Apricots Broccoli Cantaloupe Carrots Collards Mango	Romaine lettuce Spinach Squash Sweet potatoes Sweet red peppers
Calcium	Bone/teeth formation and maintenance	Osteoporosis (bone loss)	Artichoke Broccoli Chinese cabbage Clams Collards Hummus Kale, spinach	Legumes Molasses Mustard greens Nuts Orange juice (fortified) Squash Turnip greens
Vitamin C	Immune function (fighting infection)	Scurvy—a disease that causes bleeding gums	Berries Broccoli Brussels sprouts Citrus fruits (oranges)	Dark green leafy vegetables Kiwi Peas Peppers (yellow) Tomatoes

Figure 8-7. An overview of vitamins—impact and sources (used with permission from the *Lifestyle Medicine Handbook*; 2nd edition; Frates, et al.; Monterey, CA: Healthy Learning; 2021)

Nutrient	Primary Role in Your Body	Outcome of Deficiency	Good Plant Sources	
Cobalamin (vitamin B12)	Nervous system functioning	Anemia and nerve damage	Fortified cereals Fortified nutritional yeast Tofu	**Food sources should not be relied upon for adequate B12. Supplementation is recommended for those individuals who are eating a predominantly plant-based diet.*
Vitamin D	Bone health	Rickets (softening of the bones)	Mushrooms Tofu	**Sunlight is perhaps the best source.*
Folate (vitamin B9)	Tissue growth	Anemia Birth defects	Asparagus Baked potatoes Beans Beets Broccoli Brussels sprouts Cabbage Collard greens Corn	Mustard greens Nuts Oranges Romaine lettuce Spinach Sweet potatoes Wheat-grain breads and cereal
Iodine	Regulates metabolism	Hypothyroidism	Baked potatoes Cranberries Dried prunes	Dried seaweed Green beans White bread
Iron	Moves oxygen through your body	Iron deficiency Anemia	Apricots Beans Broccoli Dried fruit, e.g., prunes, raisins Green pepper	Prune juice Pumpkin, sesame, or squash seeds Rice Soybeans Spinach Tofu
Magnesium	Muscle contraction	Convulsions Heart arrhythmias Weakness tremor Tetany	Baked potato Beans Black-eyed peas Green leafy vegetables	Nuts Whole grains
Niacin (vitamin B3)	Metabolism	Pellagra, which is marked by diarrhea, dementia, and skin disorder	Avocado Brown rice Green vegetables	Peanuts Sunflower seeds
Potassium	Fluid balance Muscle contraction	Heart arrhythmias Muscle weakness	Apricots Avocados Baked potatoes Bananas Cantaloupe Dates Honeydew melon Kiwi Nuts	Oranges and orange juice Peaches Prunes Raisins Spinach Tomatoes Winter squash
Thiamine (vitamin B1)	Metabolism Cell function	Beriberi (affects heart and circulatory system)	Black beans Black-eyed peas	Sunflower seeds Wheat germ
Sodium	Fluid balance, muscle and nerve function	Muscle cramps Fatigue Nausea	Not found in unprocessed plant foods	

Figure 8-7. An overview of vitamins—impact and sources (used with permission from the *Lifestyle Medicine Handbook*; 2nd edition; Frates, et al.; Monterey, CA: Healthy Learning; 2021) (cont.)

Supplements

If you are following a completely plant-based diet, you need to speak with your physician about the role of supplements. For example, if you are consuming a 100 percent plant-based diet, you are at risk for deficiency of vitamin B12, or cobalamin. Some plant-based foods may contain small amounts of B12, but they are not reliable sources. The safest way to ensure that you are obtaining adequate B12 is to take a supplement daily or twice weekly. The general recommendation is 1,000 mcg twice a week or 200-300 mcg per day. You may need to be tested for your levels of B12 in case they are very low and require a different dose or type of supplement.

Another vitamin that sometimes requires supplementation is vitamin D. If you get sun exposure, you may not need this supplement. The recommendation is a daily intake of 1,000-2,000 IU per day in order to achieve optimal vitamin D status. Vitamin D enhances calcium and phosphorus absorption and is important for the health of your bones and teeth. Vitamin D also acts to support the health of our immune system and central nervous system. Furthermore, there is evidence that vitamin D may play a role in insulin regulation and supporting glucose control. It has even been found to support lung function and heart health. In addition, vitamin D may play a role in the prevention of colon, prostate, and breast cancers. In terms of emotions, low levels of vitamin D have been connected to low mood or depression. Your primary care physician can check your vitamin D levels and help you normalize your levels with supplementation if needed.

Another element that may be lacking in your body is the mineral iron, which is found in both plant-based foods (non-heme iron), as well as in animal products (heme iron). In order to optimize absorption of non-heme iron, it is best to consume it along with vitamin C-rich foods, such as bell peppers, citrus fruits, and carrots. Non-heme iron is found in many plant sources, including spinach, lentils, peas, beans, broccoli, and tofu.

Yet another essential element that may be at an insufficient level in your body is omega-3 fatty acids, which are essential for good health. Omega-3 fatty acids are primarily found in fish, but flaxseeds, chia seeds, hemp seeds, walnuts, and soybeans are also excellent plant-based sources. These plant-based sources provide the parent omega-3 fatty acid, alpha-linolenic acid (ALA). In turn, some of the ALA gets converted into eicosapentaenoic acid (EPA) and docosahexaenoic acid (DHA) in the body. Plants in the ocean make most EPA and DHA, and thus the omega-3 fatty acids in fish come from the plants they consume. If you follow an exclusively plant-based diet, it is important to ensure sufficient intake of plant-based sources to reach the recommended levels of EPA and DHA.

Iodine is an essential mineral that is added to some table salt (iodized salt) and is also naturally found in certain foods. If you eat a plant-predominant diet and do not use iodized salt, you need to include foods that contain iodine, such as sea vegetables (kelp, wakame, and nori), lima beans, and prunes. If you don't regularly get iodine from iodized salt or food sources, discuss supplementation with your physician.

The specific aforementioned dietary supplements mentioned can be beneficial to your health. However, taking additional dietary supplements can also involve health risks. It is important to be aware that the Food and Drug Administration is not authorized to review dietary supplement products for safety and effectiveness before they are marketed. If you wish to take a new supplement, it would be advisable to review your decision with your doctor.

Additional information on supplements is also available from the following sources:

- National Institutes of Health: Office of Dietary Supplements ods.od.nih.gov/
- National Center for Complementary and Integrative Medicine nccih.nih.gov/
- Dietary Supplement Fact Sheets https://ods.od.nih.gov/factsheets/list-all/
- Food and Drug Administration Information on Dietary Supplements: fda.gov/food/dietary-supplements/

Food Labels

Food labels help you understand a food's composition to determine if you want to include it in your diet. When you see ingredients lists that have unrecognizable names, it often indicates the item is highly processed. Usually the fewer ingredients a label has, the less processed the food and the higher the nutrient density. Reviewing nutrition labels allows you to gain a better understanding of your food, especially while working toward healthier eating.

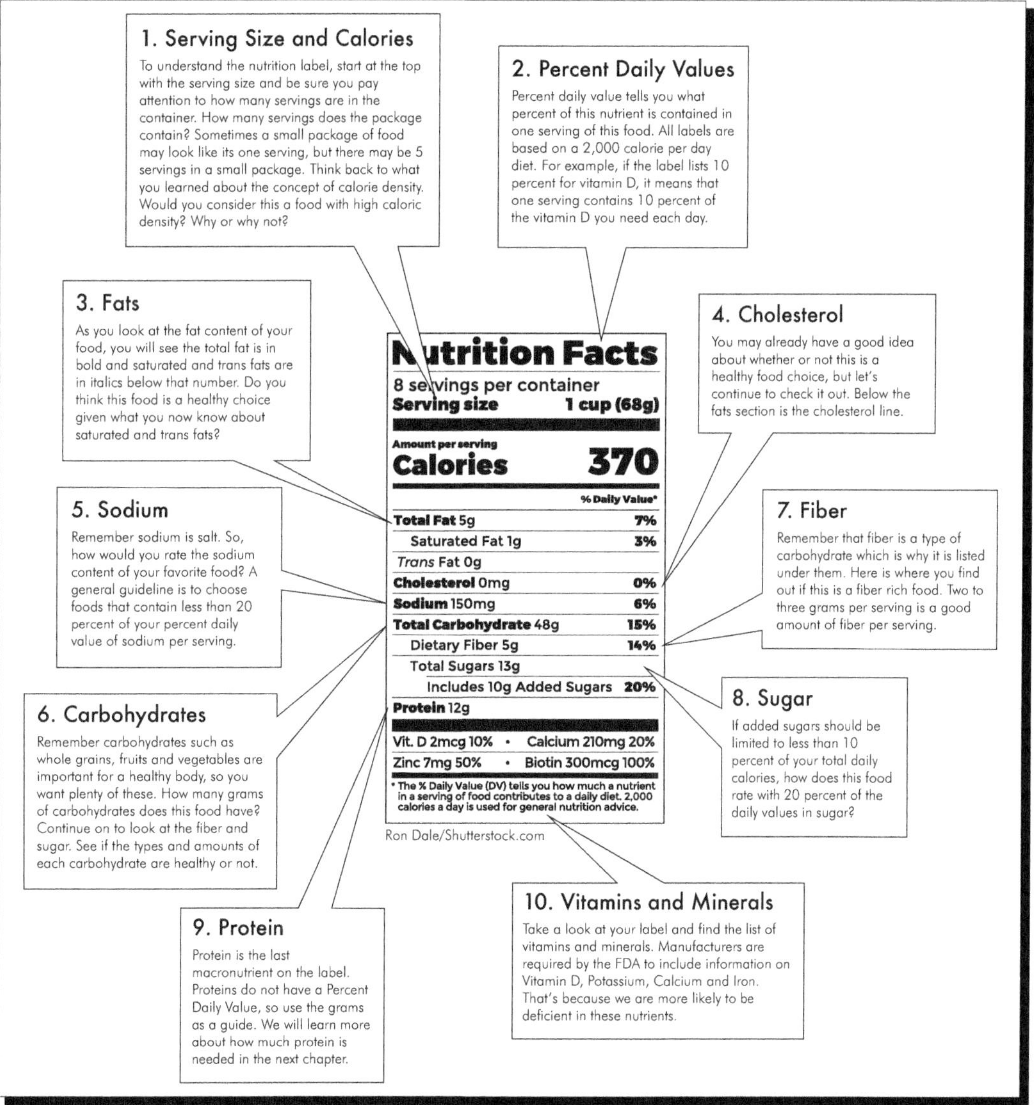

Figure 8-8. An overview of a sample food label (used with permission from *The Teen Lifestyle Medicine Handbook*; Beth Frates et al.; Monterey, CA: Healthy Learning; 2021)

❑ Reflection Time:

Do you look at food labels when you go shopping? If not, do you want to begin doing so? Why or why not?

❑ Reflection Time:

What is most important to you when looking at a food label?

Food Processing Spectrum

Foods that are unprocessed or minimally processed typically have more health benefits than foods that are highly processed. Unprocessed and minimally processed foods are typically filled with fiber, phytonutrients, vitamins, and minerals.

Foods layered in added sugar, fat, and salt tend to be excessively rewarding in your brain and release large amounts of dopamine. They are often referred to as hyper-palatable foods. Food scientists and engineers work hard to craft just the right ratios of sugar, fat, and salt, so that the food triggers the greatest reward signals in your brain and makes people come back repeatedly for the same taste.

Unprocessed or Minimally-processed	Moderately-processed	Highly-processed
CORN on the cob, plain and simple, is unprocessed. **Corn off the cob** is essentially unprocessed as well.	**Polenta** is made from cornmeal and water. **Corn tortillas** are made primarily of corn. Avoid versions with added oil and refined flour.	**Frosted Flakes** should be self-explanatory here. **Tortilla chips** are very high in fat and salt.
POTATOES contain <1 cal/gram and have both fiber and protein. They will fill you up for few calories. Not all "white" foods are "highly refined". White bread is highly refined, but white potatoes are an excellent, unrefined choice.	**Homefries** may have added salt and oil, but mostly still resemble potatoes.	**Potato chips** are loaded with oil and salt and contain 6 cal/gram. **Smiley fries** are very cute, but are highly refined and look nothing like potatoes anymore.
WHEAT... is not very palatable in its unrefined form. **Shredded wheat** often has one ingredient... wheat. Avoid versions that contain salt or are frosted with sugar.	**100% whole grain pasta** has few ingredients. If it does not say **100%**, it probably contains refined flours also. Choose **100% whole grain bread** with 5 ingredients or less and no added oil.	**Breakfast cereals** may appear healthy on the box, but often have added salt, sugar, and oil. **Crackers** are highly refined, and often contain many ingredients
Brown **RICE** is rice in its natural form, filled with vitamins, minerals, and fiber. Take a closer look: Hull, White rice, Rice bran, Rice germ	**White rice** is missing the bran and germ layers... where vitamins, minerals, and fiber are stored! Plain **rice cakes** may contain some salt, but generally have few ingredients other than puffed rice.	**Fried rice** is typically made with salt, oil, and calorie-dense sauces **Rice-based snacks** tend to have many ingredients and no longer resemble rice in its natural form.
Steel cut **OATS** are made by chopping oat groats into pieces. They take longer to prepare and have a chewy texture. **Old fashioned oats** are made by rolling out oat groats.	**Instant oats** (also known as **quick oats**) are pre-cooked, dried, and then rolled and pressed. They cook in "1 minute" as they claim and have a more porridge-like texture.	Don't be fooled! These **granola bars** contain refined flours, oil, and several types of sugar. **Instant oatmeal** is highly refined and loaded with sugar.

Source: Beth Motley MD, DipABLM, Family Medicine/Lifestyle Medicine, Prisma Health-Upstate

Figure 8-9. A comparison between unprocessed, moderately processed, and highly processed foods

❏ Reflection Time:

On the spectrum from highly processed foods, to minimally processed foods, to whole foods, where do most of your foods fall?

❏ Reflection Time:

How can you move along the spectrum toward more whole foods or more minimally processed foods?

❏ Reflection Time:

What are some examples for possible substitutions you could make when trying to eat more unprocessed or minimally processed foods?

Sugar Cycle

When you reach for candy or a cookie, you get an immediate surge in blood sugar, which helps you to feel energized and "happy." This may be pleasing to your mind, but it's alarming to your pancreas. When blood sugars are high, the pancreas works to pump out insulin to lower the blood sugar levels and bring the blood sugar into the cells. Of note, insulin is a fat-storing hormone. After insulin does its job by reducing the amount of sugar in the bloodstream, the person is often left hungry again. The cycle will continue, if they reach for another food that is high in sugar.

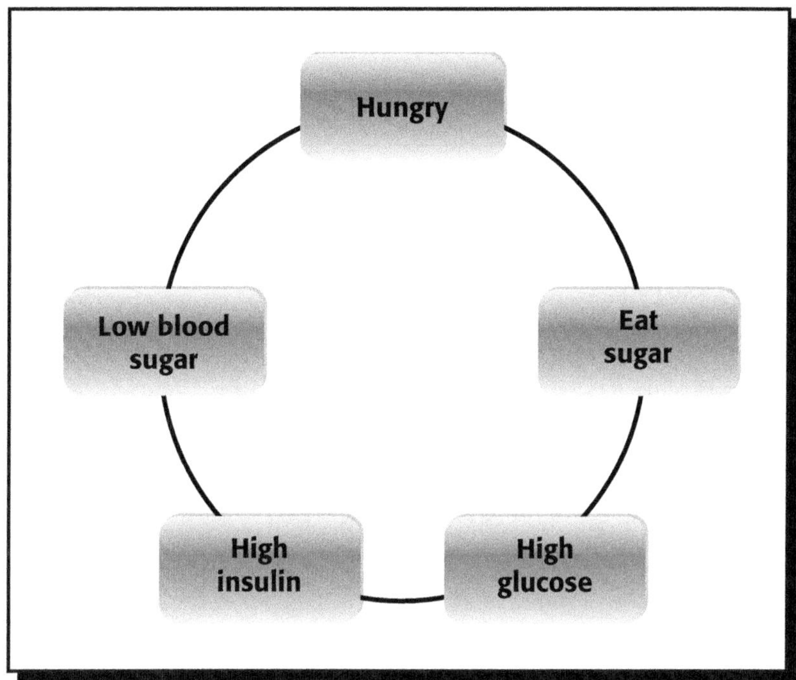

Figure 8-10. Sugar cycle (used with permission from *Lifestyle Medicine Handbook*; 2nd edition; Beth Frates et al.; Monterey, CA: Healthy Learning; 2021)

❑ Reflection Time:

Have you ever experienced the sugar cycle? What happened? How did you feel?

____

____

____

____

____

____

____

____

____

❏ Reflection Time:

How can you avoid the sugar cycle? What can you eat instead?

____

____

____

____

____

____

____

____

Macronutrients

Macronutrients include the carbohydrates, fats, and proteins that the body needs in relatively large amounts.

CARBOHYDRATES

❏ Limit and Avoid:

- Simple carbohydrates—refined and highly processed carbohydrates, such as sugar, white bread and pasta, candy, cookies, cakes, jelly, and packaged goodies
- Refined carbohydrates can increase triglycerides, risk of diabetes, and reduce HDL (the good cholesterol).
- Note that fruits and vegetables contain simple carbohydrates but are still recommended because of the fiber, phytonutrients, vitamins, and minerals that they contain.

❏ Prefer:

- Complex carbohydrates (whole grains)—whole wheat, quinoa, amaranth, bulgur, brown rice, wheat germ, oat bran, and oatmeal
- Higher intake of fiber from whole grains is associated with a decreased risk of diabetes and coronary heart disease.

FATS

There are several types of fat, including:

- Saturated fat: typically found in animal products and is less healthy
- Unsaturated fat: typically found in plant-based foods and is considered more healthy than saturated and trans fats.

- Trans fat: the unhealthiest type of fat that is found in small amounts in animal products and is also manufactured for processed foods. Since it is associated with many chronic diseases, there are significant efforts to ban its use in processed foods. Trans fat is a type of fat made in a factory (trans fats do not occur in food naturally) and are most often in processed foods.
- Cholesterol: manufactured in the body. It is a waxy, fat-like substance that is found in all the cells in the body.

❏ Avoid:

- Trans fats
- Solid fat and added sugar (SoFAs)

❏ Limit:

- Saturated fats (meats, full fat dairy, packaged desserts)

❏ Enjoy in Moderation:

- Monounsaturated fats (olive oil)
- Polyunsaturated fats (corn oil, sunflower oil, soybean oil)
- Omega 3 fats (fish—salmon, mackerel, herring, tuna; walnuts, flaxseeds)
- Omega 6 fats (oils—palm, sesame, soybean, sunflower, corn)
- Keep omega 3 intake greater than omega 6 intake

Consuming trans fat—the unhealthiest type of fat that is found in small amounts in animal products and is also manufactured for processed foods—should be avoided.

Africa Studio/Shutterstock.com

PROTEIN

> *"Eating healthy protein sources, like beans, nuts, fish, or poultry, in place of red meat and processed meat can lower the risk of several diseases and premature death."*
>
> —Dr. Frank Hu
> Chair of the Harvard
> Department of Nutrition

There are two sources of protein—plants and animals:

- Plant-based: beans, tofu, vegetables (avocados), quinoa, nuts, seeds, and non-dairy milks, such as almond, rice, and cashew
- Animal-based: fish, meat, turkey, chicken, dairy, and game meats

Protein Sources: A Head-to-Head Comparison

A food's worth is not judged by grams of protein alone! Look at the bigger picture.
Each serving below is **100g** (about **½ cup** or **3.5 oz**).

Chicken
Breast, meat only, baked

Nutrition Facts
Serving Size 100g (½ cup)

Amount per serving	
Calories 164	Calories from Fat 32
	% Daily Value
Total Fat 4g	5%
Saturated fat 1g	5%
Cholesterol 85mg	28%
Sodium 74 mg	3%
Total Carbohydrate 0g	0%
Dietary Fiber 0g	0%
Protein 31g	

Salmon
Atlantic, baked

Nutrition Facts
Serving Size 100g (½ cup)

Amount per serving	
Calories 208	Calories from Fat 121
	% Daily Value
Total Fat 13g	21%
Saturated fat 3g	15%
Cholesterol 55mg	18%
Sodium 59mg	2%
Total Carbohydrate 0g	0%
Dietary Fiber 0g	0%
Protein 20g	

Steak
Trimmed to 1/8" fat, baked

Nutrition Facts
Serving Size 100g (½ cup)

Amount per serving	
Calories 189	Calories from Fat 100
	% Daily Value
Total Fat 11g	17%
Saturated fat 4g	22%
Cholesterol 41mg	14%
Sodium 53mg	2%
Total Carbohydrate 0g	0%
Dietary Fiber 0g	0%
Protein 21g	

Nutrition facts from www.NutritionData.com.

Beans
Black, boiled

Nutrition Facts
Serving Size 100g (½ cup)

Amount per serving	
Calories 132	Calories from Fat 5
	% Daily Value
Total Fat 1g	1%
Saturated fat 0g	1%
Cholesterol 0mg	0%
Sodium 1mg	0%
Total Carbohydrate 24g	8%
Dietary Fiber 9g	35%
Protein 9g	

Cholesterol is only found in animal-based foods. These foods are also our main source of saturated fat, which our bodies can turn into cholesterol. Fiber helps to lower our cholesterol and is only found in plant-based foods.

How much protein does the average person need each day?
Multiple your body weight (kg) by 0.66 to calculate your **Estimated Average Requirement (EAR)**.

	125 lb	175 lb	225 lb	275 lb
Estimated Average Requirement (EAR)	**38 g**	**52 g**	**67 g**	**82 g**
Average intake by U.S. adults	68-86 g	96-120 g	122-153 g	150-187 g

Beth Motley M.D.
Family Medicine/Lifestyle Medicine
Greenville Health System/Univ of South Carolina

Figure 8-11. Nutrition facts for four different sources of protein (used with permission of the American College of Lifestyle Medicine)

❑ Reflection Time:

Where do you typically get your protein?

____

____

____

____

____

____

____

❑ Reflection Time:

Have you tried any plant sources of protein? What was your experience with these foods?

____

____

____

____

____

____

____

Food and Your Brain

Fortunately, the same high-quality dietary pattern that supports heart health is beneficial for your brain, as well as for the rest of your body. Foods containing omega-3 fatty acids, antioxidants, and B vitamins are particularly important for optimal brain function. Healthy foods support your mental function and mood, as well as decrease the risk of dementia.

Food impacts your brain, as well as the rest of your body. Harvard Health[3] encourages you to incorporate the following foods into your diet, as they have been associated with "better brainpower:"

- Green veggies, such as kale and spinach may slow cognitive decline.
- Fatty fish, such as salmon, have high levels of omega-3 fatty acids that are linked to lower beta-amyloid levels (a protein piece connected with Alzheimer's disease).
- Berries, such as blueberries and strawberries, have high levels of pigments called flavonoids that can help improve memory.
- Tea and coffee—recent research suggests that drinking these beverages may support mental function.
- Nuts, especially walnuts, have been shown, in some studies, to possibly improve memory.

❑ Reflection Time:

Do you think that your current food choices impact your emotional and cognitive health? Explain.

❑ Reflection Time:

Do you notice any changes physically, emotionally, or cognitively when you eat certain types of foods? Explain.

HEALTHY EATING FOR A HEALTHY WEIGHT

Food nourishes your body and mind. It also helps you to achieve and maintain a healthy weight. This section addresses several key concepts and principles that may assist you with achieving or maintaining a healthy weight. If you are overweight, underweight, struggle with an eating disorder, have a medical condition that you want dietary support for, or just want help with eating more healthfully, ask your doctor for a referral to a registered dietitian. They can support you with specific food recommendations around your health needs.

Nutrient Density & Calorie Density

You can think of your food in terms of caloric density and nutrient density. After a review of Figures 8-12 and 8-13, you will see that many plant foods are on the lower end of the calorie-density spectrum but have very high nutrient density. On the opposite end of the spectrum, you'll find foods high in added sugars and fats that are calorie dense but not necessarily nutrient dense.

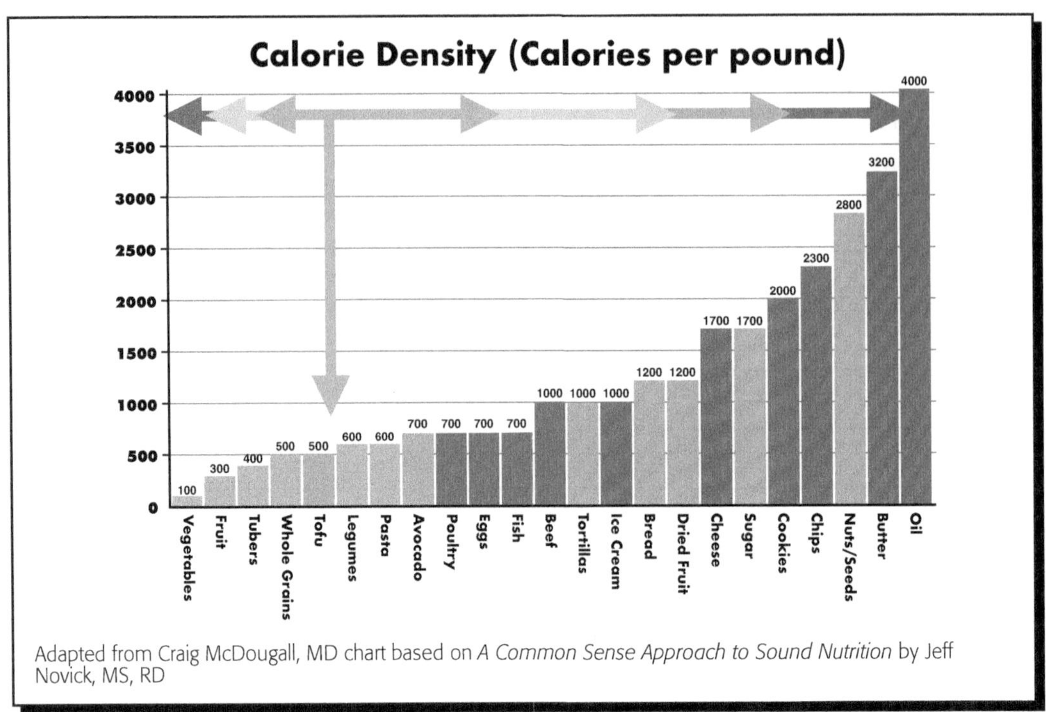

Adapted from Craig McDougall, MD chart based on *A Common Sense Approach to Sound Nutrition* by Jeff Novick, MS, RD

Figure 8-12. Calorie density chart (used with permission from the *Lifestyle Medicine Handbook*; 2nd edition; Beth Frates, et al.; Monterey, CA: Healthy Learning; 2021)

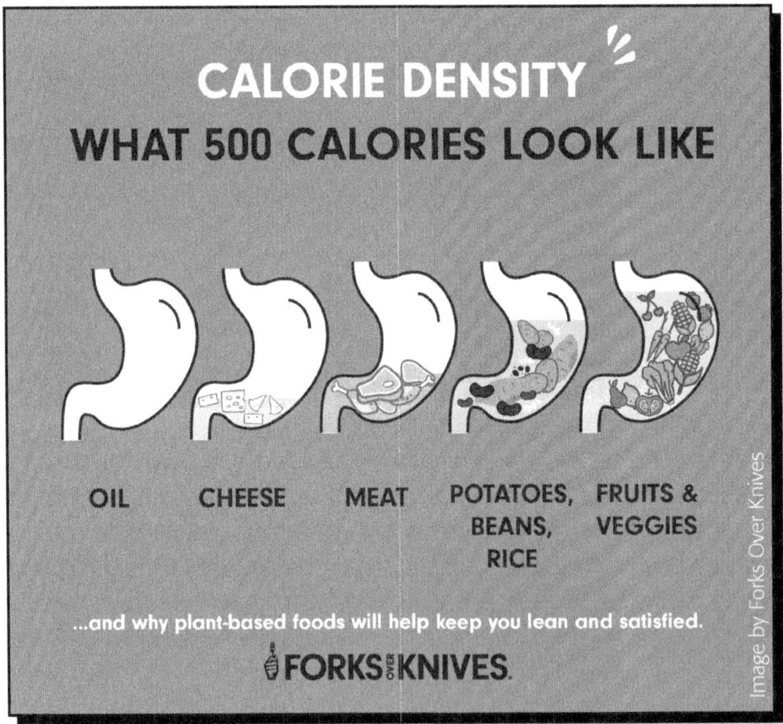

Figure 8-13. What 500 calories look like

Choosing more low-calorie density/high-nutrient density foods (fruits and vegetables) and fewer high-calorie density/low-nutrient density foods (meats, cheese, sugars, and oils) will keep you full, satisfied, and healthier. It will also help you with achieving and maintaining a healthy weight, if you are overweight or want to maintain your current weight.

❑ Reflection Time:

What foods do you enjoy that are nutrient dense?

❑ Reflection Time:

What foods do you eat that are non-nutrient dense?

❑ Reflection Time:

What could you do to increase the nutrient density of your typical food choices?

❑ Reflection Time:

Do you feel different when you eat nutrient-dense versus non-nutrient-dense foods? Explain.

____

____

____

____

____

____

____

____

____

Satiety

Satiety is experiencing fullness. There are different signals for feeling hungry and experiencing satiety. The hypothalamus in your brain regulates your appetite. There are two hormones involved—ghrelin and leptin. Ghrelin increases your appetite, while leptin suppresses it. When you don't get enough sleep, ghrelin levels go up and leptin levels go down. Your hypothalamus is sensitive to changes in your lifestyle.

It takes 20 minutes for the brain to get the signal that it is full. Eating slowly will help to ensure that your brain receives the proper signals from your stomach. Eating at regular times, with three meals and two snacks a day, helps to avoid excessive hunger and reaching for simple carbohydrates that can throw you into the sugar cycle previously described. Another signal for fullness is a distended stomach that happens after drinking water or filling up on fiber or fruits and vegetables. In addition, the following tips can help you control your food intake:

- It takes about 20 minutes to feel full; accordingly, eat slowly and mindfully.
- Eat at regular times (three times a day with two snacks) to keep your blood glucose steady.
- Fill up with fiber-rich and nutrient-rich foods
- Drink enough water before every meal.
- Get enough sleep; ghrelin (appetite-increasing hormone) increases with a lack of sleep.
- Avoid getting into the sugar cycle.

Portion Distortion

Over the last few decades, portion sizes have dramatically increased, especially at restaurants. To achieve and maintain a healthy weight, be mindful of portion.

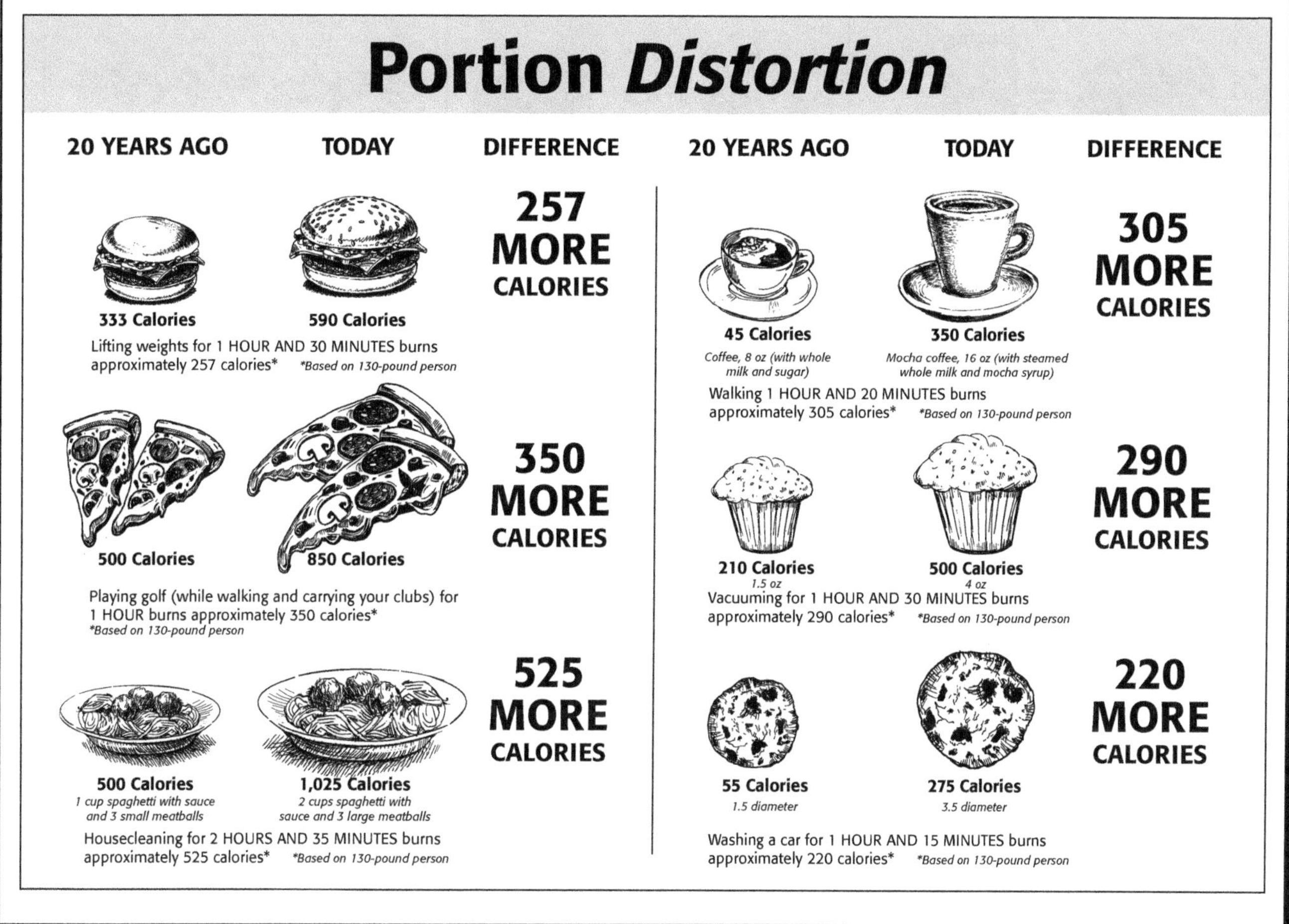

Figure 8-14. An example of how portion distortion has affected six common foods (used with permission from the *Lifestyle Medicine Handbook*; 2nd edition; Beth Frates, et al.; Monterey, CA: Healthy Learning; 2021)

Serving Sizes

When trying to increase or decrease your intake of certain types of foods, it is helpful to understand what a typical serving looks like. Having this frame of reference allows you to more easily match your desired behaviors with your actual food consumption.

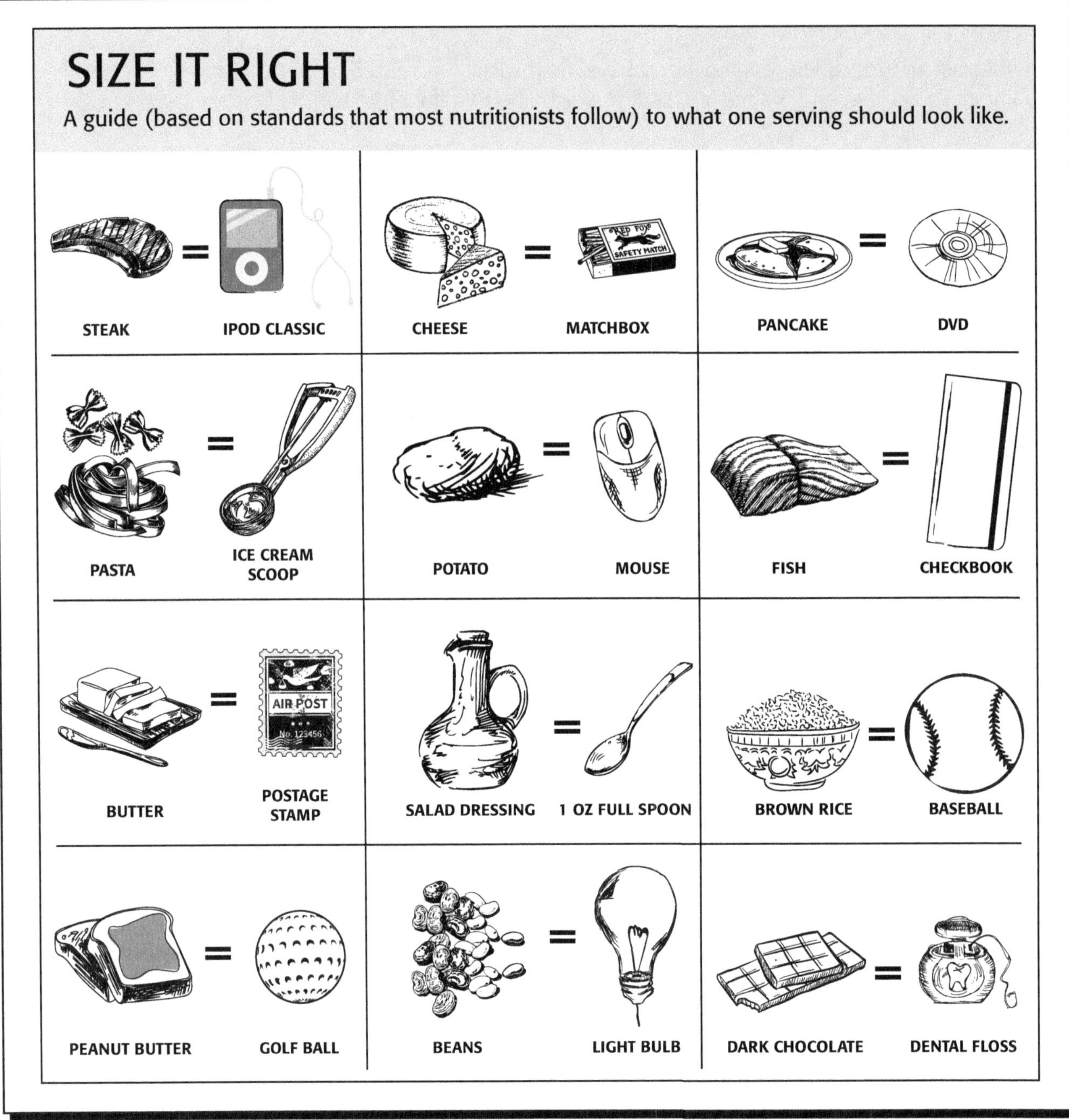

Figure 8-15. A guide (based on standards that most registered dieticians and nutrition professionals follow) to what one serving should look like (used with permission from the *Lifestyle Medicine Handbook*; 2nd edition; Beth Frates, et al.; Monterey, CA: Healthy Learning; 2021)

HAND SYMBOL	EQUIVALENT	FOODS	CALORIES
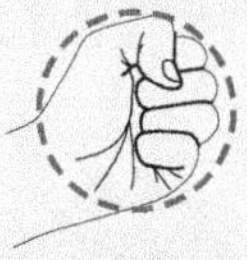	**Fist** 1 cup	Rice, pasta Fruit Veggies	200 75 40
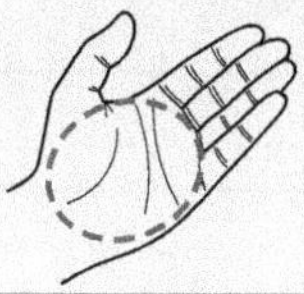	**Palm** 3 ounces	Meat Fish Poultry	160 160 160
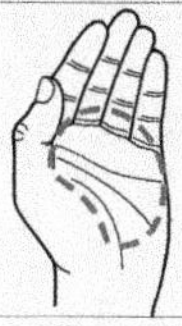	**Handful** 1 ounce	Nuts Raisins	170 85
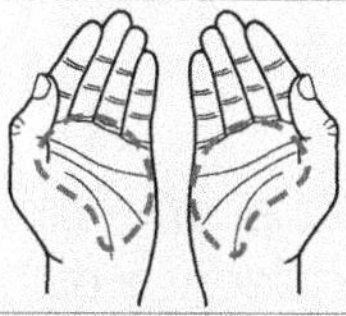	**2 Handfuls** 1 ounce	Chips Popcorn Pretzels	150 120 100
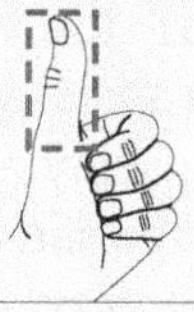	**Thumb** 1 ounce	Peanut butter Hard cheese	170 100
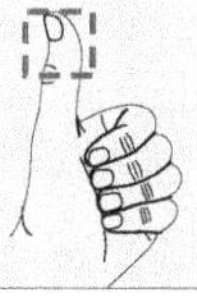	**Thumb tip** 1 teaspoon	Cooking oil Mayonnaise, butter Sugar	40 35 15

Figure 8-16. An example of a hand-based portion size chart (used with permission from the *Lifestyle Medicine Handbook*; 2nd edition; Beth Frates, et al.; Monterey, CA: Healthy Learning; 2021)

❑ Reflection Time:

Did anything surprise you about the typical serving sizes in Figures 8-15 and 8-16? Explain.

____

____

____

____

____

____

____

____

❑ Reflection Time:

Are there certain foods that you have a difficult time with portion control? If yes, what are they and how can you limit your intake moving forward?

____

____

____

____

____

____

Fueling Up With Fiber: The Role of the Gut Microbiome

The World Health Organization (WHO) recommends that people consume between 25 and 29 grams of fiber each day. Fiber lowers the incidence of type 2 diabetes, heart disease, stroke, and colon cancer. When you eat fiber, the friendly bacteria in your gastrointestinal tract ferment it. This process produces short-chain fatty acids, including acetate, propionate, and butyrate. These short-chain fatty acids play key roles in regulating your metabolism, immune system, and cell proliferation. In addition, consuming fiber creates a diverse microbiome, which is also important for health.

Another important factor for health is a healthy intestinal lining, with well-functioning epithelial cells, and a layer of mucus for a barrier. The mucosal layer and epithelial cells act as a filter for stopping opportunistic microbes from entering your body's systems and causing inflammation. Inflammation is the common denominator associated with diabetes, cardiovascular disease, and obesity, as well as many other chronic conditions. Working on ways to increase the friendly bacteria in the intestines helps your health in many ways. Fermented foods such as yogurt, sauerkraut, and tempeh also support intestinal health. In that regard, for a diverse gut microbiome, it is good to consume a variety of fiber rich foods as well as fermented foods.

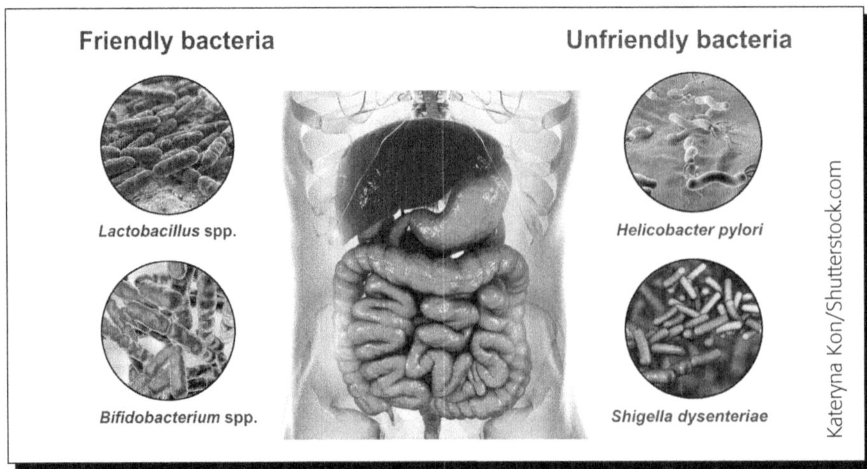

Figure 8-17. Gastrointestinal bacteria

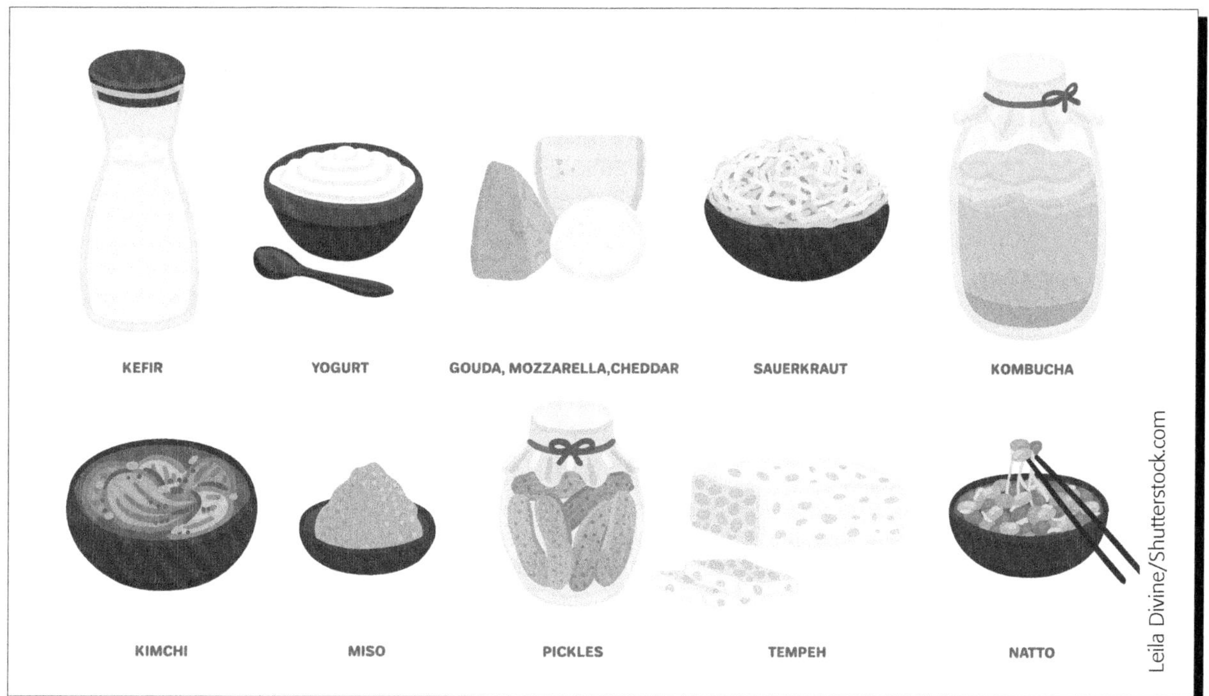

Figure 8-18. Fermented foods

Intermittent Fasting

In some cases, it's not just the quality and quantity of the food, but also the timing. For many people sticking with a strict three meals a day and two snacks eating pattern helps them to stay satisfied and full throughout the day with a steady state of blood glucose. Other people are looking to lose weight or combat aging through lifestyle. For these reasons, intermittent fasting often comes into the eating equation. Intermittent fasting has helped many individuals lose weight. Some people can sustain an intermittent fasting schedule for months and years, while others struggle with it after two to three months.

There are different intermittent fasting schedules that can work. The most straightforward and most sustainable for most people is the 12-12 schedule. This involves eating for 12 hours and fasting for 12 hours. Then, there are a variety of other options, such as eating for 10 hours and fasting 14 hours. There is also research on the 8-16 schedule, which is eating for eight hours and fasting for 16. This could be eating between 7 a.m. and 3 p.m., or eating between 1-9 p.m., or a different combination that works for an individual.

The benefits of this type of intermittent fasting are numerous, including increasing human growth hormone as much as five-fold, which could help with fat loss and muscle gain. Research also reveals that intermittent fasting may help with cellular repair and autophagy, a process by which cells clear out the "trash," i.e., old, degenerative, and dysfunctional proteins. These proteins can build up in cells, if they are not removed. Lastly, intermittent fasting might have an impact on gene expression and encourage longevity genes to be expressed.

Intuitive Eating

When you are in tune with your own body's physiological signals, you can listen to your hunger and thirst signals. Remembering that people have natural ways to indicate that they have eaten enough with the satiety signals reviewed previously, you can work to let your body's signals steer your eating patterns. With intuitive eating, you eat when you feel hungry, not when you feel stressed.

Stress eating is a coping strategy that many people utilize daily, as well as during the nighttime. Many people eat at night, either from boredom, habit, or to keep them energized, while they work late into the night. Food is fuel. One thing to be mindful about, in addition to how you are fueling your body, is when you are fueling your body. If you follow the circadian rhythm, you are awake 16 hours and asleep eight hours. Listening to your body for sleep and for eating is similar. You have signals for sleep and signals for hunger, as well as for satiety.

Interoception is the sense and understanding of what is going on inside your body. Slowing down to actually feel your body—when you are hungry or when you are thirsty is key. In fact, some people mistake thirst for hunger, meaning they think they are hungry, when they are thirsty. So, grabbing a glass of water is a good way to check to see if it is thirst or if it is hunger you are feeling. Investigations will play a role in this instance, when you are learning how to "read" your own body language and inner signals. Being in tune with your hunger signals will help you to nourish your body, when it is ready and wanting nourishment.

Mindful Eating

Mindful eating is related to the philosophy of mindfulness, which refers to the practice of being fully aware of your thoughts, feelings, and sensations during the present moment. When you eat mindfully, you use all your physical and emotional senses, as you enjoy your food. A mindful approach to eating means that you make your food choices, based on what will nourish your body. The following is a useful exercise to practice mindful eating.

❑ Mindful Eating of a Raisin

To practice mindful eating, you can use a raisin (or another food, such as a piece of dark chocolate). You will use all your senses as you savor this small piece of food. Take your time.

- #1—Put the raisin in your and feel it. It is small but has texture. Look at it carefully and examine all the tiny crevices. See the color and variations in color with the light. Did you select a black or yellow raisin? Smell the raisin. Does it have its own scent?
- #2—Now place the raisin in your mouth, but do not chew it yet. Feel the weight of it on your tongue. Move it around with your tongue. Feel the saliva accumulate in your mouth.
- #3—Next, bite into the raisin. Just take one bite. Taste that one bite. Let the raisin sit in your mouth while you savor the flavor.
- #4—Chew the raisin and hear yourself chewing. Listen to the sound of your mouth, as it manages the raisin. Chew slowly and then more quickly. Be aware of the speed of your chewing. Also, be aware of how hard you are biting down on that raisin. Try to bite softly and then more firmly.

- #5—Notice when you swallow and how you swallow. Listen to the sound of swallowing.
- #6—When the entire raisin is gone, you are done.

❑ Reflection Time:

How long did that exercise take? Try it again if you like. What did you learn?

Overcoming Common Barriers

OBSTACLE—LACK OF ACCESS OR LACK OF FUNDS

Strategies:

- Cook meals at home.
- Explore food pantries or SNAP (Supplemental Nutrition Assistance Programs), if you qualify.
- Talk to a local social worker or health/patient navigator.
- Support community-sponsored agriculture.
- Web search "healthy eating budget" for great tips.
- Remember that frozen and canned (limiting salt) vegetables are better than no vegetables.
- Plant your own vegetables like carrots, lettuce, zucchini, and tomatoes.
- Eat less meat or use other less-expensive protein sources, such as beans.
- Purchase healthy foods in bulk.
- Shop for in-season produce.
- If you have too many fruits and vegetables, freeze and use later.
- Pack your lunch rather than eating out.
- Use coupons.
- Stick to your grocery list.
- Don't shop when you're hungry.

Total Cost Per Week

- Approximately: $30-$50 per person, per week
- Removing spices (as only have to buy every few months) saves $1 per week.

Other ways to make the weekly menu cheaper:

- Buy in the biggest size packages available, or from the bulk bins.
- See if you are eligible for WIC, CalFresh or similar programs in your area.
- Buy dried beans and cook yourself rather than canned (saves over $4 per person per week).
- Buy frozen fruits and vegetables, and/or whichever are discounted (fresh or frozen).
- Substitute other nuts in recipes for peanut butter or other cheaper nuts.
- Repeat some of the cheaper meals on the menu - many are less than $1 per serve!

BREAKFAST

Tofu Potato Scramble

- 1 medium potato, cooked, diced
- ½ cup soft tofu
- 1 large tomato, diced
- 1 cup fresh or frozen spinach (thawed)
- 2 large mushrooms, diced
- ½ tsp curry powder, to taste
- ½ cup homemade soy cottage cheese (see staples)

Mix all ingredients together, cook in a non-stick pan, stirring, until warmed through and vegetables are soft.

Breakfast Nutrition:
457 Calories.
35g Protein.
15g Fat.
54g Carbohydrates.
Price per serve: $1.24 - $1.68

Hummus

- 1 x 16 oz chickpeas (canned or cooked from dry). 4 oz dry = equivalent to a 16 oz can (roughly 8 oz yield beans when strained, or 1.5 cups).
- 2 Tbsp lemon juice (or juice of one lemon)
- ¼ cup soy milk
- Cumin spice (optional)

Blend or food process until smooth.

Price per ¼ cup serve:

- Dry chickpeas: Approximately 16c per serving

- Canned chickpeas: Approximately 35c per serving

Spice containers can be purchased for 99 cents in most stores. One serving is approximately 2 cents.

LUNCH

Mexican Rice Bowl

- 1 cup cooked brown rice
- ½ cup cooked or canned pinto beans, drained
- ½ cup fresh or frozen corn, thawed
- ½ cucumber, diced
- ¼ cup bought salsa (or homemade with chopped tomato, onions, lime, garlic, cilantro, and peppers)
- ½ avocado, chopped
- ½ tsp Mexican Spice mix, to taste

Mix cucumber and salsa, set aside. Warm pinto beans and corn with spice. Top rice with bean mix, avocado, and salsa mix, and serve.

Lunch Nutrition:
573 Calories.
17g Protein.
13.5g Fat.
102g Carbohydrates.
Price per serve: $1.07 - $2.58

DINNER

Potato Chickpea Curry

- 1 large potato, diced
- ½ cup cooked or canned chickpeas, drained
- 1 cup fresh or canned tomatoes, diced
- 1 carrot, diced
- 1 cup fresh or frozen broccoli, chopped
- ½ tsp curry powder, to taste
- ¼ cup homemade yogurt (see staples)

Mix together all ingredients except yogurt, and cook until soft. Stir in yogurt to serve.

Dinner Nutrition:
485 Calories.
22.5g Protein.
6g Fat.
92g Carbohydrates.
Price per serve: $1.09 - $1.94

Figure 8-19. A sample overview of how to eat on a budget (used with permission from ACLM–*Eating on a Budget*)

OBSTACLE—UNHEALTHY SOCIAL INFLUENCES OR LACK OF FAMILY SUPPORT

Strategies:

- Involve your family in the process.
- Choose recipes with your children and partner.
- Shop together.
- Cook as a family.
- Eat family meals.
- Discuss food as fuel.
- Offer to let your children try your food.
- Do taste tests together as a family.
- Don't let others sabotage your healthful choices.
- Bring healthful foods to group gatherings.
- Try a "meatless Monday."
- Develop a support system.

❏ Reflection Time:

Who can support you on your journey toward healthier eating?

❏ Reflection Time:

How can they support you?

OBSTACLE—LACK OF RELIABLE KNOWLEDGE OR COOKING SKILLS

Strategies:

- Explore the resource section at the end of this chapter.
- Take a cooking class.
- Experiment with recipes.
- Buy cookbooks or borrow one from the library.
- Watch an online cooking video.

OBSTACLE—INCONVENIENCE OR LACK OF TIME

Strategies:

- Plan and prepare.
- Make a shopping list.
- Do batch cooking.
- Freeze healthy items for busy nights.
- Try a meal delivery service.
- Chop vegetables in bulk.
- Keep vegetables and fruits precut and in clear containers.
- Keep healthy foods readily accessible.
- Travel to the office or in your car with healthy snacks.
- Bring your lunch with you.

OBSTACLE—HABIT OR BEING ACCUSTOMED TO LESS-HEALTHY FOODS

Strategies:

- Try foods from various cultures.
- Explore websites, books, and social media for recipes.
- Try a variety of spices.
- Experiment with new grains, vegetables, and fruits.
- Try different cooking methods and find what you like.
- Remember that repeated exposure is often necessary to enjoy new foods.
- Recognize that your tastes will change, as you decrease eating highly processed foods.
- Eat mindfully and avoid distracted eating.
- Find healthier alternatives to some of your favorite less-healthy foods.

OBSTACLE—HISTORY OF FAILED HEALTHY EATING ATTEMPTS

Strategies:

- Focus on progress, not perfection.
- Remember your effort is a life-long journey.
- Recognize that small changes make big differences.
- Celebrate your successes.
- Involve others who are supportive.
- Increase your chances of success with including health professionals on your team, such as a registered dietitian, a wellness coach, a certified personal trainer, etc.

❑ Reflection Time:

What barriers and obstacles do you envision may get in your way of healthy eating?

❑ Reflection Time:

What strategies can you brainstorm for overcoming some of these barriers?

❑ Reflection Time:

What resources do you have available to you?

Get Rolling Through MOSS: Motivation, Obstacles, Strategies, and Strengths

MOSS is an acronym to help you create a plan to increase healthy movement or eating.

"A rolling stone gathers no moss, but it gains a certain polish."

—Oliver Herford
English Writer and Artist

❑ Question (motivation):

Why are you motivated to eat healthier?

❑ Question (obstacles):

What obstacles are you likely to encounter?

❑ Question (strategies):

What strategies can you use to overcome these obstacles?

❑ Question (strengths):

What strengths can you draw upon as you work toward your goal? Consider strengths that you've used to overcome previous challenges and your support system, including your healthcare team, family, and friends.

SMART Goal

In order to take what you have learned about healthy eating and put it into action, create a SMART goal for yourself (refer to Chapter 4 page 55 for detailed information concerning what a SMART goal entails).

❑ SMART Goal Time:

What is your SMART goal for nutrition? (Specific, Measurable, Action-oriented, Realistic, Time-sensitive)

Health Food Options

There are several possible dishes you can make that are healthy, including the following (Figures 8-20 to 8-25).

AMERICAN COLLEGE OF Lifestyle Medicine

GREEN SMOOTHIE GUIDE

1 LEAFY GREENS
Choose 1-2 cups, fresh or frozen

Spinach, kale, Swiss chard, arugula, parsley, cilantro (free to add other veggies like cauliflower, zucchini, carrots, beets or pumpkin)

2 FRUIT
Choose 1-2 cups, fresh or frozen

Blueberry, strawberry, raspberry, pear, pineapple, banana, apple, mango, cherries, peaches, etc.

3 PROTEIN
Choose 1 serving

Hemp seeds (2-3 Tbsp), plant-based protein powder (½-1 scoop) organic silken tofu (1/2 cup), white beans or chickpeas (1/2 cup), unsweetened soy or pea milk (1 cup, counts as liquid too)

4 FAT & FIBER
Choose 1-2 tablespoons

Flax meal, chia seeds, walnuts, avocado, nut butter

5 BOOSTERS
Optional, Choose ¼ - 1 teaspoon

Spirulina, cinnamon, turmeric (+ black pepper), nutmeg, vanilla extract, Medjool date, ginger, cayenne, cacao powder, cacao nibs, mint

6 LIQUID
Choose 1-2 cups

Filtered water, unsweetened plant milk (soy, pea, almond, cashew, oat, rice), unsweetened coconut water, green tea, ice for thickness

Figure 8-20. Green smoothies (used with permission of the American College of Lifestyle Medicine)

HOW TO MAKE A FILLING SALAD

1 LEAFY GREENS
Start with a hefty base of leafy greens, 2 to 3 cups

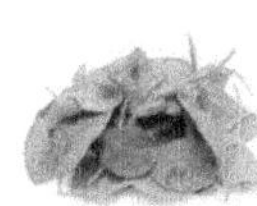 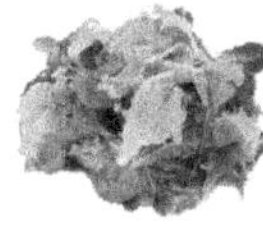   

Baby spinach, chopped kale, Swiss chard, arugula, shredded cabbage, lettuce, spring mix, shaved Brussels sprouts, etc.

2 VEGETABLES
Add texture and color with a variety of vegetables, raw, steamed or roasted, unlimited

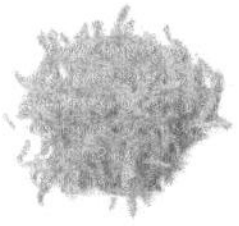   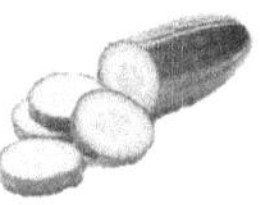 

Artichoke hearts, asparagus, bell peppers, broccoli, carrots, cauliflower, cucumber, microgreens, mushrooms, onion, snap peas, summer squash, tomatoes, etc.

3 SMART CARBS
Add filling fiber with whole grains, starchy vegetables, and/or fruit, ½ cup

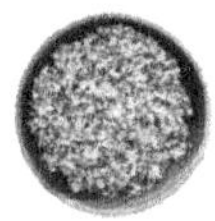  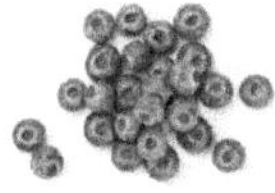  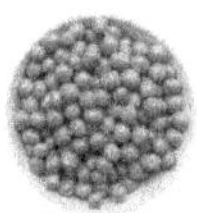

Quinoa, brown or wild rice, farro, barley, potatoes, yams, winter squash, corn, peas, mango, apples, berries, citrus segments, pomegranate seeds

4 PROTEIN
Add hearty plant protein with beans and legumes, ½ cup

  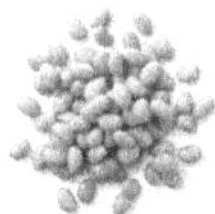  

Chickpeas, black beans, kidney beans, white beans, green peas, lentils, edamame, organic tofu, organic tempeh

5 TOPPINGS
Add crunch & flavor with nuts, seeds, fresh herbs, and/or fermented foods, 1-2 tbsp

   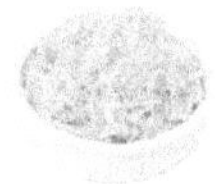 

Almonds, walnuts, pistachios, pecans, pumpkin seeds, hemp seeds, nutritional yeast, sundried tomatoes, olives, basil, chives, cilantro, parsley, sauerkraut, kimchi, etc.

6 DRESSING
Add flavor with a squeeze of citrus, a dollop of dip, or a drizzle of dressing

 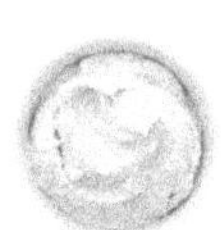  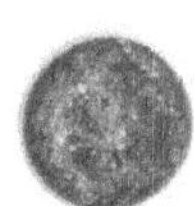 

A squeeze of lemon, lime or orange juice, guacamole, balsamic vinegar, white wine vinegar, salsa, hummus, oil-free dressing

Figure 8-21. A filling salad (used with permission of the American College of Lifestyle Medicine)

AMERICAN COLLEGE OF Lifestyle Medicine

HOW TO MAKE A NOURISH BOWL

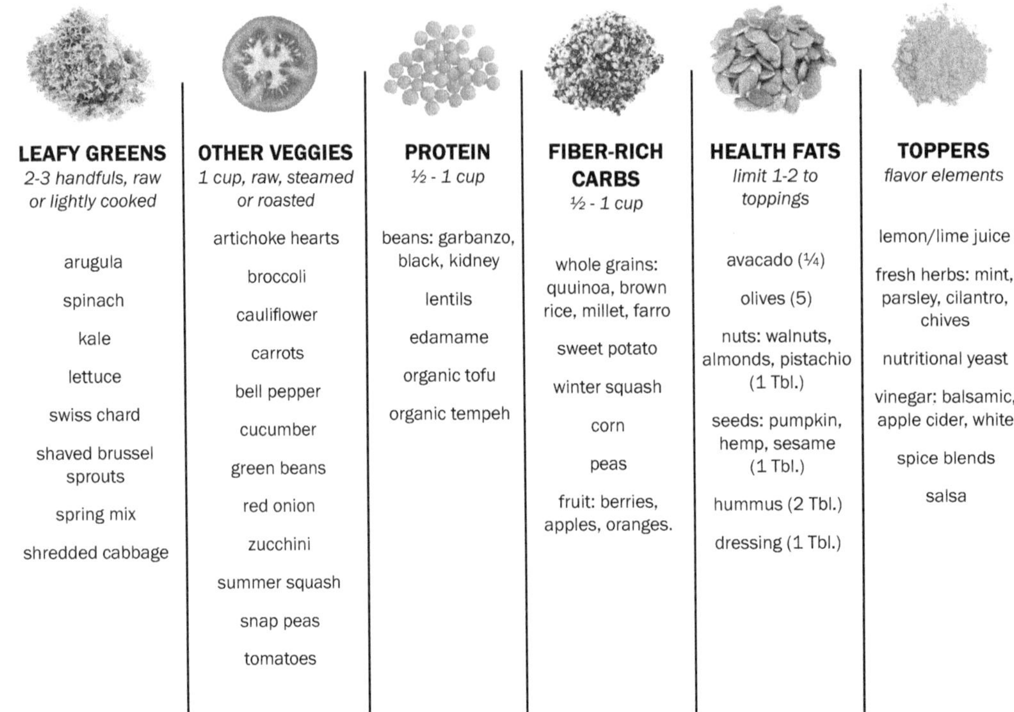

LEAFY GREENS *2-3 handfuls, raw or lightly cooked*	**OTHER VEGGIES** *1 cup, raw, steamed or roasted*	**PROTEIN** *½ - 1 cup*	**FIBER-RICH CARBS** *½ - 1 cup*	**HEALTH FATS** *limit 1-2 to toppings*	**TOPPERS** *flavor elements*
arugula	artichoke hearts	beans: garbanzo, black, kidney	whole grains: quuinoa, brown rice, millet, farro	avacado (¼)	lemon/lime juice
spinach	broccoli	lentils	sweet potato	olives (5)	fresh herbs: mint, parsley, cilantro, chives
kale	cauliflower	edamame	winter squash	nuts: walnuts, almonds, pistachio (1 Tbl.)	nutritional yeast
lettuce	carrots	organic tofu	corn	seeds: pumpkin, hemp, sesame (1 Tbl.)	vinegar: balsamic, apple cider, white
swiss chard	bell pepper	organic tempeh	peas	hummus (2 Tbl.)	spice blends
shaved brussel sprouts	cucumber		fruit: berries, apples, oranges.	dressing (1 Tbl.)	salsa
spring mix	green beans				
shredded cabbage	red onion				
	zucchini				
	summer squash				
	snap peas				
	tomatoes				

Nourish bowls are a simple way to assemble a meal utilizing already prepared food or ingredients you have in your pantry. A mix of dark leafy greens, protein, carbohydrates, vegetables, and healthy fats will provide you with energy and help you feel fuller for longer. Try different herbs, spices and sauces to add variety throughout the week.

Burrito Bowl
Romaine + grilled peppers + roasted sweet potato + black beans + salsa, cilantro, & lime juice

Mediterranean Bowl
Arugula + chopped tomato, cucumber, & red onion + garbanzo beans + quinoa + avacado + lemon juice

Asian Peanut Bowl
Massaged kale (with lime juice) + sliced cucumber & shredded carrots + edamame + brown rice + chopped peanuts + lime juice

Tofu Nicoise
Bibb lettuce + steamed green beans & sliced tomato + baked tofu + steamed new potatoes + sliced olives + Dijon dressing

Tahini Bowl
Spring mix + roasted broccoli & cauliflower + farro + lentils + mint & lemon tahini dressing

Figure 8-22. A nourish bowl (used with permission of the American College of Lifestyle Medicine)

OVERNIGHT OATS

Flavorful and filling, these overnight oats are easy to prepare and perfect for busy mornings. Small but mighty, chia seeds are fiber-filled and packed with healthy omega-3 fats, giving these oats some serious staying power.
Serves 2

INGREDIENTS

Oats

- 1 banana, mashed
- 1 cup rolled oats
- 2 tbsp chia seeds
- 1 tsp ground cinnamon
- 1 ¾ cup unsweetened plant milk
- 1 banana, sliced

Optional toppings

- Sliced strawberries
- Chopped walnuts
- Chopped peanuts
- Maple syrup

INSTRUCTIONS

1. In an airtight container, combine the mashed banana, oats, chia seeds, cinnamon and plant milk. Stir well, then cover and place in the fridge overnight.
2. In the morning, divide oats evenly into two bowls. Top each both with half a sliced banana and any additional toppings, such as sliced strawberries or chopped walnuts.

Figure 8-23. Overnight oats (used with permission of the American College of Lifestyle Medicine)

THREE-INGREDIENT BEAN BURGERS

A fork, a bowl, and three ingredients- the easiest bean burgers you'll ever make! Hint: make a big batch of these burgers and freeze them. When you're ready to eat them, simply reheat them in the oven or pop them in the toaster until warm throughout. **Makes 8 burgers**

INGREDIENTS

- 2 15-oz. cans black beans, drained and rinsed
- ½ cup quick oats
- ½ cup barbecue sauce
- Optional: salt and pepper to taste, additional herbs and spices (fresh rosemary, parsley, chili powder, cumin, etc.)

INSTRUCTIONS

1. In a large bowl, combine all ingredients and mash with a fork until a chunky dough forms. You want to leave some whole beans, but you want the dough to be mashed enough that it sticks together well. Taste and add salt/pepper/seasonings to your liking. If you have time, refrigerate the dough for 30 minutes.
2. Preheat oven to 400F. Divide and shape dough into 8 patties. Arrange on a parchment paper-lined baking sheet. Bake for 8 minutes, flip, and bake for another 5-6 minutes until a golden brown crust forms.
3. Serve with sliced tomato, pickles, onion, and your other favorite burger toppings. Refrigerate leftovers for up to one week or freeze in an airtight container for up to 3 months.

NOTES

- Swap the black beans for different beans. Try kidney, pinto, or cannellini beans.
- If you don't have quick oats, simply pulse rolled oats in a blender or food processor.
- Swap the barbecue sauce for other sauces for an entirely different cuisine. Try peanut sauce, a combination of ketchup and mustard, or a tahini-lemon sauce.

Figure 8-24. A three-ingredient bean burger (used with permission of the American College of Lifestyle Medicine)

CHICKPEA OF THE SEA

This flavorful chickpea salad only takes 5 minutes to make and there is no cooking involved, making it the perfect recipe for healthy lunches! **Serves 4**

INGREDIENTS

- 1 (15 ounces) can low-sodium chickpeas, drained and rinsed
- 1 tbsp Dijon mustard
- ¼ cup hummus or plain plant-based yogurt
- ¼ tsp old bay seasoning
- 1 large carrot, diced
- 1 celery stalk, diced
- ¼ cup red onion, diced
- ¼ cup diced celery
- ¼ cup toasted sunflower seeds
- Salt and pepper to taste

For serving, per person

- 2 romaine lettuce leaves or 2 slices whole-grain bread, lightly toasted
- Sliced red onion, tomato, avocado and/or lettuce

INSTRUCTIONS

1. In a medium bowl, mash drained and rinsed chickpeas with a fork. Add the remaining ingredients and stir to combine.
2. Prepare desired toppings, such as sliced red onion, tomato or avocado.
3. If serving as a sandwich, toast bread and serve between slices with toppings.
4. If serving with romaine lettuce leaves, top leaves with chickpea mixture and toppings.
5. To round out the meal, pair with baby carrots or a piece of fruit.

Figure 8-25. Chickpea of the sea (used with permission of the American College of Lifestyle Medicine)

References

❑ Cited References:

1. Merriam-Webster. www.mw.com.
2. Dietary Guidelines Advisory Committee. *Dietary Guidelines for Americans 2015-2020.* Government Printing Office; 2015.
3. 5 Foods Linked with Better Brainpower. https://www.health.harvard.edu/healthbeat/foods-linked-to-better-brainpower. Accessed July 14, 2021.

❑ Book Resources:

- American Heart Association. *The New American Heart Association Cookbook*, 9th ed. New York: Harmony Books; 2019.
- Bittman M, Katz D. *How to Eat: All Your Food and Diet Questions Answered.* Boston, MA: Houghton Miffin; 2020.
- Editors of America's Test Kitchen. *The Complete Mediterranean Cookbook: 500 Vibrant, Kitchen-Tested Recipes for Living and Eating Well Every Day.* Boston, MA: America's Test Kitchen; 2016.
- Greger M, Stone G. *How Not to Die.* New York: Flatiron Books; 2015.
- Greger M. *How Not to Diet.* New York: Flatiron Books; 2019.
- Greger M, Stone G. *The How Not to Diet Cookbook.* New York: Flatiron Books; 2017.
- Group EW. Dirty Dozen: The Fruits and Vegetables with the Most Pesticides. Retrieved from https://www.ewg.org/foodnews/dirty-dozen.php
- Hart A. *Jar Salads: 52 Happy, Healthy Lunches to Make in Advance.* Collingwood, Victoria, Australia: Smith Street Books; 2016.
- Heller M. *The Everyday Dash Diet Cookbook.* New York: Grand Central Life & Style; 2013.
- Hensrud DD. *The Mayo Clinic Diet,* 2nd ed. Rochester, MN: Mayo Clinic Press; 2017.
- Katz D. *The Truth About Food: Why Pandas Eat Bamboo and People Get Bamboozled.* Independently Published; 2018.
- Katzen M. *Moosewood Cookbooks*, 40th ed. Berkeley, CA: Ten Speed Press; 2014.
- Laforet M. *The Vegan Holiday Cookbook.* Toronto, Canada: Robert Rose; 2017.
- Mariotti F (ed.) *Vegetarian and Plant-Based Diets in Health and Disease Prevention.* Cambridge, MA: Elsevier Academic Press; 2017.
- Naidoo U. *This is Your Brain on Food: An Indispensable Guide to Surprising Foods That Fight Depression, Anxiety, PTSD, OCD, ADHD, and More.* New York: Little, Brown Spark; 2020.
- Ottolenghi Y. *Plenty: Vibrant Vegetable Recipes From London's Ottolenghi*. San Francisco, CA: Chronicle Books; 2011.
- Palmer S. *The Plant-Powered Diet: The Lifelong Eating Plan for Achieving Optimal Health, Beginning Today.* New York: Experiment Publishing; 2012.
- Seale S. *The Full Plate Diet: Slim Down, Look Great, Be Healthy!* Austin, TX: Bard Press; 2010.
- Shah R, Davis B. *Nourish: The Definitive Plant-Based Nutrition Guide for Families—With Tips & Recipes for Bringing Health, Joy, & Connection to Your Dinner Table.* Boca Raton, FL: Health Communications; 2020.

- Sherzai D, Sherzai A. *The 30-Day Alzheimer's Solution: The Definitive Food and Lifestyle Guide to Preventing Cognitive Decline.* San Francisco, CA: HarperOne; 2021.
- Shiue L. *The Spicebox Kitchen*. New York: Hachette Books; 2021.
- Stern B. *HeartSmart: The Best of HeartSmart Cooking.* Toronto, Canada: Penguin Random House Canada; 2006.

❑ Other Resources:

- Academy of Nutrition and Dietetics—eatright.org
- American College of Lifestyle Medicine: Section on Resources & Scientific Evidence—www.lifestylemedicine.org
- American Heart Association—www.heart.org
- American Institute for Cancer Research—www.aicr.org
- Colin Campbell's Nutrition Studies—nutritionstudies.org
- Dietary Guidelines for Americans: U.S. Department of Agriculture and U.S. Department of Health and Human Services. *Dietary Guidelines for Americans,* 2020-2025. 9th Edition. December 2020. Available at DietaryGuidelines.gov.
- Eat Lancet—eatforum.org
- FDA Section on Dietary Supplements—www.fda.gov/food/dietarysupplements
- Full Plate Living—www.fullplateliving.org
- Harvard Health Blogs—health.harvard.edu/blog
- Healthline.com
- National Center for Complementary and Integrative Health (NCCIH): Section on Dietary and Herbal Supplements—www.nccih.nih.gov/health
- Nutrition Facts—nutritionfacts.org
- Office of Dietary Supplements, National Institute of Health—www.ods.od.nih.gov
- Oldways—oldwayspt.org/traditional-diets/mediterranean-diet
- The Mediterranean Dish—www.themediterraneandish.com
- The Nutrition Source: Harvard TH Chan School of Public Health—www.hsph.harvard.edu/nutrition
- The Vegetarian Resource Group—vrg.org
- True Health Initiative—www.truehealthinitiative.org

❑ Healthy Recipe Resources:

- American Heart Association. *The New American Heart Association Cookbook*, 9th ed. New York: Harmony Books; 2019.
- Bean A. *The Runner's Cookbook*. London, England: Bloomsbury Sport; 2018.
- Bittman M, Katz D. *How to Eat: All Your Food and Diet Questions Answered.* Boston, MA: Houghton Miffin; 2020.
- Editors of America's Test Kitchen. *The Complete Mediterranean Cookbook: 500 Vibrant, Kitchen-Tested Recipes for Living and Eating Well Every Day*. Boston, MA: America's Test Kitchen; 2016.
- Greger M, Stone G. *The How Not to Die Cookbook.* New York: Flatiron Books; 2017.
- Greger M, Stone G. *The How Not to Diet Cookbook*. New York: Flatiron Books; 2017.

- Hart A. *Jar Salads: 52 Happy, Healthy Lunches to Make in Advance.* Collingwood, Victoria, Australia: Smith Street Books; 2016.
- Heller M. *The Everyday Dash Diet Cookbook.* New York: Grand Central Life & Style; 2013.
- Katz D. *The Truth About Food: Why Pandas Eat Bamboo and People Get Bamboozled.* Independently Published; 2018.
- Katzen M. *Moosewood Cookbooks*, 40th ed. Berkeley, CA: Ten Speed Press; 2014.
- Laforet M. *The Vegan Holiday Cookbook*. Toronto, Canada: Robert Rose; 2017.
- Mariotti F (ed.) *Vegetarian and Plant-Based Diets in Health and Disease Prevention.* Cambridge, MA: Elsevier Academic Press; 2017.
- Ottolenghi Y. *Plenty: Vibrant Vegetable Recipes From London's Ottolenghi.* San Francisco, CA: Chronicle Books; 2011.
- Palmer S. *The Plant-Powered Diet: The Lifelong Eating Plan for Achieving Optimal Health, Beginning Today.* New York: Experiment Publishing; 2012.
- Sherzai D, Sherzai A. *The 30-Day Alzheimer's Solution: The Definitive Food and Lifestyle Guide to Preventing Cognitive Decline.* San Francisco, CA: HarperOne; 2021.
- Shiue L. *The Spicebox Kitchen*. New York: Hachette Books; 2021.
- Stern B. *HeartSmart: The Best of HeartSmart Cooking*. Toronto, Canada: Penguin Random House Canada; 2006.
- USDA. What's Cooking? USDA Mixing Bowl: A Collection of Recipes for Schools and Child Care Centers. Blog series. https://www.usda.gov/media/blog/2015/02/23/whats-cooking-usda-mixing-bowl-collection-recipes-schools-and-child-care

CHAPTER 9
GOALS

"Knowledge is power: You hear it all the time, but knowledge is not power. It is only potential power. It only becomes power when you apply it and use it."

—Jim Kwik
Author and Brain Coach

PAVING the Path to Wellness: Questions for Goals

For each of the following five statements, choose the number on the frequency scale that best relates to you (frequency: 1= never, 2= rarely, 3= sometimes, 4= often, 5= routinely).

- I set long-term goals for myself, share them with someone, and review them___
- I set three-month goals for myself, share them with someone, and work toward them___
- I set monthly goals and share them with someone___
- I set weekly goals and share them with someone___
- I set daily goals for myself and keep myself accountable for them___

Subtotal—goals: _____

Gustavo Frazao/Shutterstock.com

Live and Learn: Brian Parker (PAVING Program Participant)

At age 54, I had a hemorrhagic stroke. I was initially unable to walk and talk. As I progressed in recovery, I set a goal that I was going to walk as much as I used to again. I used to go on long walks every morning, and these walks kept me healthy. I knew this was an important goal for me, but each initial step was frightening. I got overwhelmed, so I set a smaller goal to take each step with thoughtfulness. Slowly, I was able to appreciate each step and develop an awareness and gratitude of the places my steps took me. Step by step, I walked daily.

Walking and hiking have become essential to my well-being. I am now able to hike in the woods and have rediscovered an appreciation of the world around me. By setting a goal for the future, I have found myself more able to be in and appreciate the present.

Basic Definitions and Terms

- Goal—The object of a person's ambition or effort; an aim or desired result[1]

"Goals are dreams with deadlines."[2]

—Diana Scharf-Hunt, PhD
Author

Goal-Setting Theories

Over the years, a number of theories and theses have been developed to help better understand what drives a person to achieve a particular goal or outcome, including the following commonly accepted measures:

GOAL-SETTING THEORY

In their book *A Theory of Goal Setting and Task Performance,*[3] American psychologists Dr. Edwin Locke and Dr. Gary Latham explain that a major source of motivation comes from working toward achieving a goal. In addition, attaining a goal improves future performance that can be used toward subsequent goal achievement.

❑ Reflection Time:

Can you remember a time when you were successful with achieving a goal, and that success improved your future performance or inspired you to create another goal? Explain.

____

____

____

____

____

____

____

____

4C-F MODEL OF GOAL-SETTING AND MOTIVATION

Drs. Edwin Lock and Gary Latham's 4C-F Model of Goal-Setting recommends that you set goals that are clear. Clarity is the first C. To help you set clear goals, "SMART" goal-setting is addressed later in this chapter. Your goals should also have the right amount of *challenge* and *complexity, the two other Cs.* On the other hand, if they are too challenging and complex, you are more likely to give up. If they don't have any challenge, you may become bored and fail to meet your goal.

Receiving regular and meaningful feedback on your progress toward your goals is also important to success. Feedback is the F in the 4C-F model. The last component of the 4C-F Model of Goal-Setting is *commitment–the fourth C.* You are more likely to commit to a goal, if you are intrinsically motivated rather than only extrinsically motivated.

Extrinsic motivation comes from outside of you and often involves rewards, punishments, or opinions of others. Intrinsic motivation aligns with your internal drives, priorities, and purpose. Sometimes, your motivation has both extrinsic and intrinsic components. Success is more likely, when your goals are intrinsically motivated and connect with your purpose, priorities, and vision for your life.

❑ Reflection Time:

Consider one of your current goals. What is your motivation for your goal? Is it intrinsically motivated, extrinsically motivated, or does it contain components of both? Explain.

❑ Reflection Time:

Is there anything that you could do to your goal to make it more intrinsically motivated and relevant to you? Explain.

MOTIVATIONAL INTERVIEWING

Motivational interviewing[4] involves exploring a person's reason for wanting to change with acceptance and compassion. Motivational interviewing highlights the discrepancy between where you are and where you want to be. When coaching yourself to meet goals, it's important to ask yourself open-ended questions that invite deeper exploration into your dreams, desires, and motivators. Everyone needs affirmation for previous successes and for past attempts at reaching goals, even if they were not successful. Reminding yourself of past successes, small or large, is important for continued motivation, the key component of motivational interviewing.

❑ Reflection Time:

Think about a behavior that you would like to start and describe that behavior.

❑ Reflection Time:

Describe the difference between your current behavior in that area and your desired behavior.

Decisional balance involves exploring the pros and cons of your current, as well as your new behavior, in order to help propel you forward.

❑ Reflection Time:

- Describe the pros of continuing your current behavior.

- Describe the cons of continuing your current behavior

- Describe the pros of changing and doing the new behavior.

- Describe the cons of changing and doing the new behavior.

❑ Reflection Time:

What insight did you gain after reflecting on the discrepancy between your old behavior and your new desired behavior, as well as the pros and cons of both behaviors?

ADULT LEARNING THEORY

According to the Adult Learning Theory,[5] which was developed by American educator Dr. Malcolm Knowles, adult learners are goal-oriented. Through mastery of developmental tasks, adults solve problems, fulfil their social role, and achieve their goals. In addition to being goal-oriented, Dr. Knowles also stated that adults are self-directed, autonomous, and full of life experience and knowledge that help them learn. Adult Learning Theory also states that adults learn with a focus on relevance and attaining practical knowledge that can be immediately applied.

One of the key pieces to remember is autonomy. People want to choose their own path. They want to select the choice that is right for them. This book is providing lots of opportunities for you to pick your path, choose the option that suits you best, and brainstorm your own solutions. The MOSS framework is utilized to help you have a sense of control over the process, a sense of ownership and autonomy. No two wellness journeys are the same, because people are all different and unique.

❑ Reflection Time:

Is there knowledge that you could learn to improve your chances of goal-success? Explain.

7 HABITS OF HIGHLY EFFECTIVE PEOPLE

Steven Covey,[6] a well-known American educator, author, and thought-leader on productivity and time-management skills, recommends focusing on "beginning with the end in mind" when setting a new goal. Envisioning your future and how you want to be living and working, ten or twenty years from now, will help guide you in creating yearly, monthly, and weekly goals. Connecting your priorities, purpose, and values with your vision will prepare you for success in crafting SMART goals that propel you forward and upward to higher ground.

In addition, Covey talks about putting "first things first." It's very important to determine what's most important to you in life, in this moment, and what is most precious, what you cherish in the here and now. Making sure that your actions align with these priorities is critical. The "think win/win" that Covey promotes is a helpful strategy whenever you are collaborating with others and your goals include and embrace the goals of family, friends, and colleagues. You are seeking a "win/win" for anyone with whom you collaborate.

Covey's "seek first to understand" is another good rule to be used in PAVING the Path to Wellness. Everyone wants to feel loved and understood. When involving others in projects, the first thing you need to do is understand where they are coming from and try to walk in their shoes, with empathy and compassion.

When working with others, focus on using your strengths, as well as the strengths of your friends, colleagues, and loved ones. Doing so will help everyone enjoy the process, project, and the product even more, because you are coming from a place of strength, and you are able to find flow. Everyone has different strengths and gifts, and everyone thrives when using them. Seeking to synergize by using your strengths will help you enjoy collaborations with others.

Later in the PAVING the Path to Wellness program, time-outs are addressed. Similarly, Covey discusses "sharpening the saw." In other words, everyone needs to take breaks to function at their highest level, to improve, to gain new perspectives, to build new skills, and to grow at any age and stage in life.

TRANSTHEORETICAL MODEL OF CHANGE

The Transtheoretical Model of Change,[7] which was developed by American psychologist Dr. James O. Prochaska, is also called the Stages of Change Model. It includes the following stages of change:

- Pre-contemplation
- Contemplation
- Preparation
- Action
- Maintenance

Although they are presented in this linear fashion, people commonly circle back to previous stages before progressing again as they try to achieve their goals. On occasion, a sixth stage of termination, lapse, or relapse is also included in the model. Following is a brief overview of each of the six stages, as well as relevant questions for each stage.

- *Pre-Contemplation:* When you are in the pre-contemplation stage, you are not even considering changing your behavior. During this stage, you should practice self-compassion.

❑ Reflection Time:

Are you in pre-contemplation for any behaviors? If so, are you practicing self-compassion? Explain.

____

____

____

____

____

____

____

____

- *Contemplation:* During the contemplation stage, you think about what things would be like, if you made the behavior change but have not yet begun to prepare to make the change.

❑ Reflection Time:

Is there a behavior that you are contemplating changing? If so, what is it?

____

____

____

____

____

____

____

____

- *Preparation:* In the preparation phase, you actively make plans and prepare to begin the behavior soon. During this phase, you benefit from finding support, writing SMART goals, setting a target start date, and identifying obstacles, as well as strategies for overcoming them.

❑ Reflection Time:

Are you preparing to adopt any new healthy behavior? If so, what plans are you making?

- *Action:* During the action phase, you are performing the new behavior. This is the time to celebrate your accomplishments, review your rewards, reflect upon your motivation for this new behavior, and to create future goals.

❑ Reflection Time:

Think of a new behavior of yours. What is it? How quickly did you progress through the previous stages of change? Was it linear or did you circle back to previous steps in the process before entering the action phase?

❑ Reflection Time:

Do you want to celebrate, reflect on your motivation, or create future goals around your new behavior, now that you are in the action stage? Doing so could help you move into the maintenance phase.

- *Maintenance:* In the maintenance phase of a behavior, you want to continue the behavior and hopefully not experience a lapse or relapse. To increase your chances of staying in the maintenance phase, you can incorporate variety, seek mentors, and/or be a mentor to someone else.

❑ Reflection Time:

Explain how you are currently maintaining one or two healthy behaviors that you enjoy.

- *Termination, lapse, or relapse:* You may continue your new behavior forever, or there may come a time when the behavior no longer serves you, and you want to purposefully terminate it. You may experience a lapse or relapse, where you stop the desired behavior. If this happens, remember that it is common to move between the various stages. Use what you will learn in the rest of the chapter around goal-setting to get back on track. On occasion, you don't reach termination. As such, you are in constant maintenance and working to maintain the healthy habit.

Live and Learn: Dr. Beth Frates

Utilizing the Frates COACH Approach™ can really help when counseling patients with substance use disorders. Lifestyle medicine practitioners enjoy the process more and so do the clients when they employ compassion, openness, appreciation, and honesty. When I ran my pilot wellness group for stroke survivors and caregivers, I experienced a very challenging situation. On the very first day, the patients and caregivers strolled in and last to arrive was a gentleman wheeling his wife into the room. He looked very stressed and frustrated.

After situating her at the table, he headed for the door. Quickly I said, "Oh excuse me. You don't have to leave. We would be delighted if you joined us. It is up to you. You are welcome to participate in the discussion. Rolling his eyes, he replied "Okay."

At the time, I thought everything was going along smoothly. We had reviewed all the reasons why people have strokes, and everyone shared their own personal stories. Then, we went over risk factors for stroke. Each person shared the risk factors that they knew they had. Even the caregivers shared this information.

Everything went well, until we got to Mr. Escape (the gentleman who tried to run off after getting his wife situated). Mr. Escape paused when it was his turn. Basically, he squinted his eyes, looked straight at me, and slammed his hand on the table and then announced, in a low, loud voice, "I smoke, and I'm not quitting!" It was a belligerent response. Thankfully, I had studied behavior change and was already using health coaching methods in my interactions at this time.

This scenario was ripe for the Frates COACH Approach™. I remember feeling angry when he seemed to be angry with me. It's a natural reaction to go into protective mode when someone attacks you or you feel you are being attacked. This scenario could have fallen into a negative, vicious cycle. I also remember thinking, "Take deep breaths. Pause. Think."

I knew I needed a break—a time-out, so I reached into my purse pretending to look for something special. While rummaging around in my purse, I was taking time to pause and collect my thoughts. I knew that everyone in the group was watching me, wondering how I would respond. I was searching for empathy, and I found it.

With the Frates COACH Approach™, I needed to focus on curiosity. What was making him so angry, and why does he want to keep smoking? I figured he had tried to quit many times previously without success, and, was likely frustrated. Probably, everyone had tried to wrestle him down to make him quit smoking. I imagined that he had received countless lectures on why he needed to quit, and he didn't want one more. I needed to be open. I thought, although I may not successfully empower him to quit today, as he might not be ready, I must be open to however the conversation flows. In addition, I must be appreciative that he is talking to me and that he chose to stay in the room to participate in the group instead of racing out the door. (COA—curious, open, appreciative)

Mostly, I knew I needed to express compassion and thus, I was searching for my empathy, while rummaging through my purse. Lastly, I needed to be honest. (CH—compassion and honesty) He said he was not going to quit, but I still needed to find a way to empower him to consider quitting later and to tell him that one of the best things he could do for himself was to quit smoking. I am a healthcare provider, and I must express the facts.

After scrambling around in my purse for a minute or two, I pulled out one of my business cards. Then, I used motivational interviewing. I used a reflection, "I hear you. You are smoking, and you are not going to quit." Then, I asked permission to share some information, "May I say something?" To date, no one has answered "no" to this question. I basically gave him autonomy—the choice to listen to me or not.

After giving me permission to say something, I proceeded with "I know you are not ready to consider quitting smoking right now, not today. However, it is one of the best things you could do for your health. The smoke has a negative impact on you and the secondhand smoke has a negative impact on your wife. So, when you are ready to quit, please do give me a call. No matter when that time comes. I will be here for you. Here's my cell phone. I would be delighted to help you, when you are ready."

After that, I handed him my card. He was quiet and looked a bit confused. The rest of the group was staring in complete silence. For the next few weeks, I did not ask Mr. Escape about his smoking.

During the subsequent sessions, I did discuss the risks of smoking and the impact of second-hand smoke, which is part of the curriculum in the stroke prevention wellness group. I did not look at Mr. Escape or do anything that I felt might make him uncomfortable. Four weeks later, Mr. Escape entered the wellness group stating, "I have an announcement to make." I normally started the meetings with a greeting and a check-in with everyone, but Mr. Escape seemed eager to share something, so I let him start our session. He said, "I cut down on my cigarettes. I have a plan to quit in a month." WOW!

The whole room started clapping. I kept my facial expression and body language steady and solid. In contrast, all the members of the stroke group cheered and jumped out of their chairs. They all wanted what was best for him and his wife. I calmly and quietly asked him one question, "How does that feel?" He answered, "Great!" I learned that when someone is in a pre-contemplative state to change a behavior, empathy is one of the best possible therapeutic tools.

COACH APPROACH™

C = Curiosity

O = Openness

A = Appreciation

C = Compassion

H = Honesty

Appreciative Inquiry Spiral Model

As noted previously, what you appreciate, appreciates. Deep within yourself, you have a positive core. Everyone has strengths and gifts. Everyone has experienced some success in their past. Working from this positive core allows you to move forward toward higher levels of fulfillment, enjoyment, and well-being. Always remember your positive core. You all have inner wisdom and true beauty inside that's longing to be expressed and shared with this world. May this be the time you appreciate, accept, and acknowledge this fact.

With the Appreciative Inquiry process, you work to define your positive core, to discover what it is you're striving for, and to dream of the possibilities that might become reality. At that point, you then narrow it down and design a program through the SMART goal-setting process that you can achieve. Ultimately, you will need to deliver on your promises to yourself that are represented by these goals. You keep repeating this 5-D cycle of Appreciative Inquiry, as illustrated in Figure 9-1.

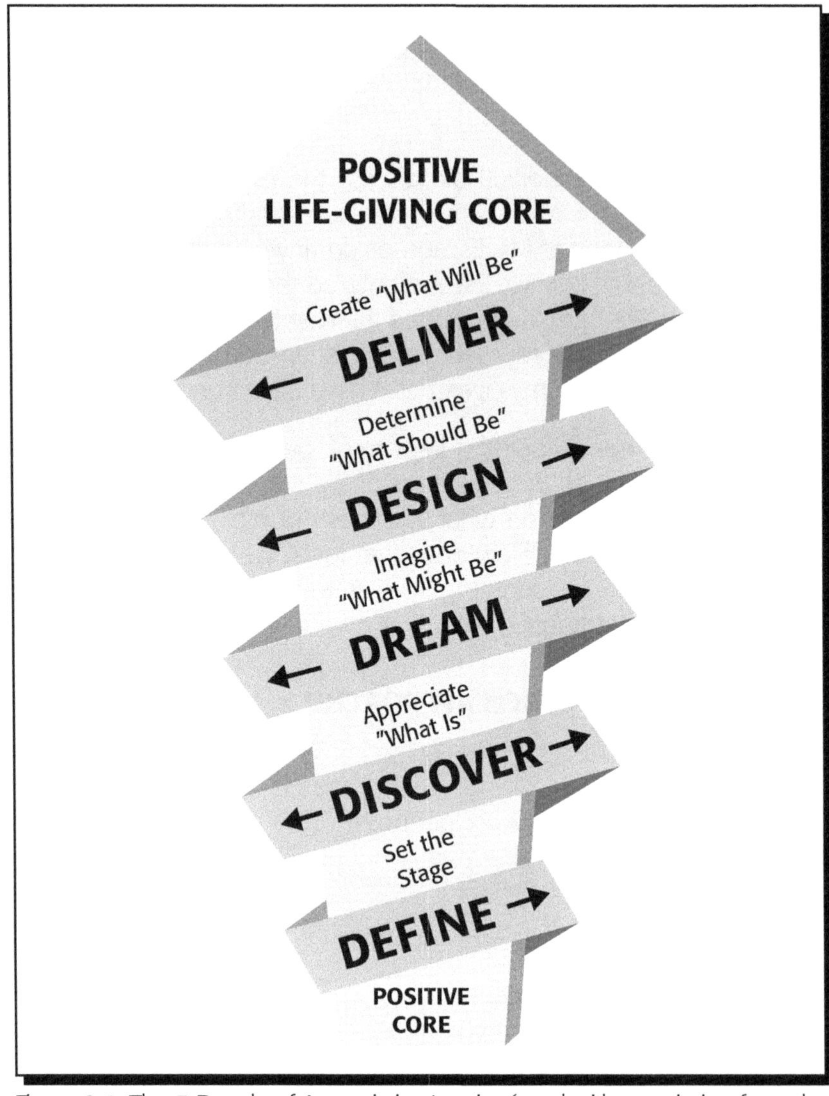

Figure 9-1. The 5-D cycle of Appreciative Inquiry (used with permission from the *Lifestyle Medicine Handbook*; 2nd edition; Frates, et al.; Monterey, CA: Healthy Learning; 2021)

Building Confidence

There are several steps that you can undertake to enhance your level of confidence, including the following:

- Remember past successes.
- Recall your strengths.
- Brainstorm strategies around obstacles.
- Appreciate the positive.

In that regard, American psychologist, who specialized in positive psychology, Dr. Charles Snyder developed the Hope Theory,[8] which stated that hope consists of both cognitive and effective elements. According to this theory, you build confidence by setting inspiring goals and identifying pathways to change. Snyder identified at least three steps that people relate to hope:

- You need to have focused thoughts.
- You need to develop strategies in advance to achieve your goals.
- You need motivation to undertake the effort required to reach your goals.

Setting SMART Goals

Setting SMART goals can increase your chances of success (refer to Chapter 4 for a detailed overview of SMART goals). In goal-setting with the ladder of behavior change, the sides of the ladder represent the person's *priorities, principles, visions, and values*—the framework around which to base your SMART goals. The rungs of the ladder are the individual SMART goals, both short- and long-term, which lead a person toward their ultimate vision or dream. Motivators, both intrinsic and extrinsic, serve as the driving force that propels individuals forward along their climb to success.

Effective and inspiring goals entail two features:

- Goals that are intrinsically meaningful.
- Goals that match your values and passions.

Take a few minutes to reflect on your priorities, key principles, core values and vision for yourself. Then, consider a goal that will help you achieve this vision. Also consider your motivators for achieving this goal. Then, use the SMART goal format to refine your goals.

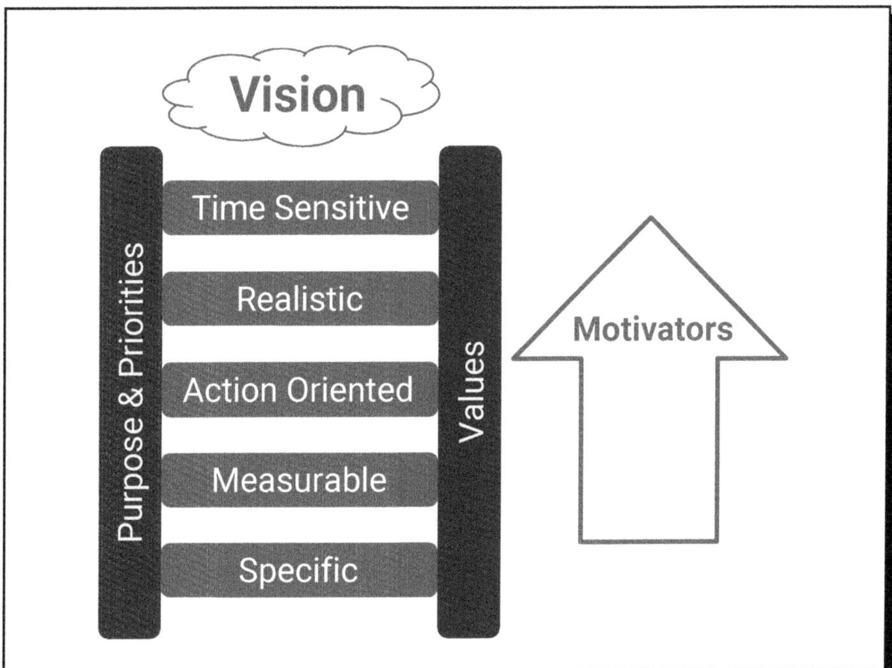

Figure 9-2. The ladder of behavioral change

SPECIFIC

Specific goals are clear and often address the "who, what, when, where, why, and how" issues. In that regard, consider an area of your life that you want to focus on with a new goal and answer the following questions to work on specificity:

❑ Reflection Time:

Who is involved with your goal?

❑ Reflection Time:

What do you need to do first, second, and third to achieve your goal?

❑ Reflection Time:

When will the steps to your goal be completed (part of T—time-bound)?

❑ Reflection Time:

Where will you complete your goal?

❑ Reflection Time:

Why do you want to complete this goal (part of R—relevance)?

❑ Reflection Time:

How will you complete this goal?

"If you have a why, you will find your how."

—Beth Frates, MD
Physician and Author

MEASURABLE

There are different ways to measure progress toward a goal, for example, employing a quantitative aspect, such as exercising for 30 minutes, reaching out to three friends, or eating six servings of vegetables daily.

❑ Reflection Time:

How will you measure and track your progress?

❑ Reflection Time:

How will you know when you've reached your final goal or even the various steps along the path toward your goal?

❑ Reflection Time:

Is there a phone application, journal, whiteboard, chart, computer program, or other system that you will use? What would a progress chart look like for your goal?

ACTION-ORIENTED

Goals should be action-oriented if you want to succeed. Although most people want to "be healthy," having a goal that is passive, rather than active, makes success more difficult. A goal may have several actionable items that are part of the goal. They should be actions that you could put on a to-do list and cross them off when you complete them.

❑ Reflection Time:

What are the actions that you need to take in order to achieve your goal? Consider listing several actions, rather than just the final, cumulative action.

REALISTIC

Having a goal that challenges you is essential, but it is also important that it is attainable. Goals that are too difficult are associated with frustration, while goals that are too easy can lead to boredom. If you realize that your goal is not as attainable as you would like for it to be, this may indicate that you need to learn a new skill in order to achieve it.

❑ Reflection Time:

Reflect on your goal. Is it too challenging? Is it too easy? Explain.

____

____

____

____

____

____

____

____

❑ Reflection Time:

Do you want to change your goal, so that it has the right balance of challenge while still being attainable? If so, update your goal below.

____

____

____

____

____

____

____

❑ Reflection Time:

Are there any skills that would increase your chances of being successful with achieving your goal that you don't already have or that you would like to improve? If so, what are those skills?

____

____

____

❑ Reflection Time:

How can you gain these skills? It may involve doing online research, talking to a healthcare provider, or taking a class.

TIME-SENSITIVE

Creating SMART goals involves putting a deadline on your goal. Goals can have any timeframe from what you want to complete in the next hour to what you want to finish during your lifetime. Short-term goals can include daily, weekly, and monthly goals, whereas long-term goals include year-long or even decades-long goals.

❑ Reflection Time:

Consider the timeline for each of your goals. You can change the timeline or put shorter- or longer-term goals in place around it to support your progress. Do you want to change the timeline for your goals or add any other shorter- or longer-term goals?

SMART Goal Summary

After working through the various components of the SMART goal system, you now have a SMART goal to clearly state to yourself.

❑ Reflection Time:

Write your SMART goal in the space provided.

____

____

____

____

____

____

____

____

Confidence in Your Ability to Achieve Your Goal

Before starting to work toward your goal, pause to consider your confidence in achieving your goal.

❑ Reflection Time:

How confident are you that you can meet your goal (1—no confidence; 5—somewhat confident; 10—extremely confident)?

____

____

If you scored below a 7, revise your goal to increase your confidence in being successful.

❑ Reflection Time:

Your revised goal is:

____

____

____

____

____

❑ Reflection Time:

Your level of confidence in being able to achieve your revised goal is:

Always remember that success breeds success and will help motivate you to continue to reach toward your goal.

Goal Accountability

Accountability increases your chances of success with meeting your goals. Some people share their goals with another person whom they believe will support them in achieving their goals. Others use smart devices, phone applications, or journals to help keep them accountable.

❑ Reflection Time:

Now that you have a clear goal, is there a supportive person with whom you could share your goal, who could motivate and assist you through accountability? Who is that person?

❑ Reflection Time:

When and how will you let them know you would like help with accountability?

Celebrating Goal Achievement

Working toward your goal will likely take hard work and dedication. You deserve to celebrate your success, as well as all progress toward achieving your goal. You don't have to wait until the end. Celebrating success is encouraging and will help you continue to succeed.

❏ Reflection Time:

List some ways you could celebrate your progress and success. Be creative!

____

____

____

____

____

____

____

❏ Reflection Time:

How do you want to celebrate your progress, once you reach your final goal?

____

____

____

____

____

____

____

bejo/Shutterstock.com

Motivation

Motivation can be extrinsic or intrinsic. Extrinsic motivation comes from outside of you and often involves rewards, punishments, or others' opinions. Intrinsic motivation aligns with your internal drives, priorities, and purpose. On occasion, your motivation has both extrinsic and intrinsic components. Success is more likely when your goals are intrinsically motivated and connect with your purpose, priorities, and vision for your life.

❏ Reflection Time:

What is your motivation for your goal? Is it intrinsically motivated, extrinsically motivated, or does it contain components of both?

❏ Reflection Time:

Is there anything that you could do to your goal to make it more intrinsically motivated and relevant to you?

Goal-Supporting Habits

Creating healthy habits increases your chances of achieving your goals. Habits are patterns of behavior that you do without as much effort, as when you first performed the behavior. You often engage in habits without thinking about them. As you repeat your desired behavior, it becomes easier for you to continue to engage in the behavior. You form and reinforce the neural connections in your brain that allow you to do the behavior.

Imagine that you are hiking through the woods, and you know where you want to go, but nobody has ever traveled the path that you are taking. The first time you walk through the woods, it takes considerable effort to travel to your destination. You may have to clear branches, step over many obstacles, and search for how to get to your final destination. Now, imagine that you are following a trail that has been used by hundreds of people before you who were also traveling to the same destination. It is much easier to travel, as branches have been cleared, and the path goes around the obstacles. Next, imagine that someone paves a path by laying stepping stones along the trail. You can walk to your destination by following the clear path with much less mental and likely physical effort.

Your brain creates similar paths through repetition. You can use the science of healthy habit formation to achieve your goal. Even when the initial behavior seems difficult, you can remind yourself that you are PAVING your Path to Wellness.

❑ Reflection Time:

How can you use positive self-talk and healthy habit formation to support you in achieving your goals?

____

____

____

____

____

____

____

Katy Milkman, professor and author of *How to Change: The Science of Getting from Where You Are to Where You Want to Be,*[9] recommends "piggybacking," which is when you stack a habit that you would like to start with a routine habit. When you are working to establish a new habit, you can pair it with an existing habit, so that it is easier to remember. For example, if your doctor prescribes a new medication that you need to take every morning, and you are worried about forgetting to take it, you could pair it with an activity that is already a habit. You (hopefully) brush your teeth every morning and could begin taking your medicine immediately after brushing your teeth. Eventually, it will become a habit to automatically do these two behaviors together.

Milkman also describes "temptation-bundling," where "want" activities that are instantly gratifying are paired with "should" behaviors that are good for your overall health. This coupling increases your chances of successfully achieving your goal.

❑ Reflection Time:

Is there a way to pair or "temptation-bundle" a new desired habit with a current habit of yours to increase your chances of success? Explain.

____

Goals Beyond Lifestyle

While having goals that center around a healthy lifestyle are wonderful, think about other ways to use goal-setting in your life.

❏ Reflection Time:

Do you have goals for your family or business? Explain.

❏ Reflection Time:

Does your purpose align with the goals of a non-profit organization or faith community? If so, would you like to become more involved with exploring and possibly supporting their goals? Explain.

❑ Reflection Time:

Would you like to set goals to learn a new hobby, sport, or instrument, or improve your current hobby activities, sports, or musical instrument? Explain.

____

____

____

____

____

____

❑ Reflection Time:

Would you like to create goals around travel? Explain.

____

____

____

____

____

____

____

If you don't have goals, you are more likely to wander aimlessly. On the other hand, if you have goals, you are more likely to move along your desired path. While you will still encounter obstacles, you are more likely to eventually attain success.

Insight from Previous Goal Attempts

Just because you had a previous goal that you were unsuccessful in achieving does not mean that it was a bad goal nor that you shouldn't try again. "Failed" attempts may lead to your greatest insights and growth.

❑ Reflection Time:

List three of your past successful goal attempts, as well as any insights into what increased your ability to be successful.

- ____
- ____
- ____

____

❑ Reflection Time:

List three of your past unsuccessful goal attempts as well as any insights into what contributed to the outcomes.

- ____________________
- ____________________
- ____________________

❑ Reflection Time:

Are there any of your past unsuccessful goal attempts that you would like to try again? Do you want to modify or update any of your goals? Explain.

❑ Reflection Time:

Are there additional skills that you want to learn or systems you could put in place to increase your chances of success? Explain.

Furthermore, remember that there are things beyond your control. Sometimes, it is appropriate to try attaining a goal again, while other goals may be better left behind. Joining a community that is working toward common goals or enlisting the help of a wellness coach can provide benefit for some people.

Goal-Supporting Environment

Think about how your environment supports or hinders one of your goals. For example, if your goal is to eat healthier food, but your kitchen environment does not have cooking utensils or healthy ingredients, you are unlikely to be successful. Conversely, a kitchen that has supplies to prepare and cook healthy meals, as well as a pantry stocked with healthy cooking ingredients, will increase your chances of success.

❑ Reflection Time:

How might your environment increase (or decrease) your chances of success in achieving your goal?

❑ Reflection Time:

How can you change your environment to better support your goal?

Goal-Supporting Schedule

Successfully achieving certain goals may necessitate modifying your schedule. Consider a typical weekday schedule and then a typical weekend day schedule.

❑ Reflection Time:

How does your schedule support or hinder your ability to achieve your goals?

❑ Reflection Time:

Do you want to modify your schedule to better support your goal success? If so, how?

As you work toward goals, remember that you are PAVING a Path to Wellness through your goal attempts. Focus on progress rather than perfection. Celebrate the successes and look for the valuable lessons learned from unsuccessful goal attempts. Enjoy the journey, as well as the learning and growing that will occur along the way. Examples of SMART, as well as not SMART, goals include the following:

❑ SMART Goal Examples:

- For a month, I will walk five times a week for 30 minutes during my lunch break.
- For the next week, I will eat five servings of fruit and vegetables per day, one for each main meal and two snacks.
- I will research yoga class schedules in nearby studios on Wednesday afternoon, after work.

❑ Not-SMART Goal Examples:

- I will lose 20 lbs.
- I will exercise more.
- In one month, I will be ready to run a marathon.
- I will eat more fruit and vegetables.

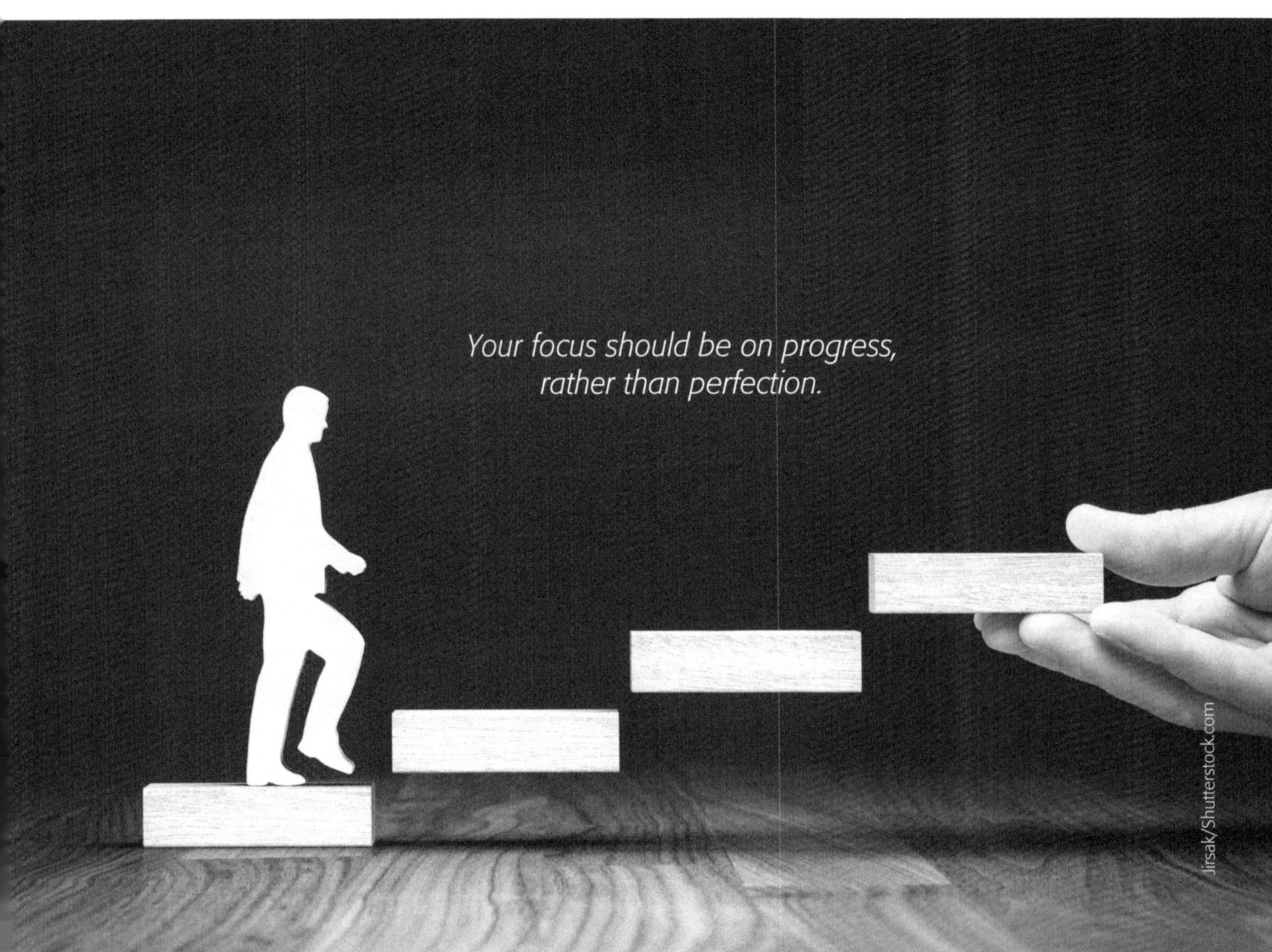

References

❑ Cited References:

1. Simpson JA, Weiner ES, Proffitt M, editors. *Oxford English Dictionary Additions Series.* London, England: Oxford University Press; 1997.
2. Scharf-Hunt D, Hait P. *Studying Smart: Time Management for College Students.* New York: HarperPerennial; 1990.
3. Locke EA, Latham GP. *A Theory of Goal Setting & Task Performance*. Hoboken, NJ: Prentice-Hall, Inc; 1990.
4. Miller WR, Rollnide S. *Motivational Interviewing: Helping People Change*. New York: Guilford Press; 2012.
5. Knowles MS (1978). Andragogy: Adult learning theory in perspective. *Community College Review*. 5(3):9-20.
6. Covey SR, Center CL. *The Seven Habits of Highly Effective People: Restoring the Character Ethic.* New York: Simon and Schuster; 1993.
7. Grimley D, Prochaska JO, Velicer WF, et al. The Transtheoretical Model of Change. In TM Brinhaupt and RP Lipka (eds) *Changing the Self: Philosophies, Techniques, and Experiences* (pp. 201–227). Albany, NY: State of New York Press; 1994.
8. Milkman K. *How to Change: The Science of Getting From Where You Are to Where You Want to Be.* New York: Portfolio Books; 2021.
9. Snyder CR, Lopez SJ, Shorey HS, Rand KL, Feldman DB. Hope theory, measurements, and applications to school psychology. *School Psychology Quarterly.* 2003;18(2):122.

❑ Book Resources:

- Arloski M. *Wellness Coaching for Lasting Lifestyle Change*. Duluth, MN: Whole Person Associates; 2009.
- Ben-Shahar T. *Happier: Learn the Secrets to Daily Joy and Lasting Fulfillment.* New York: McGraw-Hill Education; 2007.
- Burnett B, Evans D. *Designing Your Life: How to Build a Well-Lived, Joyful Life.* New York: Knopf; 2016.
- Covey S. *The 7 Habits of Highly Effective People: Powerful Lessons in Personal Change,* revised ed. New York: Free Press; 2004.
- Drucker PF. *Managing Oneself.* Boston, MA: Harvard Business Press; 2007.
- Drucker PF. *The Effective Executive: The Definitive Guide to Getting the Right Things Done.* New York: Harper Business; 2006.
- Duhigg C. *The Power of Habit: Why We Do What We Do in Life and Business.* New York: Random House Trade Paperbacks; 2014.
- Grimley D, Prochaska JO, Velicer WF, et al. The Transtheoretical Model of Change. In TM Brinhaupt and RP Lipka (eds) *Changing the Self: Philosophies, Techniques, and Experiences* (pp. 201–227). Albany, NY: State of New York Press; 1994.
- Matthews J. *The Professional's Guide to Health and Wellness Coaching.* San Diego, CA: ACE; 2019.
- Milkman K. *How to Change: The Science of Getting From Where You Are to Where You Want to Be.* New York: Portfolio Books; 2021.

- Miller WR, Rollnide S. *Motivational Interviewing: Helping People Change*. New York: Guilford Press; 2012.
- Moore M. *Coaching Psychology Manual,* 2nd ed. Philadelphia, PA; 2016.
- Rippe J (ed). *Lifestyle Medicine*, 3rd ed. Boca Raton, FL: CRC Press; 2019.
- Sharf-Hunt D, Hait P. *Studying Smart: How to Do Your Work and Do It Well, How to Survive the Pressure...and Still Have Time for Fun*. New York: Harper Paperbacks; 1990.
- Whitworth L, Kimsey-House K, Kimsey-House H, Sandahl P. *Co-active Coaching–New Skills for Coaching People Towards Success.* London, England: Breasley Publishing; 2007.

❑ Other Resources:

- Calendar, to do lists, sticky notes, dry-erase boards
- Accountability–check your progress, utilize the buddy system, use tracking systems (written logs, apps, devices, internet sites, social media), collaborate with a caregiver, spouse, or friend.
- Measurement–"What gets measured, gets managed" (Peter Drucker)–journaling, logs, pedometer, heart rate monitor, scale, blood tests, number of fruits and veggies, number of push-ups, hours spent sleeping

CHAPTER 10
STRESS RESILIENCE

"The greatest weapon against stress is our ability to choose one thought over another."

—William James
American Psychologist
and Philosopher

PAVING the Path to Wellness: Questions for Stress & Resilience

For each of the following five statements, choose the number on the frequency scale that best relates to you (frequency: 1= never, 2= rarely, 3= sometimes, 4= often, 5= routinely).

- I know how to calm myself down when I feel stress. ___
- I have two or three relaxation techniques that I use in times of crisis.___
- I am able to take a step away from a situation before I react.___
- I spend more time feeling peaceful than I do angry.___
- I have identified a happy place or time in my life that I can recall when things are tough.____

Subtotal—stress management______

sun ok/Shutterstock.com

Live and Learn: Ileana Kleponis (PAVING Program Participant)

There are many things that I remember from Dr. Frates' classes but none more so than stress reduction with deep breathing. It's a simple technique that I use over and over. Just breathing to relax, to get rid of my anxiety, to relieve my stress, to get my heart rate to slow down when it's racing.

Driving into Boston can be a very stressful experience, especially when you have an appointment to get to. One morning, according to the road sign, I knew traffic was bad and I was going to be late to my destination. I started to get anxious, but instead of getting involved in stressful thoughts, I decided to use something that I had learned in class. I decided to just breathe. Breathe in for 4, hold it for 7, and then out for 8. 4-7-8 over and over again, and it worked! As long as I could stop my anxious thinking and concentrate on my breathing, I was relaxing. No thoughts came into my head. When I arrived at my destination, I was calm.

This technique has helped me numerous times and in many situations. I practice deep breathing for a couple of minutes before going into a doctor's office. Just several repetitions of 4-7-8 helps me stay calm. I use it to try to slow my heart rate when having my blood pressure taken. When I'm waiting to meet someone for the first time, whether in person or on Zoom, it helps if I practice deep breathing. Now I take yoga classes that build on the mindfulness techniques I learned in Dr. Frates' workshop. I'm stress free when I finish the class. All I have to do is think about deep breathing.

Onchira Wongsiri/Shutterstock.com

Stress Resilience Timeline

❑ Reflection Time:

Write out or draw what your main sources of stress were during each of these phases of your life: childhood, adolescence, young adulthood, middle adulthood, older adulthood.

❑ Reflection Time:

Write or draw out what gave you strength, supported you, or helped you relax during these times of stress.

❏ Reflection Time:

Reflect on your timeline. What insights did you gain from this timeline? Have your sources of stress or your coping mechanisms changed much throughout the years?

____

____

____

____

____

____

Stress is defined by the American Institute of Stress as "physical, mental, or emotional strain or tension."[1] Stress can be good (eustress), when it motivates and energizes a person to perform. However, negative stress (distress) can cause your health to deteriorate, especially when it is chronic, and you don't have the resources to cope with it in healthy ways.

Hans Selye, considered the father of stress and the person who "coined" the term stress, explains:[2] "Yes. You see, when I created the concept, I didn't think of this difference, I called it stress. But then there was often confusion. The general public uses stress and distress as synonymous, but they are not. The stress of pain, of sorrow, of nervousness, of suffering—that's bad stress, distress. But the stress of creation, or the stress of being able to achieve by taking things in a resilient way, you don't want to eliminate that. So, there is good stress (technically 'eustress') or bad stress ('distress') but the response to any demand is stress. There is always stress, so the only point is to make sure that it is useful to yourself and useful to others."

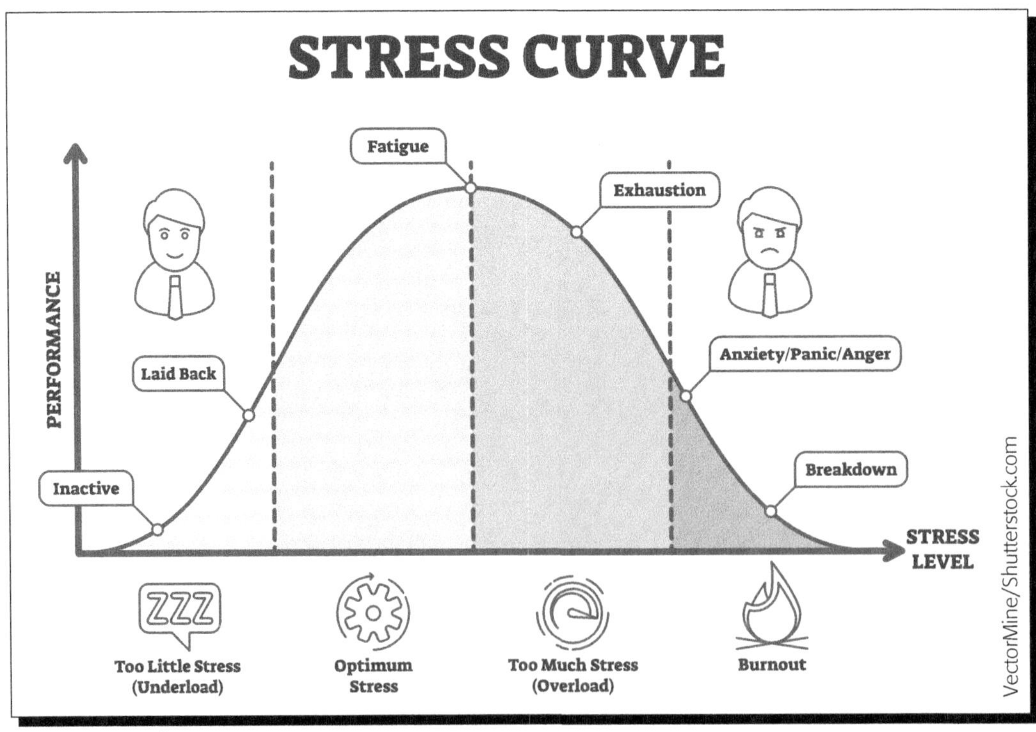

Figure 10-1. The stress curve

❑ Reflection Time:

What are some sources of positive stress in your life?

❑ Reflection Time:

Have you committed publicly to an endeavor, activity, or a goal, such as running a 5K? Eustress is associated with each of these.

❑ Reflection Time:

What are some deadlines that help you stay on track? Deadlines can help you cope with your stress in a healthy manner by making the challenge more manageable.

❑ Reflection Time:

Are there some people who can help you stay accountable on your journey? Accountability also helps stressful situations become more manageable.

❑ Reflection Time:

Give an example of when stress motivated or energized you to take action.

❑ Reflection Time:

Have you set and committed to SMART goals? How does having goals impact your stress (eustress or distress)?

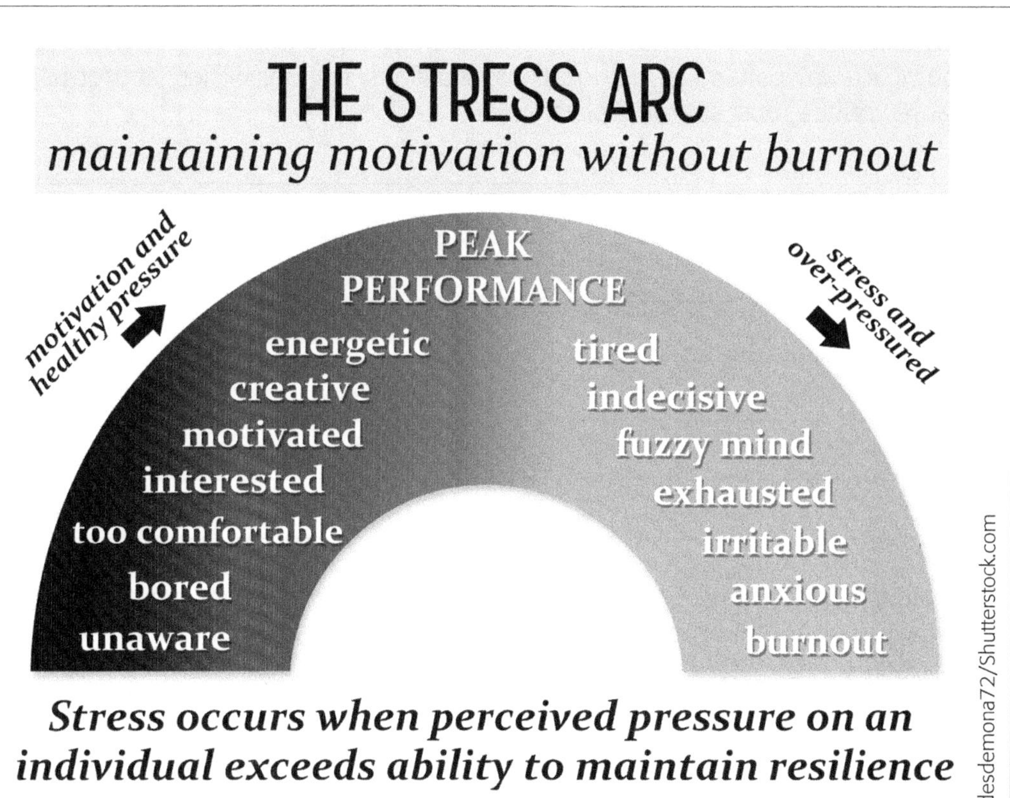

Figure 10-2. The stress arc

Your body is beautifully designed to handle short-term stressors; however, many of the stressors to which you are exposed today are prolonged or chronic, such as health concerns, financial instability, or being a caregiver.

❏ Reflection Time:

What are your sources of chronic stress?

❑ Reflection Time:

Do you notice any patterns about locations, situations, responsibilities, and/or people that cause you the most stress? Explain.

Another type of negative stress is psychological stress, which occurs when an individual perceives that environmental demands tax or exceed their adaptive capacity.[3]

❑ Reflection Time:

When considering your main sources of stress, do they exceed your current capacity to deal with them in a healthy way? Explain.

❑ Reflection Time:

What are you doing to address your stress at the present time?

❑ Reflection Time:

Which of these activities (that you are doing to address your current stress) do you consider healthy for you?

❑ Reflection Time:

Which of these activities (that you described above) do you consider unhealthy for you?

❑ Reflection Time:

Do you notice that how you think about a source of stress changes how you feel? Explain.

❑ Reflection Time:

Have there been times when you have thought something was extremely stressful, but when you took a break or tried to gain perspective in a new way, the stress was reduced by simply changing your mindset? Explain.

Stress can cause many symptoms, including:[4]

- Emotional effects: irritability, fear, nervousness, frustration, anger, insecurity, anxiety, worry, feeling scared, feeling out of control, feeling paralyzed
- Behavioral effects: poor sleep, less exercise, poor eating habits, drinking, smoking, use of risky substances, not following medical treatments, not monitoring blood sugars or fluid intake, not taking prescribed medications, social isolation, self-destructive behaviors like cutting, difficulty communicating, procrastination
- Cognitive effects: headaches, insomnia, difficulty remembering things, inability to concentrate, difficulty concentrating, poor focus, easily distracted
- Physiologic effects: increased heart rate, increased respiratory rate, sexual problems, gastrointestinal problems, frequent illnesses, weight gain or loss, increased cortisol

❑ Reflection Time:

What symptoms do you notice when you experience strain or chronic stress?

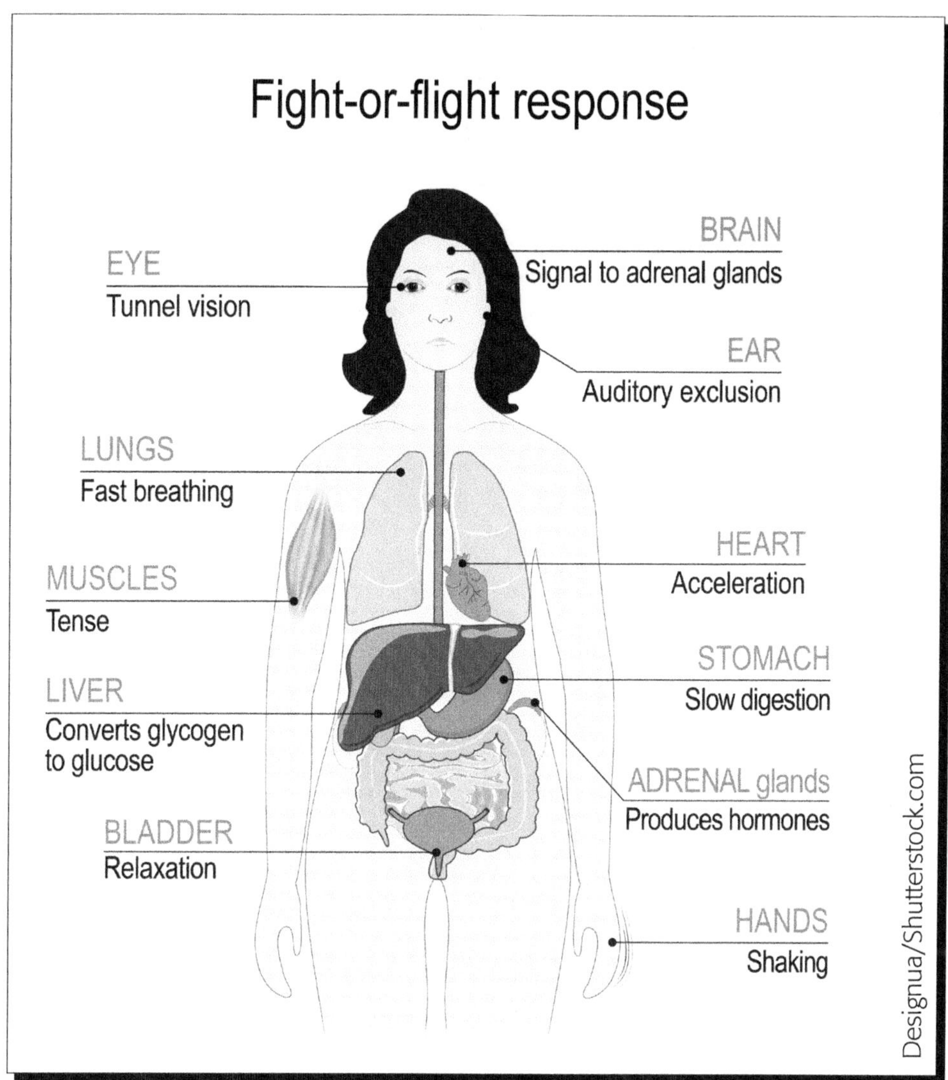

Figure 10-3. Symptoms of the fight-or-flight response

❑ Reflection Time:

What physical, emotional, and cognitive changes do you notice when you are experiencing high levels of stress?

____

____

____

____

____

____

____

____

____

❑ Reflection Time:

Is it more difficult to practice activities that support your health, such as healthy eating, exercise, and getting adequate sleep when you are experiencing high levels of stress? Explain.

___

___

___

___

___

___

___

❑ Reflection Time:

Do you notice that getting a good night's sleep, eating healthy foods, exercising, deep breathing, connecting with a friend, or other activities help you with managing your stress? Explain.

___

___

___

___

___

___

___

The fight-or-flight response describes what happens to you when you experience stress. Evolutionarily, there is a reason for the fight-or-flight response. When your ancestors encountered a predator, such as a lion, they would either fight or flee. After a long run, the lion might be gone, and they would be back to homeostasis and balance. Or, they would have fought the lion and either won, which would put them back into homeostasis. Or, they would have lost...and suffered the deadly consequences. In addition, there is also the freeze response to stress. In this case, the stress is so great, you freeze and become paralyzed by fear.

After you go into fight or flight with the lion, you then reach homeostasis again when it's all over. You may find yourself fighting with a colleague, a friend, a loved one, or a stranger in line at a store that could set off the sympathetic nervous system. If you don't take action to help resolve the issue, the stress can persist. Examples of healthy mental activities that could help you "fight" and get back into homeostasis would be discussing the issue with a trusted person, brainstorming ways to reach higher ground, compromising and negotiating a strategy for moving forward, reframing the situation to find a silver lining, positive self-talk, cognitive behavioral therapy, creating a to-do list with steps to tackle the challenge, creating SMART goals that detangle you from the stressor, treating yourself with a dose of self-compassion (speaking to yourself the way you would speak to a good friend), creating a strategy to help you make a positive out of a negative, or discussing the issue with a good friend. These mental fights mostly involve your brain.

Obviously, you aren't going to physically fight a lion, but examples of healthy activities that are like physical "fights" include physical activities such as Tai Chi, karate, jujitsu, Zumba, running, kickboxing, playing tag, dancing, and yoga, as well as activities like engaging in hobbies, doing puzzles, knitting, playing board games, and gardening. They engage your body and brain.

Instead of fighting, you can flee. You can also deal with stress through mental "flight" by performing meditation, deep breathing, mantra, prayer, mindfulness-based stress reduction (MBSR), or daydreaming. These activities give your brain a break from the stressor. You could also view funny videos, watch stand-up comedy, binge on Netflix, or converse on a different topic with a friend, colleague, or loved one. Among other forms of mental "flight" are expressive writing, journaling, writing poetry, thinking about all the things you are grateful for, listening to podcasts, and reading uplifting or calming blogs. These mental activities and ways to flee can reduce the stress by putting time and distance between you and the stressor or stressful event. This pause helps you to gain perspective as well as help you leave the sympathetic response and enter the parasympathetic state or rest and digest state.

Examples of physical "flight" or activities that use your body and brain to take a break from the stressor or stressful situation include hiking, jogging, forest "bathing," swimming, playing sports, and walking. You could also garden, play music, create music, paint pottery, wood work, volunteer at a food pantry, perform other acts of community service, write thank-you notes, meet a friend for tea or a walk, enjoy a warm bath, get a massage, drink herbal tea, mindfully eat a raisin, or chop wood.

❑ Reflection Time:

Which of these above activities are you using at the present time to manage stress in a healthy way?

❑ Reflection Time:

Which of the aforementioned activities would you like to try that you're currently not?

❑ Reflection Time:

What are some options for stress-reducing behaviors that you have that were not included in the aforementioned list?

Another weapon in your toolbox for being self-reliant is self-compassion. Self-compassion entails compassion to you in instances of perceived inadequacy, failure, or general suffering. According to Dr. Kristin Neff, in her book, *Self-compassion: The proven power of being kind to yourself,*[5] the three elements for self-compassion are the following:

- Self-kindness versus self-judgement. Instead of beating ourselves up when we make a mistake or something goes awry, we refrain from judging ourselves. We are all imperfect. We need to treat ourselves with sympathy and kindness. Be kind to yourself. Don't judge yourself. There is no place for shame, blame or guilt in the PAVING program.
- Common humanity versus isolation. Suffering and personal limitations are part of the shared human experience, common humanity. Feeling that you are the only person suffering is stressful. More than likely someone in the world is experiencing a similar feeling while you are feeling it, too.
- Mindfulness versus over-identification. You work to focus on the present moment and be mindful, without over-identifying with negative thoughts. Negative thoughts are part of life. Practice simply observing them without fixating on them. This is key to experience self-compassion.

❑ Reflection Time:

Explain how you can use the three elements for self-compassion described above in an area of your life.

____

____

____

____

____

____

____

Another tactic to address stressors and help solve problems is design thinking. In Bill Burnett & Dave Evans' bestselling book, *Designing Your Life: How to Build a Well-Lived, Joyful Life,*[6] they encourage people to be curious, try stuff, reframe problems, know it's a process, and ask for help. Accordingly, you can find innovative solutions through creating prototypes and then testing those prototypes.

❑ Reflection Time:

Is there an area of your life where you could use design thinking to address a source of stress? Explain.

____

____

____

❑ Reflection Time:

Describe three possible ways that you could address the stressor that you described in the previous question. Try to think beyond your typical ways of dealing with this source of stress. What could you try? Be curious and really think about what is causing the stress.

❑ Reflection Time:

Is there someone who you want to ask for help as you tackle this stressor? How might you reach out to them?

Resilience

Resilience is defined as being "capable of withstanding shock without permanent deformation or rupture" and "tending to recover from or adjust to misfortune or change."[7] Resilient individuals feel that they're in control of their lives. They have the confidence to tackle new adventures and challenges knowing that they will reach higher ground if they are successful or not. If they are not successful, they will learn and grow from the experience. They use a growth mindset, as described in the Attitude chapter. While you can't control your circumstances, you can control how you respond to those circumstances. As a result, you can impact your attitudes concerning a particular scenario and also the course your life takes. In other words, you have the innate ability to cope with stress (Figures 10-4 and 10-5).

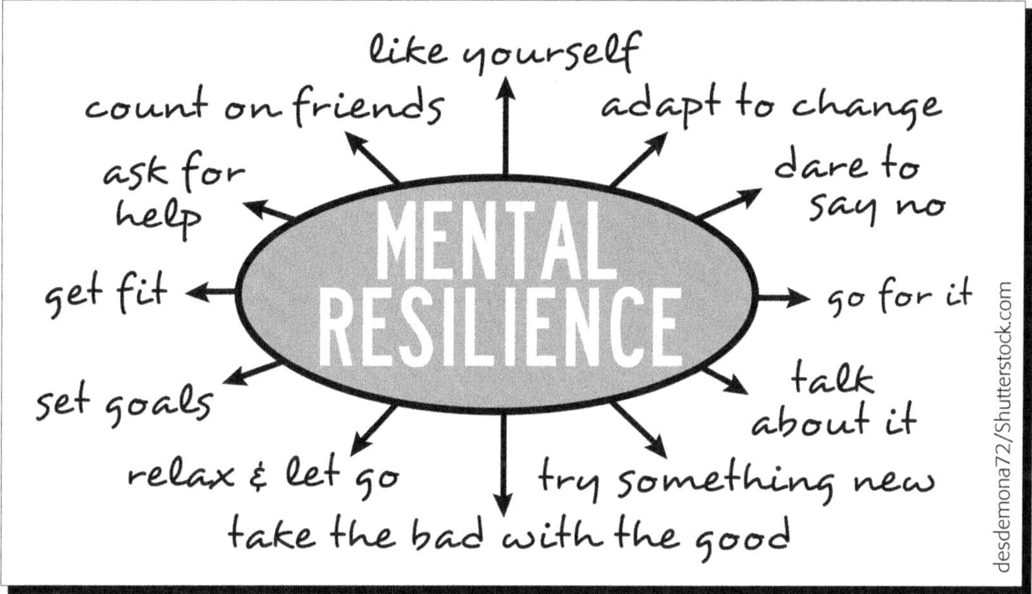

Figure 10-4. Options for developing mental resilience

Figure 10-5. Domains of resilience

❑ Reflection Time:

What does resilience mean to you?

____

____

____

____

____

____

____

____

❑ Reflection Time:

Think of times when you experienced stress and were resilient? Describe those situations.

____

____

____

____

____

____

____

____

According to Harvard Psychologist Dr. Robert Brooks,[8] although you cannot change all the stressors in life that you will encounter, you can change how you respond to stress by fostering resilience. Among the steps that can aid you in that regard are the following:

- Have a sense of purpose/meaning.
- Have a growth mindset.
- Practice mindfulness.
- Practice forgiveness.
- Cultivate optimism.
- Have supportive and meaningful relationships.
- Help, share, and serve others.
- Openly communicate.
- Exhibit gratitude.
- Be physically active.

- Practice the relaxation response.
- Engage in activities that you find enjoyable; experience fun, humor, and laughter.
- Sleep.
- Adhere to healthy eating patterns.
- Reframe and challenge your perceptions.
- Manage your expectations.
- Interact with a charismatic adult.
- Take action and have goals.
- Have an open mind; be flexible.
- Learn lessons and solve problems.
- Believe in yourself and have self-confidence.
- Live a value-based life.
- Be tolerant.
- Spend time in nature.
- Look for silver linings.
- Be flexible.
- Honor the opinions and thoughts of others, even if you don't agree, you can listen
- Select your battles wisely—is this worth a fight? How important is this to me?
- Reach out for help when you feel helpless.
- Surround yourself with people who are kind, compassionate, and helpful.

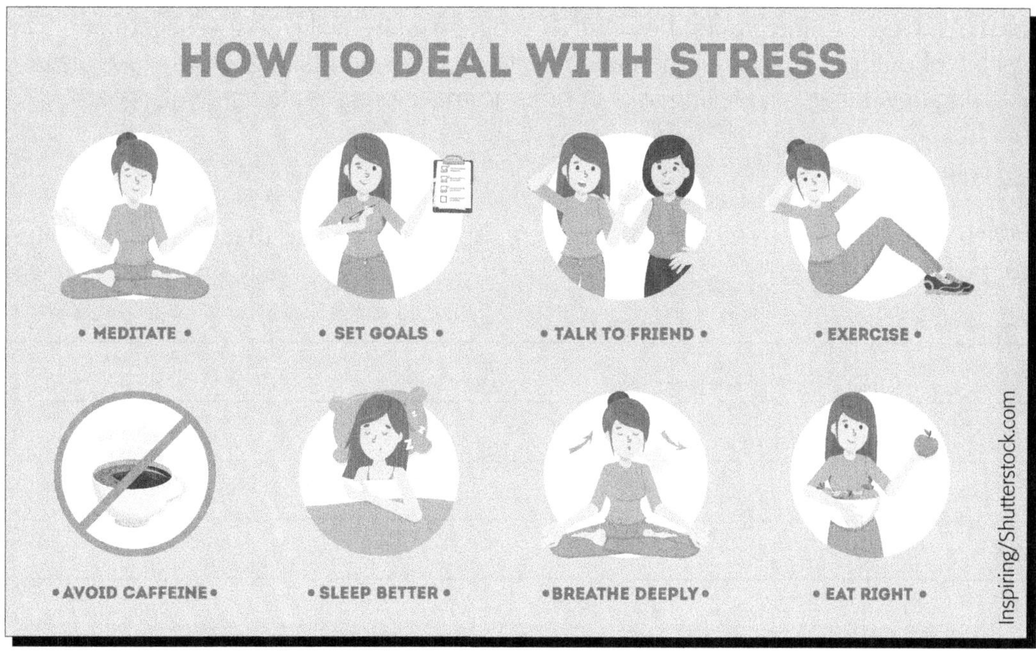

Figure 10-6. Options for dealing with stress

❑ Reflection Time:

Are there any of the aforementioned stress resiliency practices that you want to foster? Explain.

Growth Mindset

A mindset is defined as a set of assumptions, methods, or notions held by one or more people or groups of people. With regard to stress resilience, one particular aspect that you may need to address is how you view mistakes and/or failure. Mistakes are a part of life for everyone at every stage of life. The PAVING program encourages you to see mistakes and failures as opportunities to learn and grow. Everything in life won't go as you plan. The key is to adapt to your circumstances and learn from them. Remember perfection is often the enemy of progress. If you are paralyzed by the fear of making a mistake, imperfection, or the threat of an embarrasing mishap, you won't try new things or make progress. Integral to the PAVING program is the ability to investigate and try a variety of options. This experimentation invites success and failure. It may take practice in trying new things and taking risks in order to make progress toward your goals.

❑ Reflection Time:

When you experience setbacks or "failures," how can you use these as opportunities to grow?

❑ Reflection Time:

What do you think you could do to foster a growth mindset?

Caring Relationships

Another buffer against the negative effects of stress is having the support of a caring colleague, friend, or partner. Research has found that caring relationships that allow for quality emotional expression and have an orientation to learning and improving, support stress resilience.[9] There is more detail on this topic in the chapter on social support.

❑ Reflection Time:

What can you do to nurture a caring relationship in your life?

❑ Reflection Time:

How might you let this person know that they support your stress resilience?

❑ Reflection Time:

What actions can you take to be supportive of a friend who is suffering?

Gratitude

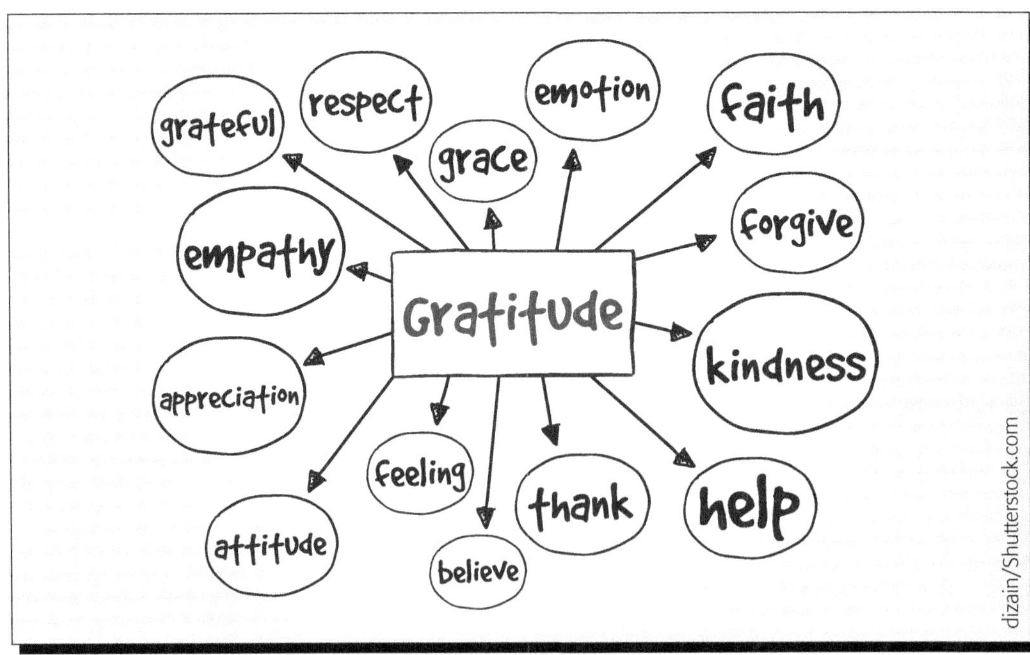

Figure 10-7. Examples of ways in which gratitude is expressed

Cultivating a sense of gratitude has been found to be one of the more straightforward ways for people to protect themselves from stress. According to American psychologist Dr. Robert Emmons,[10] gratitude is associated with increased happiness, positive emotions, strong relationships, alertness, health improvement, dealing with adversity, and making more progress toward goals. Gratitude practices also lead to increased levels of both energy and enthusiasm. Fortunately, you can cultivate gratitude in a number of ways, for example, by keeping a gratitude journal, being humble, seeing the positive—rather than the negative—in every situation, being inspired by others, assuming the positive in others, and starting each day by identifying what to be grateful for that day. More information on gratitude and attitude is in the chapter on attitude. Remember: it is impossible to be angry and grateful at the same time. If you choose gratitude, you are opening the door to deeper understanding and connection.

❑ Reflection Time:

Do you tend to put your focus on your hassles or on your blessings? Explain.

____

____

____

____

____

____

____

____

❑ Reflection Time:

For what are you most grateful, at this moment?

____

____

____

____

____

____

____

____

____

❑ Reflection Time:

How can you increase your focus on gratitude daily (gratitude journal, sticky notes, gratitude prayers, writing a thank-you note, reframing situations, talking to yourself in a more optimistic manner)?

There are many ways to manage stress that are healthy, including evidence-based peace-of-mind paths such as meditation, self-compassion, mindfulness, and relaxation. Peace-of-mind practices can decrease stress, feelings of anxiety and depression, while also improving mood and sleep quality. They are also associated with improved memory, learning, and focus.

❑ Reflection Time:

What activities or practices make you feel most peaceful?

Meditation is a type of mental exercise that typically involves active focus on the present moment and without judgement, observing thoughts and feelings from a distance. You can practice a mantra meditation exercise by doing the following:

- Setting an alarm and getting in a comfortable position
- Saying the mantra in your mind or out loud
- Breathing in and saying "I am"

- Exhaling and saying "relaxed"
- If focus is lost, refocusing non-judgmentally

Another mental exercise you can perform is 4-7-8 breathing. Although people are always breathing, they are rarely mindful of their breath. A 4-7-8 exercise will help activate your parasympathetic nervous system and increase relaxation. Practicing a 4-7-8 breathing, mindful meditation exercise can entail the following:

- Setting an alarm—no right or wrong amount of time
- Getting into a comfortable position and closing your eyes
- Noticing and feeling the sensation of your breath
- Inhaling to the count of 4
- Holding your breath to the count of 7
- Exhaling to the count of 8
- If you lose focus, without judgement, refocusing on your breath

❑ Reflection Time:

What did you notice from doing the meditation and/or 4-7-8 breathing exercises?

____

____

____

____

____

____

____

____

❑ Reflection Time:

Do you think that you could use these to increase your resilience to stress in the future?

____

____

____

____

____

____

____

____

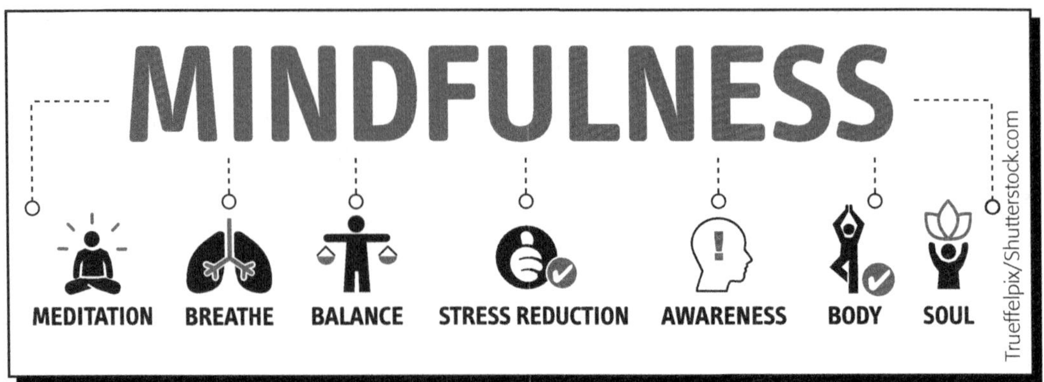

Figure 10-8. Key mindfulness factors

Another technique for calming your mind in stressful times is mindfulness. According to Jon Kabat-Zinn, the creator of the Mindfulness Based Stress Reduction (MBSR) program,[11] "mindfulness means paying attention in a particular way; on purpose, in the present moment, and non-judgmentally." Mindfulness includes being aware of what is happening in the present moment with awareness of your thoughts, feelings, and experiences in the moment. It also entails being non-judgmental. Using your five senses is a great way to get into the present moment. What do you smell, see, hear, feel, or taste?

❏ Reflection Time:

What are some ways that you could increase mindfulness moments throughout your day? Common examples include being mindful while washing your hands, eating, walking, or being in nature.

____

____

____

____

____

____

____

____

The relaxation response, a term coined by Dr. Herbert Benson, is another technique that has been shown to help people counteract the toxic effects of stress (Figure 10-9). During the "relaxation response," the body releases chemicals and the brain signals make muscles and organs slow down. Increased blood flow to the brain occurs and the body enters a deeply relaxed state. As a result, you lower your level of stress and your resting heart rate, while you increase your sense of well-being.

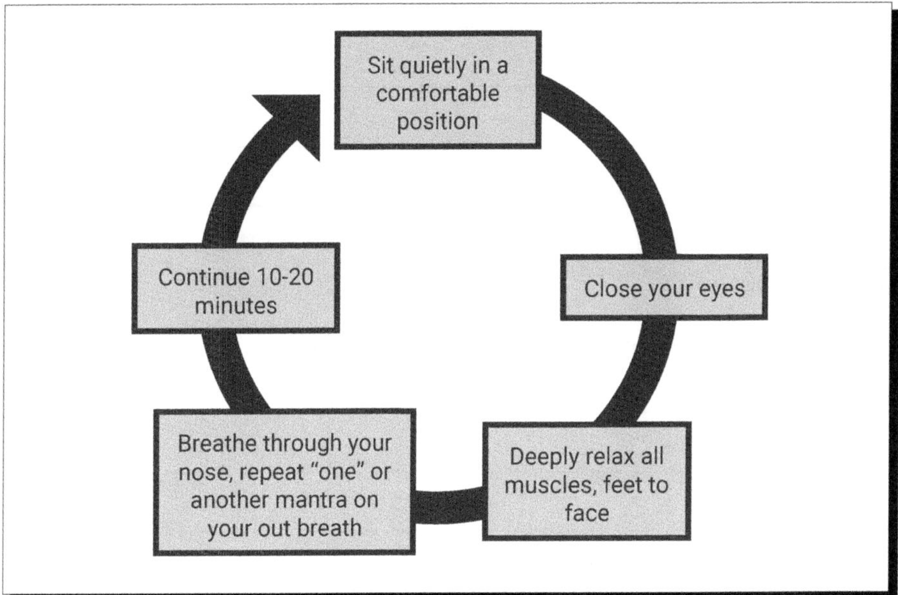

Figure 10-9. Engaging in the relaxation response

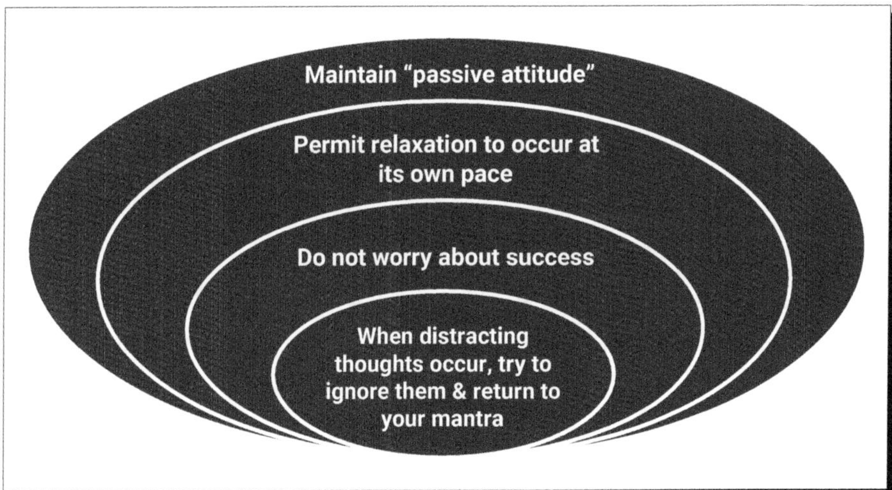

Figure 10-10. Crucial elements of the relaxation response

If you'd like to enhance your stress resilience, then trying to elicit the relaxation response can be a helpful option. Other paths to relaxation include guided imagery, progressive muscle relaxation, and repetitive movement physical activity like walking a meditation maze or just walking with full attention on each step you take.

❑ Reflection Time:

What did you experience during and after trying the relaxation response exercise?

____

____

____

____

____

❏ Reflection Time:

What can you do to increase relaxation in your daily life?

MOSS

Choose a stress resilience practice, skill or tool that you would like to incorporate into your life over the next few weeks. Then, answer the following questions:

❏ Question (motivation):

Why are you motivated to learn or try this stress resilience practice?

❏ Question (obstacles):

What obstacles are you likely to encounter?

❑ Question (strategies):

What strategies can you use to overcome these obstacles?

❑ Question (strengths):

What strengths can you draw upon as you work toward your goal? Consider strengths that you've used to overcome previous challenges and your support system, including your health care team, family, and friends.

SMART Goal

In order to take what you have learned about stress resilience and put it into action, create a SMART goal for yourself (refer to Chapter 4 page 55 for a detailed overview of what a SMART goal entails).

❏ SMART Goal Time:

What is your SMART goal for stress resilience? (Specific, Measurable, Action-oriented, Realistic, Time-sensitive)

___

___

___

___

___

___

___

___

References

❑ Cited References:

1. The American Institute of Stress. https://www.stress.org. Published June 17, 2021. Accessed July 15, 2021.
2. An interview with the "father of stress" about TM: Transcendental Meditation Blog. Transcendental Meditation Blog. http://www.tm.org/blog/people/interview-with-father-of-stress/. Accessed July 15, 2021.
3. Cohen S, Janicki-Deverts D, Miller GE. Psychological stress and disease. *Jama.* 2007 Oct 10;298(14):1685-7.
4. Wikgren S, Scott C, Rinaldi A. *Health and Wellness for Life.* Champaign, IL: Human Kinetics; 2010.
5. Neff K. *Self-Compassion: The Proven Power of Being Kind to Yourself.* New York: William Morrow Paperbacks; 2015.
6. Burnett B, Evans D. *Designing Your Life: How to Build a Well-Lived, Joyful Life.* New York: Knopf; 2016.
7. Merriam-Webster. www.mw.com.
8. Uscher J. 10 Tips to Help You Become More Resilient. WebMD. Dr. Robert Brooks, Harvard Psychologist. https://www.webmd.com/mental-health/features/overcome-obstacles-resilience. Accessed July 15, 2021.
9. Stephens JP, Heaphy ED, Carmeli A, et al. (2013). Relationship quality and virtuousness: emotional carrying capacity as a source of individual and team resilience. *The Journal of Applied Behavioral Science*, 49(1), 13–41.
10. Robert Emmons. Profile. Greater Good Magazine. https://greater good.berkeley.edu/profile/robert_emmons. Accessed July 15, 2021.
11. Kabat-Zinn J. *Wherever You Go, There You Are: Mindfulness Meditation in Everyday Life.* Hachette Books; 2009.

❑ Book Resources:

- Allen D. *Getting Things Done: The Art of Stress-Free Productivity.* Westminster, London, England. Penguin Books; 2002.
- Amen D. *The Brain Warrior's Way.* New York: Penguin Random House; 2016.
- Beiloch S. *Choke.* New York: Atria Paperbacks; 2010.
- Benson H. *The Wellness Book.* New York: Simon and Schuster; 1993.
- Eckmann TF. *101 Brain Boosters.* Monterey, CA: Healthy Learning; 2013.
- Eckmann TF, Eckmann KL. *101 Mindfulness and Meditation Practices.* Monterey, CA: Healthy Learning; 2018.
- Fabritias F. *The Leading Brain.* New York: TarcherPerigee; 2017.
- Harris D. *10% Happier: How I Tamed the Voice in My Head, Reduced Stress Without Losing My Edge, and Found Self-Help That Actually Works—A True Story.* New York: Day Streets Books; 2014.
- Kabat-Zinn J, Hanh TN. *Full Catastrophe Living: Using the Wisdom of Your Body and Mind to Face Stress, Pain, and Illness.* New York: Bantam; 2013.
- Kabat-Zinn J. *The Healing Power of Mindfulness: A New Way of Being.* New York: Hachette Books; 2018.

- Lauger EJ. *Mindfulness*, 2nd ed. Boston, MA: Da Capo Lifelong Books; 2014.
- McGonigal K. *The Upside of Stress: Why Stress Is Good for You and How to Get Good at It.* New York: Avery; 2016.
- Neff K. *Self-Compassion: The Proven Power of Being Kind to Yourself.* New York: William Morrow Paperbacks; 2015.
- Perlmutter LT. *The Heart and Science of Yoga: The American Medication Association's Empowering Self-Love Program to a Happy, Healthy, Joyful Life*. New York: AMI Publishers; 2017.
- Quach D. *Calm Clarity.* New York: TarcherPerigee; 2018.
- Rama S. *The Art of Joyful Living.* Honesdale, PA: Himalayan Institute Press; 1989.
- Rose S. *Whole Beauty: Meditation and Mindfulness—Rituals and Exercises for Everyday Self-Care.* New York: Artisan; 2019.
- Sapolsky RM. *Why Zebras Don't Get Ulcers*, 3rd ed. New York: Holt Paperbacks; 2004.
- Sood A. *Mayo Clinic Guide to Stress-Free Living.* Boston, MA: Da Capo Lifelong books; 2013.
- Storoni M. *Stress-Proof: The Scientific Solution to Protect Your Brain and Body—And Be More Resilient Every Day.* New York: TarcherPerigee; 2017.
- Wikgren S, Scott C, Rinaldi A. *Health and Wellness for Life.* Champaign, IL: Human Kinetics; 2010.
- Yoke M. *101 Nice-to-Know Facts About Happiness.* Monterey, CA: Healthy Learning; 2015.

❑ Other Resources:

- Benson-Henry Institute at Massachusetts General Hospital—www.bensonhenryinstitute.org
- Mind Body Medicine—cmbm.org
- Mindfulness Based Stress Reduction Program (MBSR)—positivepsychology.com

CHAPTER 11
TIME-OUTS

"There is virtue in work and there is virtue in rest. Use both and overlook neither."

—Alan Cohen
American Author

PAVING the Path to Wellness: Questions for Time-Outs

For each of the following five statements, choose the number on the frequency scale that best relates to you (frequency: 1= never, 2= rarely, 3= sometimes, 4= often, 5= routine).

- If I sit for over an hour, I stand up and take a break for five minutes each hour.____
- If I feel frustrated and annoyed, I take a few deep breaths to calm down. ____
- I take a vacation every year. ____
- When I am at home, I make sure to turn off my computer and put my work projects away at least for an hour at dinner time. ____
- After working on the same project for a few hours, I step away from it to get perspective on it. ____

Subtotal—time-outs: ____

Min C. Chiu/Shutterstock.com

Live and Learn: Dr. Michelle Tollefson

It seemed like every moment of my calendar was booked from the moment I woke until bedtime, often exhausted from caring for my three young children, a new puppy, and responding to student emails as a university professor. Taking time-outs seemed like a luxury that I couldn't afford.

Then, I received the phone call that changed my life forever, when I learned that a routine screening mammogram had found a tumor against my chest wall. My well-planned schedule fell apart in a moment as the next seven months were filled with multiple surgeries, chemotherapy, and more doctor's appointments than I could ever have imagined.

Initially I fought to continue my pre-breast cancer schedule as much as possible. However, as weeks of chemotherapy progressed, I realized that I needed to rely on others, as friends delivered food, and my family watched my children, while I rested and focused on my health.

Although I wish that it hadn't taken a cancer diagnosis to teach me about the importance of time-outs, I appreciate the power of time-outs to refresh me, to empower me to be more present with my family, and to give me perspective. Pausing and nurturing quiet times has allowed me to appreciate life and the people in it more deeply. Although my strength has returned, and I can make it through my days again without time-outs, I continue to prioritize these precious pauses that help bring peace to my life.

The words "time-out" can sometimes have a negative connotation. Though taking a time-out for a child may be viewed by some people as a punishment, a more positive view of a time-out, even for a child, may be taking time away from the situation that was causing stress, distress, or problematic behavior. This period not only allows for reflection and distance from the stressor, it also provides quiet time that can help reset the mind.

As an adult, stressful situations or circumstances may cause unwanted feelings or behaviors if they are prolonged. Just like children, adults can also benefit from having a time-out.

❑ Reflection Time:

What words do you think of when you hear the term "time-out"?

____

____

____

____

____

____

____

____

____

Among the words that people connect to time-outs are solitude, quiet, peace, pause, holiday, alone, stillness, reset, and private. More formal definitions of the term "time-out" include:[1]

- A short period of time during a sports event, when the game stops, and the players rest or talk to their coach
- A short period of time, when you stop doing something so that you can rest or do something else
- A short period of time, when a child must sit quietly as punishment for behaving badly

Most people are so busy being busy that they hardly stop to go to the bathroom. They are engaged in a fast-paced society, with many external demands on their time and energy. Often, they don't have scheduled "free-time," and even if they do have a canceled appointment, it is usually filled with business, as they work on their email inbox, their to-do list, or scroll social media. Being busy and talking about how busy you are is a sign of strength in society today. It's like a status symbol to be super busy. What is everyone so busy doing? What if there were a paradigm shift and speaking about how calm you felt, even in the midst of chaos, was the revered attitude? What if talking about inner peace and reaching higher ground was the norm? Instead of stressing the stressful aspects of your day, if you highlighted the solutions you came up with and the beauty you found, how would your conversations be different?

❑ Reflection Time:

Do you find it easy or difficult to take time-outs? Explain.

____

____

____

____

____

____

____

❑ Reflection Time:

If you find it challenging, what beliefs or circumstances are making it difficult for you?

____

____

____

____

____

____

____

❑ Reflection Time:

If you are successfully taking time-outs, what circumstances or beliefs are allowing you to do that?

Time-Outs as Empowerment

Some people struggle with feeling guilty for taking time-outs or worry that others think they are being lazy, selfish, or wasting time. However, you can change your way of thinking about taking time-outs by considering them to be empowerment moments.

During a discussion of time-outs during a Harvard University PAVING workshop, Michelle Guo, then a pre-med student and now a physician, raised her hand and shared her reflection on time-outs with Dr. Frates and her classmates. She said, "I think time-outs are actually empowerment moments, and if we change the way we talk about them, we'll change the way we feel about them." The words you choose to use and the labels you place on ideas, people, and projects are powerful. When you take a time-out, you are putting a space between the stimulus and your response. The gives you power. Hence, the time-out is an empowerment moment.

❑ Reflection Time:

How can you use time-outs to empower yourself?

Taking time-outs can allow you to reboot, repower, refresh, and recharge, for when you reengage with your responsibilities. For example, when you are on a plane and the flight attendants demonstrate the use of seat belts and oxygen masks, they are very clear in their instructions. They state, "Secure your oxygen mask before helping anyone with theirs." This is a very good analogy for life. Everyone needs to make sure they are safe and well so that they can help others. Self-care means taking time-out of your busyness to care for yourself. It invites you to prioritize yourself.

"If I am not good to myself, how can I expect anyone else to be good to me?"

—Maya Angelou
American Poet

❏ Reflection Time:

How can you work to you prioritize time-outs in your day?

____

____

____

____

____

____

____

____

❏ Reflection Time:

Reframe to ask yourself, how will taking a "time-out" empower me to make the most of my time when I reengage? Does this change in wording change how you feel about time-outs?

____

____

____

____

____

____

____

____

____

Time-outs don't have to involve a week-long vacation. Time-out moments can be just a minute to stretch, to take a few deep breaths. They can also involve the following:

- Examples of one- to five-minute time-out activities—walk, stretch, get a glass of water, listen to music, pet your cat or dog, do a plank, send an "I love you" message to your loved one, take a couple of deep breaths.
- Examples of 5-10 minute time-out activities—brief meditation, relaxation response, mindfulness-based stress reduction, yoga moves, tai-chi, read a few pages in a book, dance, hula hoop, call a friend, get outside, write a thank-you note, write in your journal, identify three things you are grateful for, listen to a short podcast, color in a coloring book, sing a song, give a friend or loved one a hug.

❑ Reflection Time:

List other ways you can take a time-out, if you have 1-10 minutes.

____

____

____

____

____

____

____

- Examples of 20-30 minute time-out activities—take a nap (nature's time-out for the body), meditate, take a longer walk, talk to a friend, listen to music, dance to music, dance with your partner, sit in silence, stare off into the sunset, let your mind wander, reflect, set goals, listen to a podcast, create an uplifting post on social media, write a thank-you note, walk your dog, take a swim, paddle board, do yoga, do mindfulness-based stress reduction, meditate, read a book, hug and kiss your loved one, eat a healthy snack, stretch.

❑ Reflection Time:

What are some ideas you have for taking 20-30-minute time-outs?

____

____

____

____

____

____

____

____

Time-Outs as Renewal

You can use your time in a time-out to simply relax or daydream. Alternatively, you can use the time to reflect and gain self-awareness by evaluating, analyzing, or simply considering questions about your motivation, inspiration, purpose, or inner voice. As bestselling author Stephen Covey once remarked,[2] "You can revitalize yourself and face a new day in peace and harmony. Or you can wake up in the morning full of apathy, because your get-up-and-go has got-up-and-gone. Just remember that every day provides a new opportunity for renewal—a new opportunity to recharge yourself instead of hitting the wall."

❑ Reflection Time:

In what areas are you feeling balance and equanimity?

___

___

___

___

___

___

___

___

❑ Reflection Time:

In what areas are you feeling out of control or in chaos?

____

____

____

____

____

____

____

____

❑ Reflection Time:

For the areas that feel chaotic, what needs to be in place to restore balance?

____

____

____

____

____

____

____

____

As previously noted, physical time-outs play a role in achieving and maintaining a sense of well-being. In addition, time-outs from technology are essential to staying in the present moment of your own life and appreciating the people and projects that exist currently. Too many times, people are multitasking, trying to listen to friends and family, while answering emails on their phone; being in online meetings, while scrolling through social media; or being at the dinner table on their phone, answering texts. Keep in mind that being in bed and looking through funny videos, watching late night television, or doomscrolling on your iPad, prevents you from sound sleep and really connecting with your partner. If someone comes to your home to visit you, and you can't put your phone away, what does that say to your friend? What does that say to you?

❑ Reflection Time:

How do you feel when someone is looking at their phone or screen on their computer or iPad while they are talking to you?

❑ Reflection Time:

What are things you can do to ensure that when you are with colleagues in a meeting, hanging out with friends, or eating with family members, you don't pick up your phone to check messages?

Research has been conducted that indicates that when you take breaks from work, you increase your level of productivity. This seems counterintuitive to many individuals, who feel that more time working translates to greater productivity. As it turns out, working smarter does not necessarily mean working harder or longer. In fact, working smarter can also increase your degree of accuracy. For example, researchers from the New Century Global and Cornell University studied employees for 10 weeks.[3] One group of employees received reminders on their computers to have good posture and take short breaks and the other group did not receive these messages. Those who received reminders were 13 percent more accurate in their tasks than those who did not get a reminder. In another study in the journal *Cognition*,[4] it was found that brief mental breaks kept people focused and more vigilant in their work.

Pomodoro Technique for Productivity

There is a technique for increasing productivity that chunks active work time into 25-minute bursts, followed by breaks of five minutes, called the Pomodoro technique.[5] You work on major tasks by dividing them into "pomodoro" episodes of intense work. You do three bouts of 25 minutes with a five-minute break. After that, you take a 25-minute break. The reason that it was invented is because if you give yourself infinite time to complete a task, you will fill that time with work and decrease your level of productivity. Pomodoro is Italian for tomato, and the inventor of the technique had a timer in the shape of a tomato. This factor is something to consider when scheduling a day of work.

Among the suggestions for making time-outs an integral part of your routine are:

- When you feel your focus decline, then take a walk or sit quietly and take deep breaths.
- You can set an alarm to go off every hour.
- Be aware that you only need to allot 5-10 minutes to regroup and rejuvenate.
- Do what works well for you–try experimenting (N=1).

A longer break, like a vacation, is also important for well-being. The following 12 reasons help reinforce why you should take your vacation days.[6] Taking vacations:

- Increases productivity.
- Improves performance by 80 percent.
- Boosts workplace morale.
- Helps to retain employees.
- Provides health benefits.
- Decreases stress.
- Strengthens relationships with the people with whom you travel.
- Improves mental health, decreases depression, and burnout.
- Opens your eyes to different cultures, traditions, and locations.
- Increases creativity.
- Increases motivation to work, achieve goals, and be productive up to eight weeks prior to leaving for a vacation.
- Helps you get through tough times by having something to look forward to (e.g., vacation).
- Creates memories that can last a lifetime.

Longer hours do not equal greater productivity. This has been known for a relatively long time. American automaker Henry Ford reduced the workweek of his factories from six to five days and the workweek hours from 48-40. In the process, Ford stated, "Just as the eight-hour day opened our way to prosperity, so the five-day week will open our way to a still greater prosperity."[7]

Human energy is a limited resource. People are innately built to spend energy and then recover it. They do it in 90-minute cycles (90 minutes of alertness, followed by a state of fatigue). Energy is explored in detail in its own chapter.

It is important to be aware that great ideas often come when people take a break, for example, while walking, showering, running, or after sleeping. "I thought of that while riding my bicycle," Albert Einstein once replied, when discussing his Theory of Relativity.

There are times when you may feel a need to take a break, such as the following:

- From working on a computer—after sitting at the computer for an hour
- From watching TV—after watching television for an hour
- From reading—after reading for an hour
- From sitting (remember: "sitting is the new smoking." Accordingly, get up and move at least every hour, sit on a bouncy ball, or use a treadmill desk.)
- From talking—take the time to listen to others
- After hearing bad news or reading an offensive, aggravating email
- After laughing so hard that your belly hurts
- After feeling anxious and stressing
- From fighting—after arguing with someone

When conversations get heated, you can say something like the following:

- "Let's talk about this another time."
- "Can we take a break and get back to this topic in a few minutes?"
- "I am feeling upset and agitated right now. It will be best to talk about this later."
- "Will you please excuse me?"

One sure-fire way to get out of a situation or a difficult conversation is to tell the other person that you need to go to the bathroom. This is a comment that people will not argue with you about. While you are in the bathroom, you are by yourself and can take deep breaths, can reflect, and, most importantly, can disengage from the difficult circumstances. By doing this, you also give the other person a break. This time-out is often just what people need to calm down and address the issues with greater clarity.

A time-out is often just what people need to calm down and address an issue with greater clarity.

Praethip Docekalova/Shutterstock.com

Self-Care

Self-care is what people do for themselves to establish and maintain health, as well as prevent and deal with illness. It is a broad concept encompassing:[8]

- Hygiene (general and personal)
- Nutrition (type and quality of food eaten)
- Lifestyle (sporting activities, leisure etc.)
- Environmental factors (e.g., living conditions, social habits, etc.)
- Socioeconomic factors (income level, cultural beliefs, etc.)
- Self-medication

The World Health Organization defines self-care as "the ability of individuals, families and communities to promote health, prevent disease, maintain health, and cope with illness and disability, with or without the support of a healthcare provider."[9]

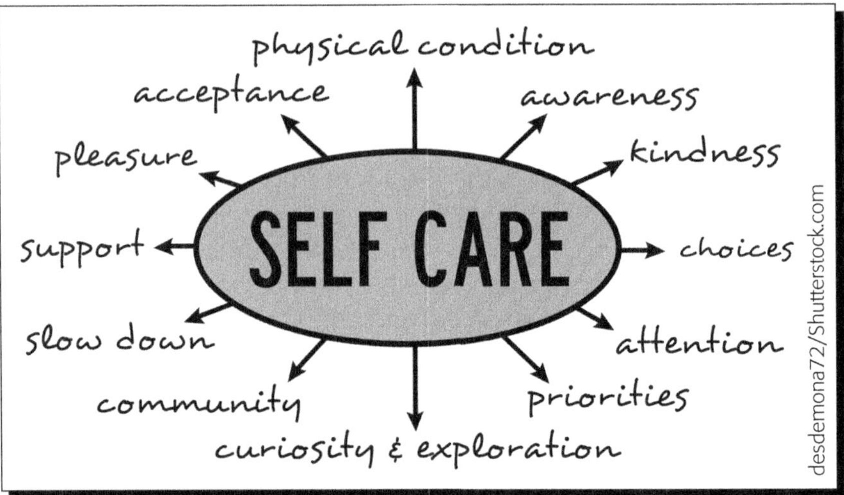

Figure 11-1. Key factors in self-care

❑ Reflection Time:

If you feel like you are experiencing any signs of burnout, please consider seeking professional help by reaching out to a mental health professional or other care provider.

MOSS

Consider how you would like to incorporate time-outs into your life over the next few weeks and then use MOSS to help you make this desire a reality. Evaluate the role that time-outs play in your life and then answer the following questions:

❑ Question (motivation):

Why are you motivated to take a particular type of time-out?

❑ Question (obstacles):

What obstacles are you likely to encounter?

❑ Question (strategies):

What strategies can you use to overcome these obstacles?

❑ Question (strengths):

What strengths can you draw upon as you work toward your goal? Consider strengths that you've used to overcome previous challenges and your support system, including your healthcare team, family, and friends.

Your support system for dealing with challenging circumstances includes your healthcare team, family, and friends.

SMART Goal

In order to take what you have learned about time-outs and put it into action, create a SMART goal for yourself (refer to Chapter 4 page 55 for a detailed overview of what a SMART goal entails).

❑ SMART Goal Time:

Detail your SMART goal for time-outs.

____

____

____

____

____

____

____

____

References

❑ Cited References:

1. Merriam-Webster. www.mw.com.
2. Covey SR. *The 7 Habits of Highly Effective People: Powerful Lessons in Personal Change*. New York: Simon and Schuster; 2004.
3. Lang SS. When workers heed computer's reminder to take a break, their productivity jumps, Cornell study finds. *Cornell Chronicle*. https://news.cornell.edu/stories/1999/09/onscreen-break-reminder-boosts-productivity. Published September 23, 1999. Accessed July 15, 2021.
4. Ariga A, Lleras A (2011). Brief and rare mental "breaks" keep you focused. Deactivation and reservation of task goals preempt vigilance decrements. *Cognition*. 118(3), 439–443.
5. Nöteberg S. *Pomodoro Technique Illustrated: The Easy Way to Do More in Less Time*. Raleigh, NC: Pragmatic Bookshelf; 2009.
6. Hoeller SC (2015, July 3). 8 reasons why Americans should take their vacation days. Business Insider. https://www.businessinsider.com/why-americans-should-take-their-vacation-days-2015-6. Accessed July 15, 2021.
7. HENRY FORD: Why I Favor Five Days' Work With Six Days' Pay. Wikisource. https://en.wikisource.org/wiki/HENRY_FORD:_Why_I_Favor_Five_Days%27_Work_With_Six_Days%27_Pay. Published December 4, 2012. Accessed July 15, 2021.

8. Webber D, Guo Z, Mann S (2015). Self-care in health: we can define it, but should we also measure it? *Selfcare Journal*, 4(5), 98–114.
9. World Health Organization. Self-care interventions for health. https://www.who.int/news-room/fact-sheets/detail/self-care-health-interventions#:~:text=What%20is%20self%2Dcare%3F,support%20of%20a%20health%20worker.

❑ Book Resources:

- Hahn TN. *How to Relax.* Berkeley, CA: Parallax Press; 2015.
- Neston J. *Breath: The New Science of a Lost Art.* New York: Riverhead Books; 2020.
- Nolan A, Schumann K, Callahan S. *Mothers Need Time-Outs Too: It's Good to Be a Little Selfish—It Actually Makes You a Better Mother*. New York: McGraw-Hill Education; 2008.
- Nöteberg S. *Pomodoro Technique Illustrated: The Easy Way to Do More in Less Time.* Raleigh, NC: Pragmatic Bookshelf; 2009.
- Payne D. *Time-Out: Adult Coloring Book.* Scotts Valley, CA: CreateSpace Independent Publishing Platform; 2015.
- Schwartz SY, Goldstein D. *Unplug: A Simple Guide to Meditation for Busy Skeptics and Model Soul Seekers.* New York: Harmony; 2017.
- Soojung A, Pang K. *Rest: Why You Get More Done When You Work Less.* New York: Basic Books; 2016.

❑ Other Resources:

- Take vacation time.
- Limit your time responding to emails.
- Take a day away from technology.
- Take mini-breaks once each hour.
- Walk around the room or up and down the stairs.
- Ride a bike.
- Track your time-outs.
- Track your creativity/productivity.

CHAPTER 12
ENERGY

"What lies behind us and what lies before us are tiny matters compared to what lies within us."

—Ralph Waldo Emerson
American Essayist

PAVING the Path to Wellness: Questions for Energy

For each of the five following statements, choose the number on the frequency scale that best relates to you (frequency: 1= never, 2= rarely, 3= sometimes, 4= often, 5= routinely).

- I have a friend who I know energizes me. ____
- I have identified at least one activity that brings me joy and energy. ____
- I am able to avoid situations and people that drain my energy. ____
- I only drink two cups of coffee a day. ____
- I don't rely on sugar/sweets or cookies for a quick energy fix. ____

Subtotal—energy: ____

fizkes/Shutterstock.com

Live and Learn: Dr. Amy Comander

During the pandemic, many of us made the abrupt shift to work from home. As a doctor, I continued to work most days in the hospital; however, on one or two days per week, I work remotely and practice telemedicine. Before and after my busy virtual clinic sessions, I also have numerous virtual meetings related to my work at the Massachusetts General Hospital Cancer Center in Waltham, or at the American College of Lifestyle Medicine, or in board meetings—such as work I do with the non-profit organization, the Ellie Fund.

On these remote work days, by the afternoon I have noticed that I feel more exhausted than usual. Why was I feeling more fatigue by the afternoon? I was at home, wearing comfortable clothing, and I did not have to deal with a work commute! Then, I read about the concept of "Zoom fatigue," which describes the tiredness, worry, or burnout associated with overusing virtual platforms of communication.[1]

I have read that Zoom fatigue is now widely prevalent, and a new phenomenon for many of us. Our brains are not "wired" for social interactions that occur through a video platform! Our routine social interactions are associated with "reward circuits" in our brains, which enable us to remain alert and engaged. A Zoom meeting is far from a normal social interaction—there are inherent audio delays, lack of real eye contact, and other non-verbal cues that our brains need to process. These factors result in increased cognitive effort and less "reward" from the social interaction.

I have found that the best antidote to Zoom fatigue is an easy one… get outside! Increasing scientific research has demonstrated that spending time in nature is critical to our health and well-being. In fact, the Japanese have a term for this *shinrinyoku*, which means "forest bathing," and refers to the importance of spending time in the woods. Research has shown that this practice on a regular basis can lower blood pressure, heart rate, and stress hormones, and thus lead to decreased anxiety, depression, and fatigue. Even if I cannot get out into the woods during the day, I have found that a brief walk in my neighborhood is refreshing. I have also found that taking a break in between video meetings, perhaps with a brief stretch or walking to the kitchen for a glass of ice water, can help me maintain my energy.

One of the best antidotes for Zoom fatigue is to get outside.

Ivica Drusany/Shutterstock.com

❑ Reflection Time:

What words come to mind when you think of the word energy? List as many words as you can.

According to the *Merriam-Webster Dictionary*, energy has a variety of definitions, including the following:[2]

- Dynamic quality: narrative energy
- The capacity of acting or being active: intellectual energy
- A usually positive spiritual force: the energy flowing through all people
- Vigorous exertion of power: effort: investing time and energy
- A fundamental entity of nature that is transferred between parts of a system in the production of physical change within the system and usually regarded as the capacity for doing work
- Usable power (such as heat or electricity)

❑ Reflection Time:

Which of these definitions of energy resonates the most with you? Why?

Most people do not consider energy when they think about wellness, even though your energy significantly impacts your level of wellness. Instead, people are really focused on time and time management. The thing to remember is that you may have time to do something, but you may not have the energy. Accordingly, honoring your energy levels is critical for balance and well-being. Recognizing what gives you energy and what drains your energy will allow you to enjoy this type of balance.

❏ Reflection Time:

List people, places, and projects that give you energy.

____

____

____

____

____

____

____

____

❏ Reflection Time:

List people, places, and projects that drain your energy.

____

____

____

____

____

____

____

____

The concept that some people can drain your energy is difficult for some people to consider. However, everyone can acknowledge that there are people in their lives who are so compassionate, understanding, and full of love that they have an ability to provide loving kindness in all interactions. This loving kindness translates into positive, powerful energy. You are blessed when you can surround yourself with these types of energizing people that can be referred to as "lilies."

The goal is to be a lily and to surround yourself with lilies. First, you need to recognize and acknowledge the lilies in your life. This would be a good time to contact those lilies and thank them for the energy they continue to provide to you. They may be completely unaware that they are lilies.

❑ Reflection Time:

How can you maximize the time that you spend with the people, places, and projects that energize you?

The opposite of the lily is more difficult to discuss. It is the leech. These people drain you. Sometimes just the thought of them is enough to tire you. Knowing when these people will be on your schedule for a meeting tends to negatively impact you prior to the meeting. Understanding what it is about the leech that drains you is important for your own self-awareness.

Being open and honest with yourself and being able to identify the leeches in your life is the first step. Being able to set boundaries for yourself, to limit your time with leeches, and in some circumstances to even remove leeches from your life, will add a tremendous amount of energy and joy to your day-to-day existence. This is not easy and takes time. Setting boundaries is a critical step to managing energy.

❑ Reflection Time:

How can you minimize time spent with the people, places, and projects that drain you of energy?

____

____

____

____

____

____

____

____

____

Almost everyone is familiar with the concept of karma: what goes around, comes around. What is the exact science involved in this? Who knows? However, being kind, respectful, a team-player, and thoughtful will allow you to experience a calm, positive energy for yourself, as well as exude this to others. People with a positive, optimistic outlook tend to be drawn to people who search for the silver lining, work to reach higher ground whatever the circumstance, try to build up others around them, and realize their words and actions leave imprints that can empower or impede others.

You can't always be positive or be around positive people. Difficult situations will arise. Death will happen. You will grieve. This is part of life. There will be times when your energy will be drained due to the natural ups and downs and rhythms of being human, such as experiencing loss of a job, relationship, money, people, projects, or health. An optimistic, positive attitude will allow you to balance out your negative experience with opportunities to heal, connect with others, open the door to new opportunities, and to thrive once again. Sometimes, life is a roller coaster.

"Life is like riding a bicycle. To keep balance, you have to keep moving."

—Albert Einstein
Theoretical Physicist

Your energy levels, and specifically working toward maintaining high levels of energy and increasing energy levels, are important for you to be able to traverse the low and to rise again. It's really a matter of balance.

"Energy, not time, is the fundamental currency of high performance."

—Jim Loehr, EdD
Performance Psychologist

Managing Energy

According to Jim Loehr and Terry Schwartz in their book *The Power of Full Engagement*,[3] managing energy to increase your level of engagement involves adhering to a new paradigm (Figure 12-1).

Old Paradigm	**New Paradigm**
Manage time	Manage energy
Avoid stress	Seek stress
Life is a marathon	Life is a series of sprints
Downtime is wasted time	Downtime is productive time
Rewards fuel performance	Purpose fuels performance
Self-discipline rules	Rituals rule
The power of positive thinking	The power of full engagement

Figure 12-1. The power of full engagement (from Loehr & Schwartz, 2005)

According to Jim Loehr and Tony Schwartz, there are four types of energy—physical, emotional, mental, and spiritual (Figure 12-2).[3]

Physical Energy	**Emotional Energy**
Self-regulation	Frequent positive emotion
Frequent active leisure	High quality connections
→ Active parasympathetic system and better recovery from stress and threat	→ Behavioral flexibility, creativity, capacity to see opportunity
Mental Energy	**Spiritual Energy**
Realistic optimism and positive self-talk	Having a "why" to live
Experiences of deep engagement	Shared and valued purpose
	Awareness of values
→ Capacity to concentrate, create, learn, bounce back	→ Greater joy, tolerance for inevitable obstacles

Figure 12-2. The four types of energy (from Loehr & Schwartz, 2005)

PHYSICAL ENERGY

Sources of physical energy are exercise, nutrition, sleep, and time-outs. When you exercise, you increase the number of mitochondria in your cells. Mitochondria are the "powerhouses" in your body. Many people feel they are too tired to exercise. If they do go for a walk or engage in some physical activity, they will likely feel energized at the end of their session. As well as helping to build muscle strength and endurance, they are also increasing their number of mitochondria, which will enhance their energy levels.

What you put into your mouth fuels you. When you follow the eating pattern similar to the Harvard Healthy plate, Mediterranean diet, or a whole-food, plant-predominant diet, you are nourishing all of your organs, muscles, nerves, brain cells, and even your gut microbiome, with phytonutrients, antioxidants, fiber, vitamins, minerals, and prebiotics. Your brain operates on glucose and physical activities requires glucose. However, you don't want to consume straight sugar and simple carbohydrates. It is better to consume complex carbohydrates like whole grains, vegetables, and other whole-foods that are digested over time and can release glucose at a steady rate, allowing optimal functioning without sugar highs and lows. Regular meals and snacks help to maintain your energy level throughout the day.

Sleep allows you to clear toxins, repair cellular damage, consolidate memories, rest and rejuvenate. Without sleep it's very difficult to feel energized during the day. Sleep is essential for energy. Naps before 3 p.m. for 20-30 minutes can help energize you, without interrupting your nighttime sleep. These relatively short time-outs act to rejuvenate your body and brain. As discussed in the chapter on time-outs, deep breaths, music, walking, and other time-out activities can be a source of energy as well. Sleep is covered in detail in its own chapter.

❑ Reflection Time:

How do you think your exercise, eating, and sleeping habits are contributing to your level of physical energy?

____

____

____

____

____

____

____

____

____

____

____

MENTAL ENERGY

Your attitude can increase your energy level. Using positivity, optimism, gratitude, and positive self-talk are strategies to bolster your energy levels. As discussed in the chapter on attitude, you are prone to automatic negative thoughts (ANTs), which can rapidly drain your energy. Firing the "gremlin" that feeds you these ANTs and hiring a "prince" or "princess" who nourishes your minds with genuine compliments, acknowledgment of your strengths, highlights your hard work, encourages you to persevere, provides self-compassion, and enhances mental energy. This is better than an energy drink filled with caffeine and chemicals that are short-lived. Treating yourself the way that you would treat a good friend provides more powerful and long-lasting sources of energy.

FLOW

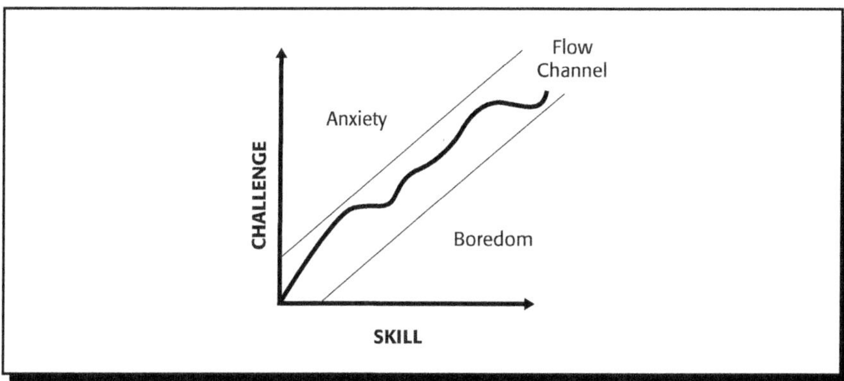

Figure 12-3. The concept of flow (used with permission from the *Lifestyle Medicine Handbook*; 2nd edition; Frates, et al.; Monterey, CA: Healthy Learning; 2021)

When you are in flow, you are energized. Flow is a concept described by Hungarian-American psychologist Mihaly Csikszentmihalyi, in his book *Flow*.[4] Basically, when you are in flow, you are fully engaged in the moment, on the task at hand, and all your attention is focused on the person or project in front of you.

People lose sense of time when they are in the state of flow. For example, for authors, this could be writing a new chapter. For musicians, this could be playing Bach's Brandenburg Concerto; for basketball players, this could be practicing free-throws; for teachers, this could be lecturing; for many people, this could be reading a good book; for some people, this could be hiking on beautiful trails. Identifying the activities that bring you the sensation of flow will increase your sense of joy in life and increase your energy levels.

When your skills meet the challenge at hand, you can find flow. If your skill levels are not up to par with the challenge, you will feel anxious. If your skill level is too high for the challenge, you will be bored.

Because boredom and anxiety can drain energy, if you find yourself in a position where your skill level does not meet the challenge, you need to chunk the challenge. This means you break the challenge into smaller parts. Other methods include bringing others into the project so that they can help you complete it comfortably. Giving yourself more time to complete a task is often an effective way to find flow. Alternatively, you may need to increase your skill level, before you can tackle the level of challenge at hand. The goal is to learn to find flow. Being in this flow channel helps you stay energized.

❑ Reflection Time:

Identify and describe a couple of activities that put you into flow.

____

____

____

____

____

____

____

EMOTIONAL ENERGY

Referring back to the chapter on attitude, you will remember the power of positivity and Barbara Fredrickson's recommendation to focus on three positive comments for every negative comment. Remaining in a positive space allows you to continue with a creative mindset and sustained motivation.

The chapter on social support reviews the power of social connections. As previously discussed, lilies and leeches have the potential to either bolster your energy or drain it. Being mindful of how your friends, family, and colleagues impact your emotional state is critical for your emotional health. Take stock of how you feel around people when you see them and when you leave after a meeting with them. Are you more or less energized?

People lose sense of time when they are in the state of flow.

Brian A Jackson/Shutterstock.com

With a growth mindset, mishaps are viewed as opportunities to learn and grow, as discussed in the chapter on attitude. A growth mindset enables you to stay energized, even when you have experienced a failure. With the goal of reaching higher ground, you can remain focused on an ultimate positive outcome, even if you are currently experiencing negative consequences. If you focus on the negative consequences, replay the failure, and go down a "rabbit-hole" of self-doubt, you will quickly lose all energy. A growth mindset helps you combat this and allows you to move onward and upward.

Everyone experiences a range of emotions throughout the day, some are positive, some are negative. In addition, some emotions are very strong, even overpowering at times. Other emotions are quiet and subtle. The following lists illustrate examples of various emotions:

Strong Positive Emotions:

- Celebratory
- Excitement
- Jocularity
- Natural euphoria
- Passion
- Pride
- Surprise
- Zeal

Strong Negative Emotions:

- Affronted
- Agitation
- Anger
- Disrespected
- Exasperation
- Fear
- Frustration
- Grief
- Guilt
- Insulted
- Jealousy
- Resentment
- Shame

Softer Positive Emotions:

- Admiration
- Affection
- Amusement
- Appreciation
- Awe
- Confidence
- Connection
- Contentment
- Elevation
- Gratitude
- Happiness
- Hope
- Inspiration
- Joy
- Love
- Optimism
- Peace
- Pride
- Relief
- Satisfaction
- Self-efficacy
- Serenity
- Tranquility
- Wonder

Softer Negative Emotions:

- Feeling judged
- Disappointment
- Disconnection
- Emptiness
- Helplessness
- Inadequacy
- Melancholy
- Misunderstood
- Sadness
- Unloved
- Unseen

SPIRITUAL ENERGY

The kind of energy from within that propels you forward, day to day and moment to moment, is your spiritual energy. It is usually derived from a strong sense of purpose, an area that will be covered deeply in the next chapter. When you are involved in work, community projects, friendships, and deep relationships that feed your soul and align with your sense of purpose, you feel energized. Identifying those people, places, and projects that are near and dear to you and spending time on or with them, helps to increase your energy levels. For example, you can think about why you are here, in this world, at this moment, and what you can do day to day, to make the world a better place in some small yet significant way. When you feel that you are living a life consistent with your values and prioritizing these values, in the moments of your days, you are living mindfully and able to express your full spiritual energy.

This chapter has presented an image that, hopefully, you'll find helpful when considering your spiritual energy. In that regard, the first thing you need to address is a vision of yourself in the future, maybe 10 or 20 years down the road. Seeing yourself using your unique gifts and talents, living freely and energetically, helps you to target behaviors and beliefs that will allow you to enjoy transcendence, as identified in Maslow's hierarchy of needs. Transcendence occurs when you're really living your purpose, working to make the world a better place, and realizing you are a small piece of a huge universe.

The ladder shown in Figure 12-4 can help you take steps toward your vision. The sides of the ladder feature purpose and priorities on one side and vision and values on the other side. Taking time to identify your purpose and list your priorities is the first step. The next step is writing out your values and the vision you have of yourself, 5, 10, or 20 years in the future. The rungs of your ladder are your SMART goals (for more information on goals, refer to Chapter 8).

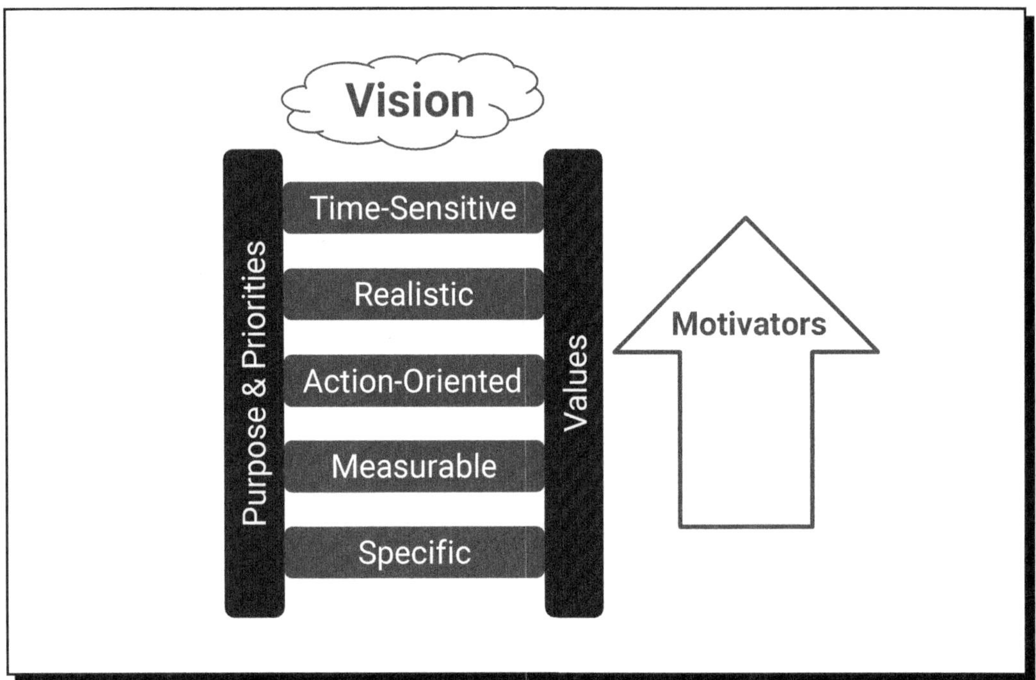

Figure 12-4. Spiritual energy

When discussing spiritual energy, religion and other forms of spirituality come into play. This is a time when you think about your connection with that which is greater than yourself. Many people believe in a higher-power, from which they get great strength.

Being in nature and forest-bathing often helps you to put things in perspective, realizing you are part of a larger ecosystem. Whether you are raising a family, teaching, working in a store, driving a bus, making bread, working as a secretary, a lawyer, librarian, or being a pet owner, a plant lover, a grandparent, a parent, or a child, you are an integral part of your small sphere, as well as the global community. Whatever your beliefs, it is a good time to explore your relationship with the universe and your part in this world. Community service and volunteering to help those in need is a powerful way to experience spiritual energy.

❑ Reflection Time:

What brings you spiritual energy?

____

____

____

____

____

____

____

____

Although a lot of people spend a great deal of energy on time management, you now know how important it is to spend time on energy management. In order to manage your energy, you need to realize when you are at your energetic peak, a point that can vary for many individuals. There is a lull, a time of decreased energy, between 2-3 p.m. for many, but this may not be you. The only way you will know is to keep an energy log. Keep a record of when you feel the most energetic and when you feel the least energetic over the course of a day and a night. For example, there are morning people who pop up, full of energy early in the morning and others who are raring to go late at night. Knowing your energy peaks and valleys will benefit your health and happiness. This is an excellent investigation to do during this PAVING program.

Longfin Media/Shutterstock.com

Everyone has people and projects that energize them, as well as those that drain them. Being clear about this is essential in order to manage your energy. Another critical concept is energy pacing and training. On occasion, there are times you need to sprint. On the other hand, life is a marathon, so managing your energy for the marathon is important. The following lists detail examples of activities that can either boost or drain your energy:

Potential Energy Boosters:

- Art
- Bingo
- Book club
- Bowling
- Cleaning
- Collecting baseball cards
- Coloring
- Cooking
- Crossword puzzles, word searches, Sudoku
- Dancing
- Deep breathing
- Doing a puzzle
- Drawing
- Exercise
- Going to a museum
- Journaling
- Jump roping
- Knitting & crocheting
- Learning
- Meditation
- Music
- Nature and getting outside
- Nourishing food
- Organizing
- Painting
- Photography
- Playing board games
- Playing cards
- Playing with your pet
- Poetry
- Positive social interactions
- Quilting
- Reading
- Rest and quality sleep
- Scrapbooking
- Sewing
- Showering
- Singing
- Skipping
- Solitude
- Spirituality
- Traveling
- Variety
- Volunteering
- Walking a dog
- Watering your plants or tending your garden
- Yoga

Potential Energy Drainers:

- Alcoholism
- All-nighters
- Arguments
- Cancer
- Childcare
- Cluttered space
- Comparing yourself to others
- Complicated relationships
- Confrontation
- Cutting
- Difficult people
- Disability
- Disagreements
- Distractions
- Doomscrolling
- Drug addiction
- Excessive social media
- Family members suffering with illness
- Feeling the need to fit in or keep up with others
- Gambling
- Gossip
- Heart failure
- Hoarding
- Human leeches
- Illness
- Insomnia
- Lack of boundaries
- Lack of engagement
- Lack of purpose
- Mental health struggles
- Mortgage payments
- Multitasking
- Neglecting yourself
- Out of control weight gain
- Overcrowded schedule
- Overdue bills & debt
- Parents with dementia
- Procrastination
- Prolonged commutes
- Prolonged sitting
- Resentment
- Teenage drivers
- Too many emails
- Too many meetings
- Too many Zoom meetings
- Too much television
- Unhealthy competition
- Unhealthy eating habits
- Video game addiction
- Workaholism
- Workplace drama

❑ Reflection Time:

List the people, places, and projects that give you energy.

❑ Reflection Time:

List the people, places, and projects that drain your energy.

❑ Reflection Time:

At what time of the day do you feel least energized?

❑ Reflection Time:

At what time of the day do you feel most energized?

____

____

____

____

____

____

____

Quick Tools for Energy:

- Keep an energy journal—find out what gives you energy:
  - ✓ Identify and use your strengths.
  - ✓ Uncover intrinsic motivation.
  - ✓ Cherish the charismatic people in your life.
  - ✓ Find your happy place.
- Take stock of your energy givers and takers:
  - ✓ Foster positive relationships and people who energize you (lilies of your life).
  - ✓ Remove energy takers from your life (leeches of your life).
- Find natural sources of energy:
  - ✓ Incorporating nature and quiet/reflection time in your daily schedule, which can replenish energy
  - ✓ Doing something you like and that fulfills you
  - ✓ Taking sufficient rest time
- Avoid unnatural sources of energy:
  - ✓ Chemical energy (caffeine, tea, energy drinks, alcohol, others)
- Evaluate your sleep, nutrition, exercise, and social-connection patterns.

Burnout is associated with exhaustion, disconnection, and feelings of inadequacy.

PEERAWICH PHAISITSAWAN/Shutterstock.com

Burnout

Have you ever felt physically and emotionally drained, exhausted and overwhelmed? If so, you may have been suffering from burnout. Burnout can occur in a variety of settings and circumstances, though the majority of research centers on work, health professional, and caregiver burnout.

Burnout is associated with exhaustion, disconnection, and feelings of inadequacy. Herbert Freudenberger, who initially coined the term burnout in 1974, defined it as "the extinction of motivation or incentive, especially where one's devotion to a cause or relationship fails to produce the desired results."[5] As such, job burnout frequently occurs when there is a mismatch between values, expectations, and resources. Energy can be drained through a lack of control, dysfunctional workplace dynamics, unclear job expectations, work-life imbalance, lack of fairness, insufficient rewards, and work overload.

❑ Reflection Time:

Is there an area of your life (e.g., job, project, relationship, responsibility) where you have noticed a decline in energy, struggle to find motivation where it used to be easy, and feel impatient, moody, easily frustrated, or dissatisfied? Explain.

❑ Reflection Time:

After reflecting on your answer to the last question, do you believe you are experiencing burnout in your job, a relationship, a project, or another area of your life? Explain.

Once you have identified an area of potential burnout, you can take steps to address it. Sometimes, burnout may occur around a project or area of your life, where you can simply walk away from the responsibility, project, or relationship. At other times, leaving the area of burnout may not be a choice. If you find yourself facing this circumstance, the following are some strategies that can assist you:

- Engage in self-care (treat your body right).
- Socially connect with others (establish strong social relationships).
- Expand your envelope (have a life outside of work).
- Make relaxing a part of your routine (take at least a 15-minute break every day).
- Communicate with your supervisor (have an ongoing dialogue with your boss).
- Be clear about your job responsibilities (know what your job entails and what others expect of you).
- Learn to say "no" (set and adhere to reasonable limits about what you can and cannot do at work).
- Don't accept boredom as an irrefutable characteristic of your job (ask for a change in duties).
- Learn to delegate (be aware that time is an irreplaceable asset).
- Realize that you can't change everything (change what you can, accept what you can't).
- Be introspective (try to ascertain the source of your discontent and then address it).
- Don't do anything rash (be cool—haste makes waste).
- Work with a purpose (understand and accept the fact that you are a difference-maker because of what you do—you make life better for others).[6]

❑ Reflection Time:

How can you take the aforementioned insights into addressing burnout and apply it to an area where you are experiencing burnout?

____

____

____

____

____

____

____

____

Health Optimization

Optimization is defined as 'an act, process, or methodology of making something (such as a design, system, or decision) as fully perfect, functional, or effective as possible.' Health optimization seeks to maximize an individual's well-being, functioning, and quality of life. The concept of optimal functioning is not a purely physical or mental state; rather, it is a representation of human potential.[6]

❏ Reflection Time:

Think of a time when you felt or performed your best. What did that look like? How did that feel?

Failure to get enough rest, skipping meals or eating poor quality foods, not engaging in physical activity, not connecting with friends, and working on evenings and weekends can lead to burnout. Exhaustion, cynicism, negativity, being short-tempered or easily distracted, apathetic, feeling depressed or anxious, problems sleeping, and irritability are common symptoms of burnout.

❏ Reflection Time:

Reflect on a time when you experienced burnout or a prolonged lack of energy. What were some of the "warning signs" that you experienced that let you know that your energy battery was low?

❏ Reflection Time:

If you notice these warning signs in the future, what could you do to recharge? Is there someone you could connect with who could help you?

Both energy management and time management are important. Often when you manage your time well, you also manage your energy well. The two factors are not the same. Some things take little time but require a lot of mental or emotional energy. Other things take lots of time but require a small investment in energy. Extra time in the day is like gold for many people. When you have this extra time, you need to think about the best way to use it. You also need to consider how you can match your energy levels with the extra time.

Time Affluence

Ashely Whillans,[7] a professor of business administration at the Harvard Business School, has noted that 80 percent of working Americans feel as though they are "time poor," i.e., they do not have adequate time to fulfill all their responsibilities. In her work, she has demonstrated that these feelings of "time poverty" are associated with lower levels of happiness, as well as with higher rates of depression, anxiety, and stress. In contrast, "time affluence" refers to the concept of feeling as if an individual has enough time on an everyday basis.

Dr. Whillans' work has shown that those who prioritize *time affluence* tend to be happier and are more inclined to pursue activities about which they are passionate. She outlines specific suggestions to help people achieve time affluence, to include:

- Planning out your future leisure time
- Scheduling time for active pursuits
- Spending more time eating and *savoring* meals
- Meeting new people
- Helping others

In addition, she recommends "buying time" by reducing your commute to work, and if possible, outsourcing chores and tasks that you dislike.

Another strategy to achieve time affluence is to manage your "time confetti," a term coined by author Bridgid Schulte.[8] "Time confetti" refers to chunks of free time that occur during the day. Those who are more intentional with "time confetti"—such as going for a walk, or getting a healthy snack, rather than scrolling through social media—will feel more connected to the present and achieve more time affluence. Those who can avoid time traps during the day and achieve more time affluence are able to carve out happier and more meaningful moments.

Artificial Sources of Energy

Artificial sources of energy, such as caffeinated beverages, coffee, tea, sodas, and energy drinks, can seem like a quick and easy solution, but they often create more problems in the long run. Caffeine has a half-life of four to six hours. If you have a caffeinated beverage at 3 p.m., half of it may be in your system at 9 p.m., which can disrupt your sleep. Sleep is essential for a healthy body and mind, which will be discussed in Chapter 13. Remember that the simple solution isn't always the best solution. Rather, the key is to work hard to use natural sources of energy throughout the day.

Jiri V/Shutterstock.com

Self-Care

How do you find time for self-care? The simple answer is that you don't *find* time, you *make* time.

Time is something you can't get more of or get back. Everyone is given the same 24 hours each day. Given your schedule, you might argue that it takes too much time to engage in all the essential lifestyle behaviors to stay healthy. Why spend so much time exercising, in exchange for a similar amount of time extended in your life? You are spending all of your "extra" time exercising! The problem with that notion is that it does not consider the quality of your life. Lifestyle medicine doesn't just extend life, it makes it better. Making time can be challenging though, especially if you already have a busy schedule.

The fact is, if you do not choose how to spend your time, someone else will choose for you. Taking control of your health is a personal decision that only an individual can make. You must make the time for self-care—you won't find more time in your day!

Using the concepts of prioritization and evaluating opportunity cost, you can determine how it is most important for you to spend your time. While self-care is not easy, the payoff is great!

Monkey Business Images/Shutterstock.com

MOSS

Assess the energy you have in your life and then answer the following questions:

❑ Question (motivation):

Why are you motivated to increase your energy this week?

❑ Question (obstacles):

What obstacles are you likely to encounter? Consider what is dragging you down.

❑ Question (strategies):

What strategies can you use to overcome these obstacles?

❏ Question (strengths):

What strengths can you draw upon as you work toward your goal? Consider strengths that you've used to overcome previous challenges and your support system including your healthcare team, family, and friends.

____

____

____

____

____

____

____

Rawpixel.com/Shutterstock.com

SMART Goal

In order to take what you have learned about energy and put it into action, create a SMART goal for yourself (see Chapter 4 page 55 for an overview of SMART goals and what they entail).

❑ SMART Goal Time:

What is your SMART goal around energy for this week?

____

____

____

____

____

____

____

____

PhotoIris2021/Shutterstock.com

Making time to control your health can be challenging, especially if you already have a busy schedule.

References

❑ Cited References:

1. Wolf CR. Virtual platforms are helpful tools but can add to our stress. *Psychology Today.* 2020.
2. Merriam-Webster. www.mw.com.
3. Loehr, J, Loehr, JE, Schwartz T. *The Power of Full Engagement: Managing Energy, Not Time, is the Key to High Performance and Personal Renewal.* New York: Simon and Schuster; 2005.
4. Csikzentmihalyi M. *Flow: The Psychology of Optimal Experience*. New York: Harper Perennial Modern Classics; 2008.
5. Frudenberge H (1974). Staff burnout. *Journal of Social Issues*. 30(1), 159–165.
6. Frates B, et al. *Lifestyle Medicine Handbook: An Introduction to the Power of Healthy Habits*, 2nd ed. Monterey, CA: Healthy Learning; 2021.
7. Whillans AV, Dunn EW, Smeets P, et al. (2017). Buying time promotes happiness. *Proceedings of the National Academy of Sciences*, 114(32), 8523–8527.
8. Schulte B. *Overwhelmed: How to Work, Love, and Play When No One Has the Time*. New York: Macmillan; 2015.

❑ Book Resources:

- Freudenberger H, Richelson G. *Burnout: The High Cost of Human Achievement.* Norwell, MA: Anchor Press; 1980.
- Loehr J, Loehr JE, Schwartz T. *The Power of Full Engagement: Managing Energy, Not Time, Is the Key to High Performance and Personal Renewal.* New York: Simon and Schuster; 2005.

CHAPTER 13
PURPOSE

"Everyone has his own specific vocation or mission in life; everyone must carry out a concrete assignment that demands fulfillment. Therein he cannot be replaced, nor can his life be repeated, thus, everyone's task is unique as his specific opportunity to implement it."

—Victor Frankl
Austrian Neurologist
and Psychiatrist

PAVING the Path to Wellness: Questions on Purpose

For each of the following five statements concerning purpose, choose the number on the frequency scale that best relates to you (frequency: 1= never, 2= rarely, 3= sometimes, 4= often, 5= routinely).

- I feel that I have a clear purpose in life. ____
- I am able to prioritize my activities and projects easily. ____
- I make sure that my activities and projects are in alignment with my values. ____
- I have identified the people and activities that are most important to me. ____
- I am using my strengths to fulfill this purpose. ____

Subtotal—purpose: ____

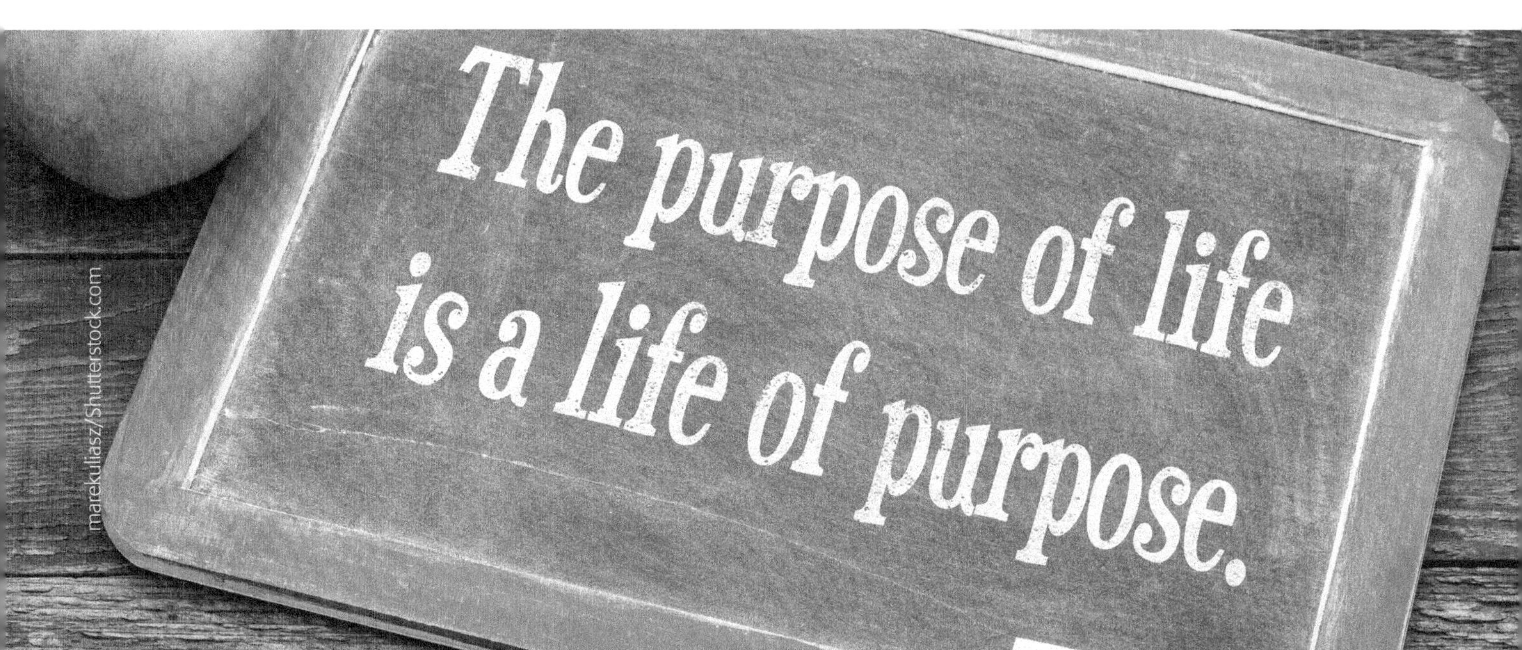

marekuliasz/Shutterstock.com

Live and Learn: Jane Stachowiak (PAVING Program Participant—18 Years Post-Stroke)

At age 32, after my stroke, I decided my life would be devoted to improvement. Helping others and myself to live better and longer, brought a deeper purpose to my life. So, the last 37 years have been a journey to clarify and support my dharma (the external and inherent nature of reality; a universal truth taught by the Buddha).

This journey has led me to explore and answer six questions.

- Who? Who am I going to serve? Beside myself I want to help as many people as I can, regardless of demographics.
- What? My desire is to provide strategies on how to take meaningful steps to enhance our lives in a variety of dimensions—physical, healthy eating, attitude, skills, stress release, social connections, spirituality, and environment. Each person's path to a better life is unique. My role with others is to instruct and/or coach. For me, I experiment and find out what works best and repeat.
- Where? Over the last four decades, I have made myself available at my workplace, colleges, wellness programs, fitness centers, stroke recovery associations, and Ayurveda groups. I support friends and family.
- When? I take advantage of opportunities. For example, when a student shares that she has been sleeping poorly, a door has opened. I can ask her questions. This allows her to reflect identifying possible causes and solutions. She is empowered to take positive steps.
- Why? Why do I want everyone to improve? A simple saying—"the more you know, the more you grow" ties nicely with W.B. Yeats' quote "Happiness is neither virtue or pleasure, not this thing or that, but simply growth." I believe in the impact of each of us on the universe. As I grow, you grow, and as you grow, I grow and that is a happy thing! Each person is influenced by other people's personal habits, attitudes, smiles, knowledge, life stories, etc. These behaviors can generate positive, negative or neutral effects. I want more happiness in all our lives.
- How? How am I going to improve today and how can I help others improve their well-being, are two questions I ask daily. One answer is to know and grow your resources. This includes but is not limited to:
  - ✓ Meditation, movement (yoga), and chanting
  - ✓ My skill sets in mindfulness, nutrition, and exercise
  - ✓ My toolbox to adapt in every situation
  - ✓ Reflection, journaling, and creating (loving myself)
  - ✓ Experiment and observe behaviors and thoughts
  - ✓ Create and maintain an environment that is conducive to growth and renewal
  - ✓ Empower with stories, lessons, quotes, and laughter
  - ✓ Awareness of habit development
  - ✓ Involvement in groups, hobbies, sports, friends, and family
  - ✓ Expansion of my world through film, books, theatre, and art

I am blessed with abilities, education, and other gifts that complement my purpose. It is a sign that my purpose suits me. Some of my talents I possessed before my stroke. Some talents were diminished by the stroke. How glad I am that I kept working at being better. It is amazing how new doors open when others close. It happens when you least expect it.

Since 1984, I have prioritized my time and energy in order to better serve others and to become better myself. What does better mean? It is not one size fits all. It is personal. Being coached on achieving that next rung on the ladder is empowering. Skills are learned that help in the future. I have had a lot of people cheering me on, as well as me cheering on thousands.

Lastly, living with my purpose has connected me for nearly 40 years with many people, books, events, workshops and experts. My purpose has directed me through my stroke with the ability to thrive—get back to work full-time, start a new department, teach meditation, coach student leaders, travel the US, Canada, and UK, and enjoy retirement. It gets me up and going each and every day.

❑ Reflection Time:

What words come to mind when you think of the word purpose? List as many words as you can.

____

____

____

____

____

____

____

Purpose Timeline

What people believe to be their purpose in life often changes as they grow older and experience life transitions. Major life changes, such as the birth of a child, death of a parent, marriage, divorce, new career, retirement, graduation from college, children leaving home, or cancer diagnosis may alter an individual's life's purpose.

Deciding upon a certain purpose in life is not a destination. Rather, uncovering your purpose in various stages of life is a journey. Exploring meaning in life and working toward goals that align with your purpose help you to pave your path to wellness.

❑ Reflection Time:

Write out or draw what you believed your purpose was during each of these phases of your life, for example:

- Teenager: I want to be a teacher.
- College: Learning about news broadcasting and deciding to be a journalist to share the news of the day with people and keep them updated with accurate information.
- Post-college: Realizing that I enjoy the camera work more than the reporting, I switch to videography and learn to approach newsworthy situations with a lens of filmmaking. I learn how to make backgrounds appealing and intriguing to the viewers.
- Mid-life: Working at the local cable station as the camera person for 15 years, becoming the manager of the station, and delivering the news in an unbiased, accurate, professional, and entertaining way is my purpose. Feeling that I am using my gifts and strengths to make the world a better place by providing important information to my community aligns with my purpose.
- Elder years: My purpose involves leaving a legacy by writing a book about camera work and videotaping for success with local news stations—a how to guide for beginners. Volunteering at the local cable station to review footage, focusing on passing life lessons to family and videotaping them and interviewing them about life and what brings them joy is my purpose.

❏ Reflection Time:

What did you want to do with your life when you were younger and why did you want to do that?

❏ Reflection Time:

What did you major in while you were in college and why? If you did not attend college, what type of activities did you pursue after high-school and why?

❏ Reflection Time:

What was your first job and why?

❑ Reflection Time:

What was your favorite job and why?

____

____

____

____

____

____

____

❑ Reflection Time:

When creating your own timeline of purpose, did you notice any specific transitions, major events, or stressors that were associated with the evolution of how your purpose changed? Explain.

____

____

____

____

____

____

____

Through the course of time, there have been many brilliant minds that have described the purpose of life. This is a subject on which many have spent a great deal of time pontificating. The following are a few of those quotes. Some may resonate with you, and others may not. Read through them and see how the words make you feel.

"The purpose of life is not to be happy. It is to be useful, to be honorable, to be compassionate, to have it make some difference that you have lived and lived well."

—Ralph Waldo Emerson
American Essayist

"If we take man as he is, we make him worse. But if we take him as he should be, then we make him capable of becoming what he can be."

—Johann Wolfgang van Goethe
German Poet

❑ Reflection Time:

Which of the aforementioned quotes resonates most with you and why?

Purpose

According to the *Merriam-Webster Dictionary*,[1] purpose is defined as:

- the reason why something is done or used: the aim or intention of something
- the feeling of being determined to do or achieve something
- the aim or goal of a person: what a person is trying to do, become, etc.

Most people would like to feel joyful, helpful, and content each day. There is a human desire to be connected to others, a desire to make a difference, and a desire to feel useful. People want to feel as if they matter—what they do matters. This gives them a sense of satisfaction, a happiness. It adds to their overall sense of well-being.

Eudemonic well-being is based upon the premise that people feel happy if their life has purpose, challenge, and growth. Other important elements for eudemonic well-being include the feeling that what you do is worthwhile, aligned with actualizing personal potential, and supports a greater good. Hedonic well-being is focused on decreasing pain and maximizing pleasure in order to achieve happiness.

❑ Reflection Time:

Write a few examples of when you typically feel happy.

❑ Reflection Time:

How do these examples connect with eudemonic well-being (your purpose, challenge, growth, greater good)?

____

____

____

____

____

____

____

____

Viktor Frankl

Viktor Frankl was a psychiatrist, author, and concentration camp survivor. Not only did he survive the atrocity of the Holocaust, but he also managed to thrive after it. He was the creator of logotherapy, a type of therapy in which a person works to make meaning out of their life experiences. Frankl believed and wrote about man's will for meaning, and man's desire for purpose in life. His work and writings have helped many people get through difficult times. He believed that we are all here, on this planet, for a reason. The following is a powerful quote from his book, *Man's Search for Meaning:*[2]

> "Everyone has his own specific vocation or mission in life; everyone must carry out a concrete assignment that demands fulfillment. Therein, he cannot be replaced, nor can his life be repeated, thus, everyone's task is unique as is his specific opportunity to implement it."

Frankl's writings have so many nuggets of useful information based upon his experiences. He not only uses quotes but also equations to help people thrive. His mathematical equation of despair equates despair with suffering without meaning. Everyone suffers, but if they find meaning in the suffering, they won't fall into the deep, dark place of despair.

MATHEMATICAL TYPE OF EQUATION FOR DESPAIR:

Despair = Suffering – Meaning (D = S – M)

Merriam Webster Dictionary[1] defines despair as "the utter loss of hope." Frankl chronicled his life and experiences as a prisoner in the Nazi concentration camps. In his writings, he noted that those who survived the longest were not necessarily the individuals who were the most physically fit. Rather, those who survived were those individuals who were able to maintain a sense of *hope* and *control* in their environment. As Frankl noted,[2] "we who lived in concentration camps can remember the men who walked through the huts comforting others, giving away their last piece of bread. They may have been few in number, but they offer sufficient proof that everything can be taken from a man but one thing: the last of human freedoms–to choose one's own attitude in any given set of circumstances–to choose one's own way." Thus, those who could find hope, even in the most difficult of circumstances, were able to achieve meaning and a sense of purpose.

Viktor Frankl's work is a source of great comfort to many to this day. Reading his short book on the search for meaning is often inspiring and can even serve as a pivotal point in people's lives, when they are at a crossroads due to a health setback, a job change, a divorce, a new relationship, changing their place of residence, a death of a loved one, or other stressful situation. Rereading the book often may provide a new perspective on his work and on your life.

Live and Learn: Dr. Michelle Tollefson

When I was diagnosed with breast cancer at age 42, I initially thought "why me?" At the time of my diagnosis, I was as healthy as I had ever been; I had a normal screening mammogram the year prior, was eating healthy, exercising, and had breastfed my three children. Within a few days, my view of my health was transformed from being a healthy physician to a cancer patient.

As an advocate for lifestyle medicine, I occasionally did news interviews. When I learned of my diagnosis, I reached out to some of my news contacts to ask if we could use my "story" to help others. Although my breast cancer diagnosis pales in comparison to Frankl's time in a concentration camp, it was still a source of suffering for me personally. It made me confront my own mortality and a life where my identity would forever be linked with cancer.

The news team worked with me to tell my breast cancer story through sharing my mammogram images on the news soon after my diagnosis, accompanied me into the operating room on the day of my mastectomy, and interviewed members of my cancer care team. Sharing my story to encourage others to get timely mammograms and to embrace healthy lifestyle behaviors, allowed me to attribute meaning to my diagnosis.

A silver lining of being a breast cancer survivor was the opportunity to participate as a member of one of the early PAVING the Path to Wellness groups for breast cancer survivors. After graduating from the program, Drs. Frates and Comander invited me to lead a PAVING the Path to Wellness group for breast cancer survivors in my native Colorado. Although I would never have chosen this diagnosis, the journey and opportunity to support other breast cancer survivors has become one of the most rewarding areas of my life, currently, and hopefully for decades to come.

❑ Reflection Time:

Can you think of a time, when you experienced suffering, which was also associated with meaning or purpose in your life? Describe how this relates to Frankl's equation.

____

____

____

____

____

____

____

____

IKIGAI (生き甲斐) is a Japanese concept that can be translated as "reason for being." As shown in Figure 13-1, *Ikigai* involves the overlap of your passion, mission, profession, and vocation. *Ikigai* may also be defined as "the reason you wake up in the morning." In researching the book by Francese Miralles and Hector Garcia, *Ikigai: The Japanese Secret to a Long and Happy Life*,[3] the authors interviewed residents of the Japanese village with the highest percentage of centenarians—one of the world's "Blue Zones." From their research, the authors found that a strong sense of *Ikigai* was key for living a longer and happier life. It is important for people to discover their own *Ikigai* in order to find meaning and satisfaction in life.

____

Figure 13-1. The overlapping elements of *Ikigai*

❑ Reflection Time:

What do you love? Consider your hobbies, people, and places that you enjoy.

____

____

____

____

____

____

____

____

❑ Reflection Time:

What does the world need? Are there certain types of injustice that you feel called to address?

____

____

____

❑ Reflection Time:

What are you good at? Consider your strengths and gifts. What would others say are your strengths?

❑ Reflection Time:

What can you be paid for or what can you volunteer your time for that connects with your purpose? If you need to receive payment for employment, explore how *Ikigai* connects with your job.

❑ Reflection Time:

Is there a way for these areas to overlap and connect to your *Ikigai* or reason for being? Explain.

____

____

____

____

____

____

____

____

A Good Life

There are numerous definitions of a good life. It varies for each individual. Yet, there are certain common themes when people describe the good life. A good life for many involves feeling satisfied, confident, useful, happy, comfortable, loved, and understood. These are merely a few aspects of feeling you are living a good life.

Research has been conducted on the good life. Author and executive life-coach Richard Leider writes extensively on the topic of the power of purpose and has described and defined the good life. According to Leider, the good life entails:

- Living in the place you belong,
- With the people you love,
- Doing the right work,
- On purpose.

People who believe they have purpose in their lives are more likely to report being happy and describe themselves as living the good life. The following are a few thought-provoking quotes from Richard Leider:[4]

- "Reimagining your life is going to be messy."
- "Pushed by pain or pulled by possibility."
- "People with a sense of purpose have learned to let life question them and have moved the focus of their attention and concern away from themselves to others. Purpose, then, is not a job or a role or a goal. It is the belief that our lives, our part in the whole of things, truly matter. Having a profound sense of who we are, where we came from, and where we're going, we choose to believe that mattering matters. It is thus a mindset—a choice. It is first and foremost the choice to choose 'life' despite the circumstances we find ourselves in. It is the choice to bring who we are—our gifts and energies—to whatever we are doing. Purpose is a cradle-to-grave, 24/7, moment-to-moment choice in our daily lives." – Richard J. Leider, *The Power of Purpose*[4]

❑ Reflection Time:

What are your reactions to these quotes?

____

____

____

____

____

____

____

Richard Leider also created a way of looking at the phases of our lives. According to Leider, there are four phases of life:[4]

PHASE I—PLATEAU:

- Life running smoothly
- Satisfied, comfortable, and safe
- May stay too long
- Doesn't require work to grow
- Give up, shut down

PHASE II—TRIGGER:

- Sudden change
- New challenges
- Diagnosis, death, job change
- Triggers = catalysts

PHASE III—LIMBO:

- Endings—transitions—beginnings
- Emotional withdrawal
- Knowing what has been lost
- Not knowing the future
- Immobilized, numb, confused

PHASE IV—REPACKING:

- Exploring solutions
- Looking for answers
- Confused and uncertain
- Energy in exploration

❑ Reflection Time:

Can you think of a time when a trigger occurred which was a catalyst for change in your life? Describe. After this trigger, you may have felt lost, numb, and confused.

❑ Reflection Time:

After this time of limbo, did you enter a repacking phase when you explored solutions and looked for answers? Explain.

❑ Reflection Time:

Are there any current life circumstances where you feel like you are in limbo or the repacking phase? What could you do to take the next step and move toward healing and meaning?

Purpose Exercise

Consider writing your own obituary. Many people have read obituaries. Some of them have written them for family members, grandparents, parents, cousins, and friends.

❏ Reflection Time:

What would you want your obituary to include?

____

____

____

____

____

____

____

____

Want to Know More?

PURPOSE AND HEALTH OUTCOMES

People with a purpose:[5,6]

- Live longer
- Have a lower risk of cognitive decline
- Have a lower risk of disability
- Have positive relations with others

EUDEMONIC WELL-BEING

Research (over eight years, 9,050 English people, average age of 65) reviewed the pattern of well-being across ages and the association between well-being and survival at older ages. Among the findings were the following:

- Highest well-being category: 9 percent died
- Lowest well-being category: 29 percent died
- On average, people in the highest well-being category lived two years longer than those in the lowest category.[7]

IKIGAI RESEARCH

A strong connection exists to one's sense of purpose. Research showed the following in a group of 73,000 Japanese men and women:[8]

- Those with a strong connection to their *Ikigai* lived longer.
- A lower level of purpose in men was correlated to earlier death and cardiovascular disease.

ALZHEIMER'S DISEASE

Research has shown that greater purpose in life is associated with a reduced risk of Alzheimer's disease and mild cognitive impairment. For example, in a study of over 900 older adults, it was found that:[9]

- People with a low sense of purpose were 2.4 times more likely to be diagnosed with Alzheimer's disease than those people who had a strong sense of purpose.
- Those with a strong sense of purpose were less likely to suffer disability and impairments in activities of daily living (ADLs).

PAIN CONTROL

Research has demonstrated that a connection exists between having a meaning in life and handling pain, including the following:[10]

- Individuals who have a higher level of purpose in life are better able to adjust to chronic pain.
- Women with a stronger sense of purpose were better able to handle heat and cold stimuli applied to their skin.

MOOD

Research has been conducted into the impact of having a sense of purpose and mental health. Among the links discovered between the two are the following:[11]

- Having a purpose helps people better manage symptoms of depression.
- Having a purpose protects individuals from a decrease in the quality of life and fosters resilience—being able to manage difficult situations.

WORK AND RETIREMENT

Research has found that an association exists between mortality and the age of retirement. Among the findings were the following:[12]

- Among retirees, a significant link exists between all-cause mortality and life purpose.
- People who retired early at age 55 were more likely to die early compared to those who retired at 65.
- The mortality rate of individuals who retired at 55 (adjusted for health factors) was twice that of their still-working colleagues
- The risk of death increased by 51 percent after retirement, particularly for those who retired early.

MOSS

Answer the following questions on life purpose, using the MOSS technique:

❑ Question (motivation):

Why are you motivated to explore your purpose and vision?

❑ Question (obstacles):

What obstacles are you likely to encounter or are getting in the way of you focusing on or finding your purpose (examples include anger, fear, grief over the loss of a loved one, etc.)?

❑ Question (strategies):

What strategies can you use to overcome these obstacles?

❑ Question (strengths):

What strengths can you draw upon as you work toward your goal? Consider strengths that you've used to overcome previous challenges and your support system including your healthcare team, family, and friends.

SMART Goal

In order to take what you have learned about purpose and put it into action, create a SMART goal for yourself (refer to Chapter 4 page 55 for an overview of what a SMART goal entails).

❑ SMART Goal Time:

What is a SMART goal related to your purpose or vision?

References

❑ Cited References:

1. Merriam-Webster. www.mw.com.
2. Frankl VE. *Man's Search for Meaning*, 4th ed. Boston, MA: Beacon Press; 2000.
3. Miralles F, Garcia H. *Ikigai: The Japanese Secret to a Long and Happy Life.* Westminster, London, England: Penguin Life; 2017.
4. Leider RJ. *The Power of Purpose: Creating Meaning in Your Life and Work.* Oakland, CA: Berrett-Koehler Publishers; 2005.
5. Boyle PA, Barnes LL, Buchman AS, et al. Purpose in life is associated with mortality among community-dwelling older persons. *Psychosomatic Medicine*. 2009 Jun;71(5):574.
6. Boyle PA, Buchanan AS, Barnes LL, et al. (2010). Effect of a purpose in life on risk of incident Alzheimer's disease and mild cognitive impairment in community-dwelling older persons. *Archives of General Psychiatry*, 67(3), 304–310.
7. Steptoe A, Deaton A, Stone, AA (2015). Subjective well-being, health, and ageing. *The Lancet*, 385(9968), 640–648.
8. Steger MF, Kawabata Y, Shimai S (2008). The meaningful life in Japan and the United States: levels and correlates of meaning in life. *Journal of Research in Personality*, 42(3), 660–678.
9. Boyle PA, Buchanan AS, Barnes LL, et al. (2010). Effect of a purpose in life on risk of incident Alzheimer's disease and mild cognitive impairment in community-dwelling older persons. *Archives of General Psychiatry*, 67(3), 304–310.
10. Smith BW, Tooley EM, Montague EQ, et al. (2009). The role of resilience and purpose in life in habituation to heat and cold pain. *J. Pain*, 10(5), 493–500.
11. Blaźek M, Kaźmierczak M, Besta T (2015). Sense of purpose in life and escape from self as the predictors of quality of life in clinical samples. *J Relig Health*, 54(2), 517–523.
12. Bamia C, Trichopoulou A, Trichopoulas D (2008). Age at retirement and mortality in a general population sample: the Greek EPIC study. *Am J Epidemiol*, 167(5) 561–569.

❑ Book Resources:

- Buettner D. *The Blue Zones Solution: Eating and Living Like the World's Healthiest People*. Washington, DC: National Geographic; 2015.
- Frankl VE. *Man's Search for Meaning*, 4th ed. Boston, MA: Beacon Press; 2000.
- Leider RJ. *The Power of Purpose: Creating Meaning in Your Life and Work.* Oakland, CA: Berrett-Koehler Publishers; 2005.
- Miralles F, Garcia H. *Ikigai: The Japanese Secret to a Long and Happy Life.* Westminster, London, England: Penguin Life; 2017.

❑ Other Resources:

- MetLife—Discovering What Matters Workbook—www.metlife.com/assets/cao/mmi/publications/studies/mmi-discovering-what-matters workbook.pdf
- YouTube—Finding meaning in difficult times (Interview with Dr. Viktor Frankl)
- YouTube—Richard Leider videos
- www.ted.com—Why believe in others

CHAPTER 14
SLEEP

"A good laugh and a long sleep are the best cures in the doctor's book."

—Irish Proverb

"The good educator insists on exercise, play, and plentiful sleep: 'the great cordial of nature.'"

—John Locke
English Philosopher

PAVING the Path to Wellness: Questions on Sleep

For each of the following five statements, choose the number on the frequency scale that best relates to you (frequency: 1= never, 2= rarely, 3= sometimes, 4= often, 5= routinely).

- I sleep seven to eight hours a night. ____
- I don't drink coffee after noon time. ____
- I have a bedtime routine in which I relax before bed. ____
- I don't sleep with my phone on in the bedroom. ____
- I take 20-minute naps when I am overtired. ____

Subtotal—sleep: ____

Live and Learn: Dr. Amy Comander

In the early months of the COVID-19 pandemic, I found myself feeling increasingly anxious, and I was staying up later than usual to watch the latest news. I had my smartphone on my nightstand, and I would scroll through my newsfeeds on Twitter and other social media platforms. I found that when I finally put my phone down, it was difficult for me to fall asleep, and when I awoke the next morning, I did not feel well rested. While at work, I felt more tired than usual in the afternoon and it was harder for me to concentrate.

After a few weeks, I decided I needed to prioritize my own health, including improving my sleep habits. I decided to make three changes to improve my sleep quality. The first change I made was to avoid the consumption of caffeine in the afternoon. I love enjoying a cup of coffee later in the day. However, I read that the half-life of caffeine typically ranges from four to six hours. Studies demonstrate that caffeine intake even six hours before bedtime can reduce sleep quality. I decided to decrease caffeine intake later in the day; now, I enjoy coffee in the morning, but not after 2 p.m.

The second change I made was to move my bedtime earlier, so as to ensure I was getting at least seven hours of sleep each night. My early morning exercise routine is important to me, so I decided to get in bed no later than 10 p.m. each night. I now set an alarm at 9:30 p.m., which reminds me to stop what I am doing and get ready for bed!

The third change I made was to avoid the use of my smartphone for one hour before bedtime. Research shows that the bright light emitted by a smartphone close to bedtime impacts our circadian rhythm, our body's natural "sleep-wake" clock. Instead of doomscrolling on my social media feed before bedtime, I now try to read a book, or listen to music.

While the pandemic has certainly brought uncertainty and anxiety for many people, including myself, these three changes in sleep habits have certainly helped me, and I have shared these tips with my patients as well.

Definition of Sleep

In the *Merriam-Webster Dictionary,*[1] sleep is defined as: A natural periodic state of rest for the mind and body, in which the eyes usually close and consciousness is completely or partially lost, so that there is a decrease in bodily movement and responsiveness to external stimuli. During sleep, the brain in humans and other mammals undergoes a characteristic cycle of brain-wave activity that includes intervals of dreaming.

Sleep Timeline

❑ Reflection Time:

Reflect on sleep throughout the stages of your life. Think about sleep challenges that have occurred, wind-down routines that you've enjoyed, and your general feelings toward sleep. Then, write out or draw what comes to mind during each of these phases of your life, for example:

- Childhood: not wanting to go to bed, because of wanting to continue daytime games, or enjoying reading a book with a parent prior to going to bed, or reciting a bedtime prayer.
- Teenager: working on homework late into the night not prioritizing sleep, falling asleep while studying for an exam and then having trouble staying awake the next day, and sleeping in on weekends, trying to recover.
- College: learning more about how much sleep you needed to be productive, possible difficulty falling asleep when your apartment mates were loud, or there was music next door, and using white noise machines and sleep masks.
- Post-college: realizing sleep's importance to feeling energetic throughout the day, experiencing sleep deprivation with a new baby, helping your baby learn good sleep habits, or enjoying reading a good book at the end of the day to relax.
- Mid-life: feeling like you had more control over your sleep schedule, not having to stay awake when your children woke up during the night, experiencing insomnia, when feeling stressed about work and couldn't fall asleep, or realizing that you could journal prior to bed and write about what you needed to focus on the next day, to improve sleep.
- Elder years: realizing how health issues negatively impacted your sleep, experiencing frustration with sleep being interrupted during the middle of the night due to needing to use the bathroom, or working with your doctor to adjust a medication that negatively impacted sleep.

❑ Reflection Time:

After reflecting on sleep throughout your lifestyle in the aforementioned activity, what insight did you gain, patterns did you notice, or reflections do you have?

____

____

____

____

____

____

____

❑ Reflection Time:

How does your current health impact your sleep? Consider medications, chronic medical conditions, and nighttime wakings to use the bathroom.

____

____

____

____

____

____

____

Benefits of Sleep

Everyone knows that they feel better after a "good night's sleep," but why? Research is ongoing, but research shows that sleep is an important time for the body to restore itself. It gives neurons (brain cells) an opportunity to shut down, remove waste products, and repair themselves. Adenosine is a neurotransmitter, a chemical in the brain, which promotes sleep and suppresses arousal. When you are awake, the levels of adenosine rise each hour, and studies suggest that the presence of adenosine is responsible for causing fatigue, the longer you stay awake. Sleep also may be an opportunity for the brain to exercise important neuronal connections that might otherwise deteriorate.[2]

In addition, growth hormone is released during deep sleep, protein production is increased, and protein breakdown is decreased while sleeping. Furthermore, hormones are balanced during sleep, including those that influence satiety and appetite, specifically ghrelin and leptin. Ghrelin increases hunger, while leptin increases satiety. Sufficient sleep leads to a balance of these two hormones.

Glymphatic System

Since 2015, there has been a great deal of interest in the glymphatic system, which is a drainage system for the brain. This system mainly functions during sleep, clearing waste products from the brain. In other words, without sleep, you can't clear your brain of neurotoxic waste products, including β-amyloid, which has been associated with Alzheimer's disease. Recent literature reports that lack of sleep may be a risk factor for Alzheimer's disease. As such, getting less than six hours of sleep a night for multiple nights could increase your risk of dementia.[3] The National Sleep Foundation recommends that 18-64 year olds get seven to nine hours of nightly sleep, and people age 65 or older get seven to nine hours.[4]

❏ Reflection Time:

How many hours of sleep do you think you need nightly to function at your best? Explain.

____

____

____

____

____

____

____

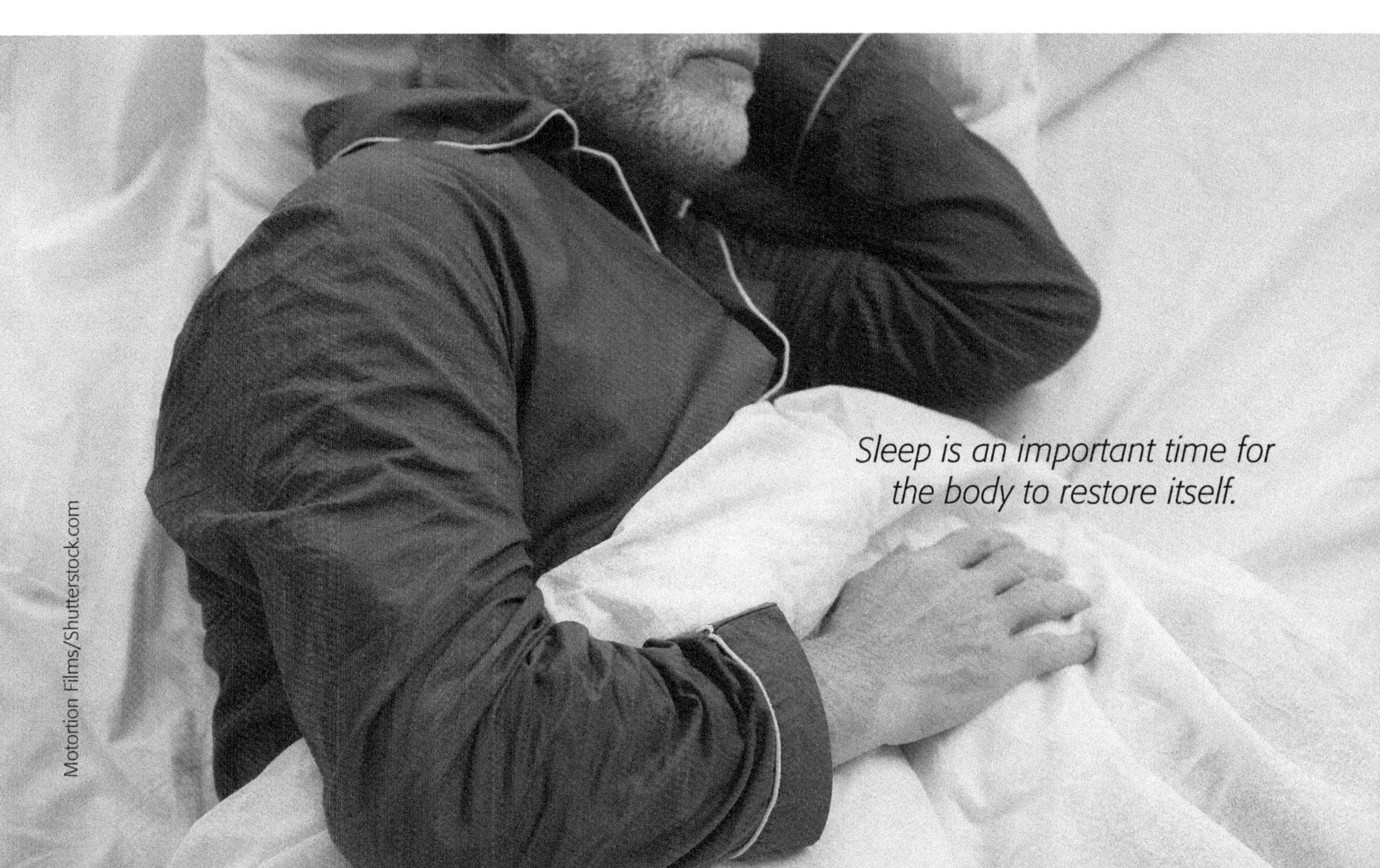

Motortion Films/Shutterstock.com

Sleep is an important time for the body to restore itself.

Sleep Signals

Your body has natural signals for sleep that are already set up for you. You just need to understand them to experience their full benefits It is easier to accomplish this if you know what your body wants to do naturally, if it is left undisturbed and uninterrupted by life's busyness. The body has three signals for sleep:

- Darkness
- Adenosine build-up
- Melatonin release

Your body is on a circadian rhythm with daylight. You are meant to be awake when the sun is shining, and asleep when it's dark outside. Thus, if you expose yourself to sunlight in the morning when you wake up, you can get into this circadian rhythm. This also means that at night, you want to be in the pitch-black darkness when possible. Using black-out curtains can help keep the room dark throughout the night and early morning hours.

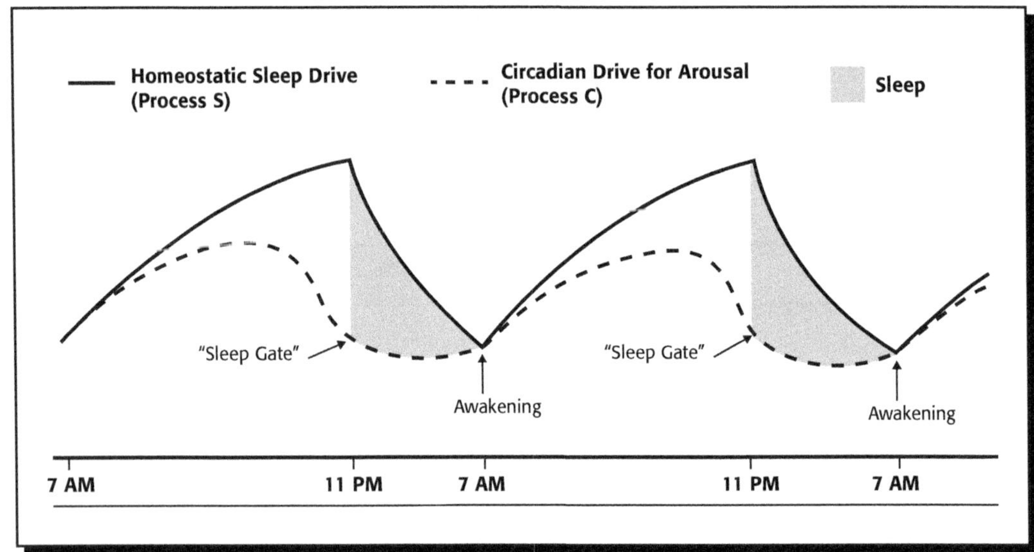

Figure 14-1. The homeostatic sleep drive and the circadian drive for arousal (used with permission from the *Lifestyle Medicine Handbook*; 2nd edition; Frates, et al.; Monterey, CA: Healthy Learning; 2021)

Throughout the course of the day, you use adenosine triphosphate (ATP), which creates a build-up of the chemical adenosine. Adenosine normally reaches a peak at 11 p.m. This high level of adenosine signals our body to sleep. To allow this build-up to occur naturally, it is important to avoid caffeine, which binds to the same receptor as adenosine and blocks the signal for sleep. Caffeine has a half-life of four to six hours, which means after you consume caffeine (coffee, tea, diet coke, coke, Pepsi, diet Pepsi and other sources), you will have half the caffeine in your system four to six hours later. If you consume a coffee or caffeinated beverage at 3pm, you may have half of it in your system at 8 or 9pm when you are getting ready for sleep. So, consuming caffeinated drinks only in the morning allows this natural build-up of adenosine to occur and signal sleep at 11 p.m.

After darkness has set in around 11 p.m., the pineal gland in the brain releases melatonin, which naturally signals your body to sleep. Melatonin also helps you fall asleep which is why some people take melatonin supplements. One way to help your pineal gland release melatonin on its own is avoiding blue wavelength light. Blue wavelength light is emitted by most technology devices, including computers, iPads, and cell phones. Televisions and some alarm clocks also emit it. Using blue wavelength blocking glasses or applications on your devices that block blue wavelength light helps minimize your evening blue wavelength light exposure. There are blue wavelength blocking glasses that you can buy as well. Staying away from devices, TV, and bright lights two to three hours prior to bed will allow this natural release of melatonin to occur and send a natural signal for sleep.

Sleep Cycle

When you fall asleep, you go through four different stages of sleep (Figure 14-2). These stages are all essential for sound sleep. You can only enjoy and experience all the stages thoroughly, when you have seven to nine hours of uninterrupted sleep, which is your goal.

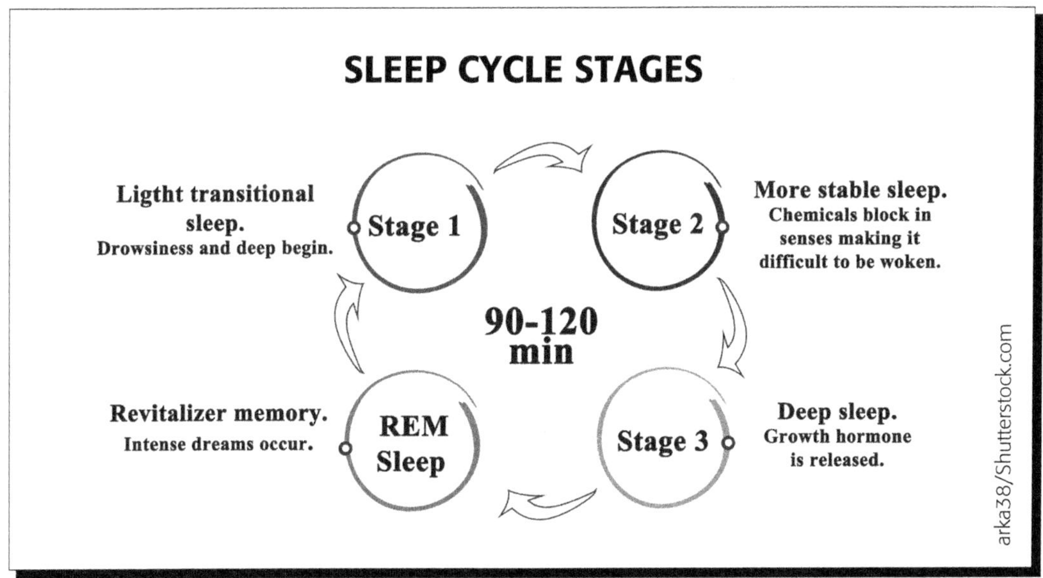

Figure 14-2. The different stages of sleep

Sleep cycles are typically about 60-90 minutes in duration, with about five sleep cycles occurring during an eight-hour sleep period. The various stages of sleep include:

- Stage 1—onset of sleep when transitioning from wakefulness to sleep.
- Stage 2—usually lasts 20 minutes: humans spend approximately 40-50 percent of their total sleep time in this stage.
- Stage 3—known as slow-wave sleep and delta sleep: it is the beginning of deep sleep.
- Stage with Rapid Eye Movement (REM)—individuals enter this stage about 90 minutes after initially falling asleep and experience multiple episodes throughout the night for a total of 1.5-2 hours.

REM Sleep = Dreams

When you sleep until you wake up naturally, instead of awakening by an alarm, you may recall more dreams. This happens because REM sleep increases throughout the night, and the longest episode is often immediately before you wake up in the morning. Usually most people wake with an alarm, which disrupts sleep before getting into this last and longest episode of REM. However, during the COVID pandemic, people worked from home and set their own schedules, allowing them to sleep longer and thus report and remember more dreams. Some people do not remember their dreams, while others remember them vividly. The interpretation of dreams is a fascinating area that has captivated psychologists for ages.

Each stage has its importance and value for health. Thus, working to enjoy uninterrupted sleep for seven to nine hours is the goal.

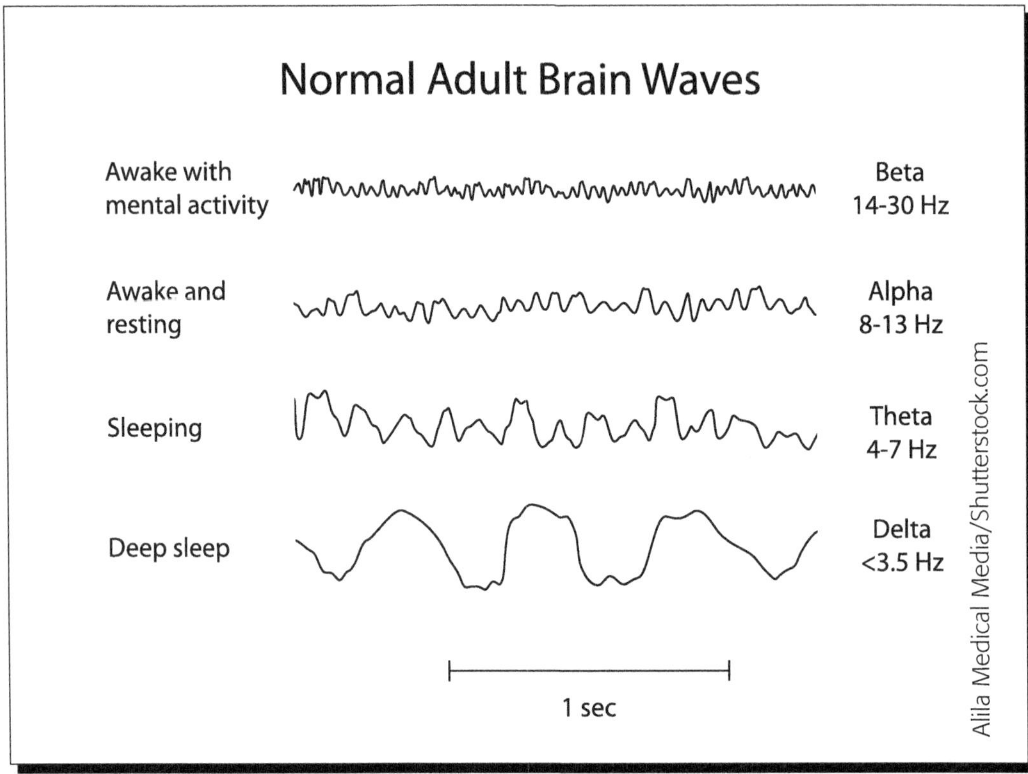

Figure 14-3. The brain waves of a normal adult

Sleep specialists can identify sleep stages by the waves the brain emits (Figure 14-3). Electroencephalograms (EEGs) are used to help understand a person's sleep patterns. This requires the placement of electrodes on the scalp that register electrical signals from the brain. It's fascinating. The brain has a certain pattern it wants to follow, and with uninterrupted sleep, it will.

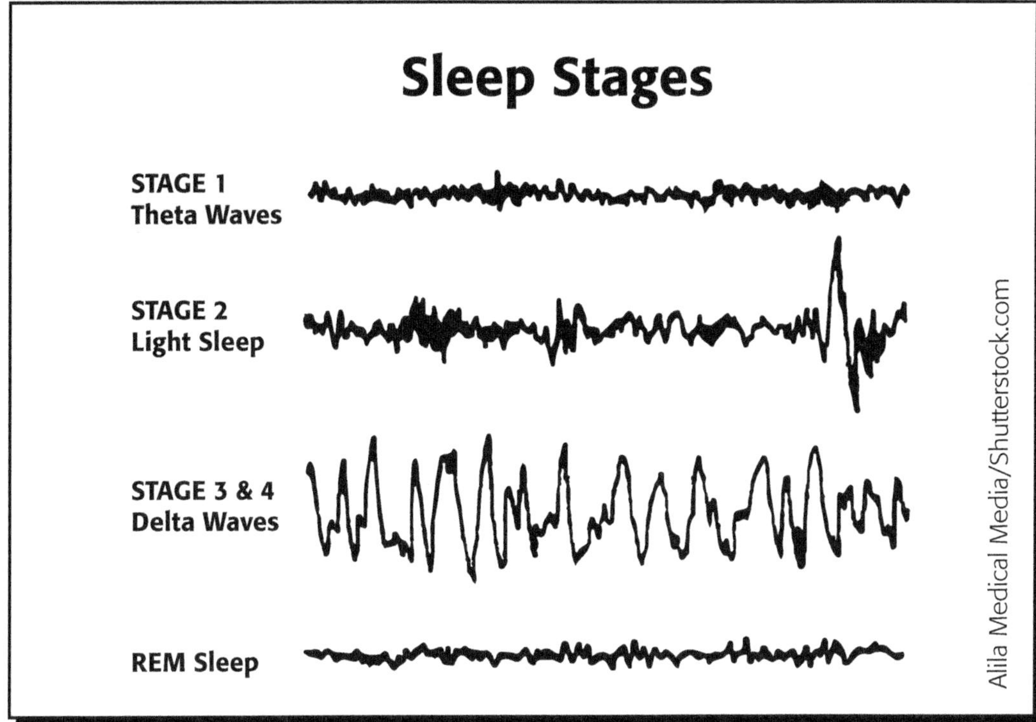

Figure 14-4. An electroencephalographic (EEG) recording of the four sleep stages (used with permission from the *Lifestyle Medicine Handbook*; 2nd edition; Frates, et al.; Monterey, CA: Healthy Learning; 2021)

As discussed in the nutrition chapter, it's important to be aware of your surroundings and how to set yourself up for success. In that regard, to increase the chances of seven to nine hours of solid sleep, keep your bedroom like a cave (i.e., quiet, cool, dark). With the bedroom quiet, you are less likely to wake up and disrupt your sleep cycles. A cool bedroom allows for your core body temperature to drop, which is another natural signal for sleep, in addition to darkness, build-up of adenosine, and release of melatonin. If your bedroom is between 60-70 degrees, optimally around 67 degrees Fahrenheit, your core body temperature will drop. To help this process, you can wear socks on your feet, allowing for vasodilation of the feet and heat to escape from the feet. When heat escapes from your feet, heat from your core follows and works to your feet, which helps create a drop in core body temperature. Another way to accomplish this naturally is to take a warm bath. Upon exiting the heat of the bath and entering your bedroom, your core body temperature will drop.

Keeping the bedroom dark and avoiding bright lights is important. As mentioned previously, the lights from the devices, like iPads, cell phones, laptops, computers, and televisions, emit blue wavelength light that blocks the release of melatonin. Darkness is a natural cue for sleep too. Keeping your bedroom as dark as possible for a full seven to nine hours will help ensure sufficient sleep.

❑ Reflection Time:

How does your environment impact your sleep? Consider your bed, bedding, room temperature, noise, and light (including light from electronic devices).

❑ Reflection Time:

How do others who live in your house impact your sleep? Consider a possible partner, children, and/or a pet's sleeping and waking habits.

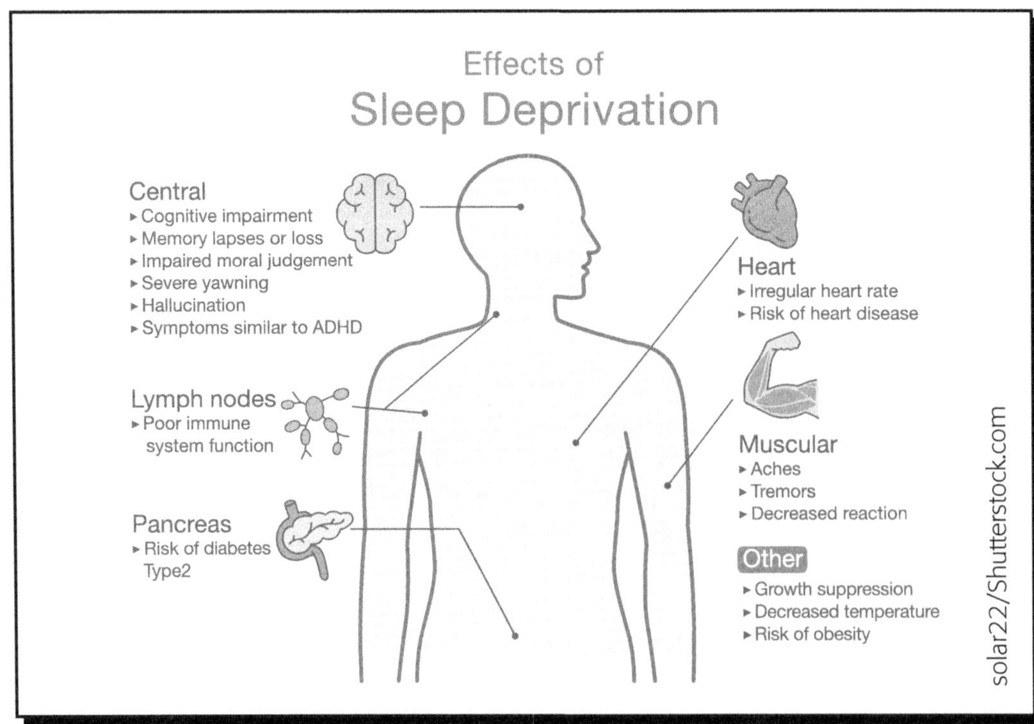

Figure 14-5. The effects of sleep deprivation

Insufficient Sleep

Insufficient sleep is associated with an increased risk of hypertension, cardiovascular disease, gastrointestinal disorders, type 2 diabetes, obesity, as well as depression and anxiety symptoms (Figure 14-5). Susceptibility to infections also increases with inadequate sleep, as do rates of accidents and injuries.

Insufficient sleep negatively impacts thinking, learning, as well as logical reasoning. Most people can remember experiencing mental "fog," when they didn't get enough sleep for several days. Your interpersonal relationships, mood, and quality of life may suffer due to lack of restorative sleep.

INSUFFICIENT SLEEP AND REACTION TIME

Research has correlated a lack of sleep with drunk driving, with regard to reaction times. From a study conducted in Australia, the scientists learned that people who are awake 18 hours have a similar reaction time to someone who has a blood-alcohol concentration of 0.05.[5] Being awake 24 hours was found to correlate with the reaction time of someone who has a blood alcohol level of 0.10. Since being legally drunk entails a blood alcohol level of 0.08, taking sleep seriously is important for your safety behind the wheel, as well as for others on the road, while you are driving.

Among the tips to avoid drowsy driving are the following:

- If you feel your eyes closing while you are driving, switch drivers if someone else in the car is awake enough to take over the wheel. If not, call someone to drive you to your destination.
- Take a break. Go outside. Get coffee.
- Call a friend and explain what is going on.
- Take a short nap in a safe location after informing someone about your location and your plans.

❑ Reflection Time:

How do you feel when you don't get enough sleep?

____

____

____

____

____

____

____

____

____

____

❑ Reflection Time:

How do you feel when you get sufficient sleep?

Figure 14-6. Common causes of insomnia

INSOMNIA, INTERRUPTED, AND INSUFFICIENT SLEEP

Several factors can cause insomnia (Figure 14-6), including the following:

- Stress
- Worry
- Anxiety
- Technology

- Physical activity and inactivity
- Beverages (caffeine, alcohol, and water)
- Food
- Bedroom—temperature, light, sound, and others (spouse, children, and/or pets)
- Medical conditions and physiologic processes (overnight bathroom needs)
- Common sleep disorders
- Obstructive sleep apnea
- Naps
- Tobacco use and nicotine

INSUFFICIENT SLEEP AND PSYCHOLOGICAL REASONS

- *Stress:* Stress can clearly have an impact on your day and night. Refer to the chapter on stress for details and techniques to reduce stress.
- *Worry:* Worry makes falling asleep more challenging. If you wake during the night and are worried about something, your mind may become focused on this issue, precluding you from returning to sleep. Consider journaling prior to bed or writing down issues that concern you, to help put aside your worries.
- *Anxiety:* According to the American Psychological Association,[6] anxiety is "an emotion characterized by feelings of tension, worried thoughts and physical changes." Although everyone experiences occasional anxiety, "people with anxiety disorders usually have recurring intrusive thoughts or concerns."

If anxiety is negatively impacting your life or you believe you have an anxiety disorder, reach out to your primary or mental health care provider. Therapy is often beneficial. Accordingly, when anxiety improves, a better night's sleep may follow.

TECHNOLOGY

- *Work projects:* Easy access to technological devices makes it difficult to "unplug" from work responsibilities. With a phone notifying you of possible emails from your boss or a client needing support, you may find that work invades your sleep time. Consider turning your phone on silent or better yet, leaving your phone outside your bedroom. You'll be setting a good example for your colleagues by putting boundaries in place to protect your sleep.
- *Blue wavelength light:* This light is emitted from devices, such as televisions, smartphones, computers, and alarm clocks, which can disrupt your sleep. Blue wavelength light blocks the release of melatonin from the pineal gland, thereby interfering with this important signal for sleep.
- *Stimulation:* In addition to emitting light, devices tend to be very stimulating and can make falling asleep more difficult, if they are used close to bedtime. It's easy to become worried by watching the news, energized by social media, or invigorated by your favorite television show. In order to prepare your mind for a restful night's sleep, consider limiting technological devices to the daytime or at least avoiding them in the hour or two before you intend to fall asleep. Instead, consider journaling, having a cup of decaffeinated tea and reading a relaxing book, or doing gentle yoga stretches, to prepare your body and mind for sleep.

PHYSICAL ACTIVITY AND INACTIVITY

A lack of exercise is associated with insufficient sleep and being tired is associated with less motivation to engage in healthy lifestyle behaviors (such as prioritizing sleep). However, vigorous exercise late in the day can make it difficult to relax and fall asleep easily at bedtime. To support adequate sleep, avoid excessive sedentary behavior and schedule your exercise sessions during the day.

BEVERAGES

- *Caffeine:* Caffeine competes with adenosine for the same receptor, but it has the opposite effect that adenosine has. Caffeine revs up cell activity. Caffeine consumption leads to adrenalin production. Although the metabolism of caffeine varies among people, the typical time to clear half of the caffeine from their bloodstream is four to six hours. Drinking caffeine in the afternoon may impair your ability to fall asleep at night.

  As mentioned previously adenosine is a chemical created while you are awake through the process of using up internal energy stores (the degrading of energy storage molecules–adenosine triphosphate (ATP)). As adenosine increases, it generates a homeostatic pressure or drive to fall sleep. During sleep the level of adenosine decreases. Seven to nine hours of sleep are needed to bring adenosine down to the baseline level that allows for full wakefulness and energy.
- *Alcohol:* Although alcohol may help you fall asleep, it interrupts your REM sleep and increases nighttime awakenings, restlessness, night sweats and nightmares. Ideally, it is beneficial to avoid alcohol for at least four to six hours prior to bedtime for optimizing sleep.
- *Water:* Although it is important to stay well hydrated throughout the day, you may want to avoid excessive liquids late at night. A full bladder at night can lead to nighttime awakenings to use the restroom, which disrupts sleep.

❑ Reflection Time:

Are you consuming any beverages that may be negatively impacting your sleep? If so, explain any changes that you want to make.

____

____

____

____

____

____

____

____

____

____

FOOD

When you are sleep-deprived, ghrelin (the hunger hormone) increases, and leptin (the satiety-feeling full hormone) decreases. Research showed that partial sleep deprivation led to an average of 385 extra calories consumed daily, with the food choices being significantly higher in fat and lower in protein.[7]

Insufficient sleep is associated with increased weight gain, especially abdominal adiposity (fat tissue around the waist), which is detrimental to health. In addition, short-sleep duration is correlated with increased snacking between meals, lower protein intake, a poor-quality diet, and greater daily caloric intake.[8]

❏ Reflection Time:

Have you noticed a change in your eating habits when you don't get enough sleep? Explain.

____

____

____

____

____

____

____

____

____

A big meal prior to bed can make it difficult to fall asleep. If you are hungry, a small snack is best. Consider trying nuts, seeds, bananas, or honey, as these are high in tryptophan, a protein found in certain foods that is sleep-promoting. Magnesium (in almonds and bananas) may also contribute to their ability to support falling asleep. Avoiding foods that are spicy or high in fat can also decrease your chances of disrupted sleep from acid reflux (indigestion/heartburn).

BEDROOM: TEMPERATURE, LIGHT, SOUND, AND OTHERS (SPOUSE, PARTNER, CHILDREN, AND/OR PETS)

Previously, the value of keeping your bedroom like a cave—quiet, cool, and dark—was discussed. Similarly, streetlights can be bright and contribute to disruptive sleep. Blackout curtains may be helpful if you live near streetlights. In addition, early morning sunlight can wake you earlier than desired, particularly in the spring and summer. As such, blackout curtains can help you stay asleep for a full seven to nine hours.

MEDICAL CONDITIONS AND PHYSIOLOGIC PROCESSES

Some medical conditions require using prescription medications that may make sleep more challenging. For example, a diuretic medication or just advancing age may cause you to need to use the bathroom during the night. If you wake to use the restroom during the night, keep the lights dim or use red lights, which will prevent the sleep disruption caused by blue wavelength light.

Physical discomfort from any source, such as arthritis or low back pain, may make it more challenging to initiate and maintain sleep throughout the night. Women who are perimenopausal often experience difficulties with sleep due to hot flashes and night sweats. Sleeping with a fan nearby and having sheets and blankets that allow for quick cooling can help with symptom management.

Common Sleep Disorders

With almost 70 million people in the U.S. having chronic sleep problems, it is important for you to increase your awareness about sleep health, address sleep disorders, and learn ways to optimize your sleep.[9] Exploring all of the over 100 sleep disorders is beyond the scope of this chapter. However, if you suffer from insomnia, hypersomnia, restless leg syndrome, nightmares or terrors, sleep apnea or other conditions that make sleep challenging, reach out to your primary care physician, as you may benefit from medical treatment or consultation with a sleep specialist.

- *Obstructive Sleep Apnea:* This is a sleep disorder in which breathing repeatedly stops and starts during sleep. With obstructive sleep apnea, intermittent throat muscle relaxation occurs, blocking the airway during sleep. This interrupts normal breathing for short periods of time, which can decrease oxygen levels in the blood causing nighttime awakenings. Several types of sleep apnea exist, but the most common type is obstructive sleep apnea.

  The most noticeable signs of obstructive sleep apnea are snoring and severe daytime sleepiness. Snoring is a signal of sleep apnea. Sleep apnea is also a risk factor for stroke. It's important to consider a sleep workup with an EEG and sleep specialist, if you or someone you love snores.

  In addition, sleep apnea has been connected with an increased risk of a variety of health-related conditions, such as congestive heart failure, hypothyroidism, kidney failure, neurological diseases (Parkinson's disease, Alzheimer's disease, and amyotrophic lateral sclerosis—ALS), damage to the brainstem caused by encephalitis, stroke, brain injury, or other factors (e.g., obesity). You need to contact your primary care physician, if you think you may have sleep apnea as you might need a sleep study and possible treatment for this condition.
- *Microsleeps:* These are short bouts of sleep that suddenly occur without notice, lasting from a fraction of a second to 30 seconds. They often happen with night-shift fatigue, staying awake overnight and are associated with excess daytime sleepiness. Microsleeps are indicators that people are not getting enough sleep. People with sleep apnea often experience microsleeps, which can lead to accidents when these individuals are driving.

- *Naps:* Naps can be beneficial and don't typically disrupt nighttime sleep, especially if they are only 20-30 minutes in length and are taken before 3 p.m. If you are tired during the day, try experimenting with a brief nap to see if it re-energizes you. For some people, naps during the day can make it more difficult to fall asleep and maintain sleep throughout the night. Try investigating to discover what works best for you.
- *Tobacco use and nicotine:* These come in many forms, such as smoking, patches, and gum. Nicotine acts as a stimulant and can keep you awake. See your primary care provider for assistance with cessation.

❑ Reflection Time:

Describe the pre-bedtime routines that you enjoy the most or that seem to work the best for you.

❑ Reflection Time:

If you could do any bedtime routine, what would you like to try? Why?

Tips for Better Sleep

There are a number of "don'ts" and "dos" for achieving a better night's sleep, including:

DON'Ts:

- Don't keep a television in the bedroom or watch television in bed on your computer or other devices.
- Don't use the computer, iPad, laptop, cellphone or other electronic devices in the bedroom or sleep with these electronic devices. Don't charge your phone in your bedroom. Find a different location.
- Don't argue or have difficult conversations immediately before bed.
- Don't do vigorous physical activity right before bedtime.
- Don't consume caffeine or caffeinated beverages in the late afternoon or evening. Stop all caffeine (coffee, tea, chocolate, even decaffeinated coffee) at least four to six hours before bedtime.
- Don't drink alcohol to help you fall asleep. Alcohol may help you get to sleep more quickly, but it will interrupt your sleep, specifically your REM sleep. Research links evening alcohol consumption with frequent wakings, less restful sleep, headaches, night sweats, and even nightmares. The recommendation is to avoid alcohol for at least four to six hours before bedtime.
- Don't drink lots of beverages of any kind close to bedtime. Liquids before bed usually means a full bladder, which translates to bathroom visits and sleep disruption. Stay hydrated throughout and drink plenty of water in the morning and early afternoon. Try not to drink two to three hours before bed.
- Don't go to bed too hungry or too full.
- Don't eat meals or snacks high in fat or protein before bed. They can be difficult to digest and thus may disrupt the sleep cycle.
- Don't take other people's pills, especially their sleeping pills. This is dangerous. There is a reason why these are prescribed.
- Don't take over the counter medications to aid sleep for more than a couple of days (e.g., antihistamines). Some people use them when they are sick with a cold or flu. However, long-term use is not recommended. Speak with your physician if you are having trouble sleeping.
- Don't take nonprescription medications before bed without checking the ingredient labels, because many pain relievers, weight loss pills, diuretics, and even cold medications can have caffeine in them.
- Don't smoke before bed or overnight, if you wake up. Nicotine acts as a stimulant, with similar effects to caffeine. People who fall asleep smoking can wake up in a fire and third degree burns all over.
- Don't take naps longer than 20 minutes nor take naps late in the day.
- Don't use a nightlight, but if you need one, use a red light or one that is as dim as possible.
- Don't become anxious and worry about not sleeping.
- Don't watch the clock minute by minute during the night.

❑ Reflection Time:

Are you engaging in any of the above habits that you would like to change? If so, what specific actions will you take to address them?

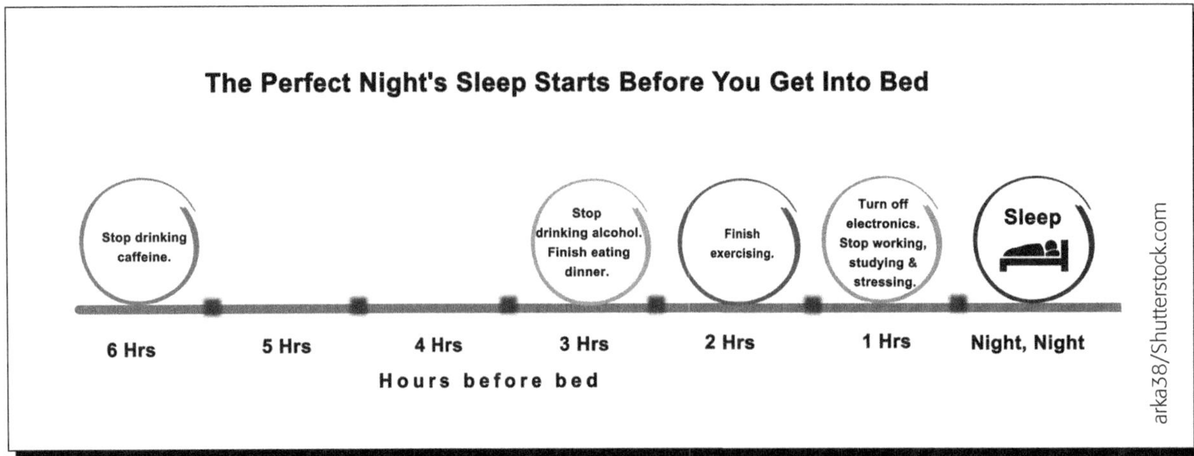

Figure 14-7. A timeline for a perfect night's sleep

DOs:

- Establish a sleep routine. Try to go to bed and get up at the same time each day. If you are working to create a new sleep routine, set a regular waking time for weekends and weekdays to start.
- Restrict the use of the bedroom to sleep and sex only.
- Move your body and exercise each day, preferably in the morning or afternoon.
- Get outside and let the sun shine into your eyes in the morning. Make sure to get natural light exposure each day.
- Keep the temperature in the bedroom cool, around 67 degrees.
- Keep the bedroom as quiet as possible when sleeping and use ear plugs or white noise, if needed.
- Keep the bedroom as dark as possible, pitch black is ideal. Consider using black-out curtains or use an eye mask.
- Wear socks to bed to keep your feet warm allowing for heat to be released peripherally, which allows for a drop in core body temperature.
- Take only short (20 minutes or less) daytime naps in the late morning or early afternoon, if desired.
- Have the lights as dim as possible for two to three hours before bed or use red lights in the bedroom.
- Finish dinner two to three hours before bed.
- Have a comfortable wind down routine that relaxes you before bed. Do relaxation exercises, mindfulness practices, or meditation; enjoy a warm bath; or drink some warm non-caffeinated drink. Note: chamomile tea is non-caffeinated and may help with relaxation.
- Consider using lavender-scented products like creams, as this scent may have slight relaxing and calming effects, when inhaled as in aromatherapy.

❑ Reflection Time:

What helps you fall asleep when you are finding it challenging to initiate sleep or resume sleeping after a mid-sleep awakening?

❑ Reflection Time:

Is there anything else that you want to experiment with and try the next time you wake during the night or have difficulties initiating sleep?

❑ Reflection Time:

Do you want to change any of these habits to improve your sleep? Explain.

Sleep Tracker

Now that you've reflected upon your relationship with sleep in the past, you need to gain a better understanding of your recent sleep habits. Understanding where you are at sleep-wise at the present time can help bring more clarity to how to support your sleep routine moving forward.

❑ Reflection Time:

Using the sleep-tracking chart (Figure 14-8), track your pre-bed routine, as well as your sleep schedule for the next week.

❑ Reflection Time:

Reflect on patterns that you found or new insight that you gained after reviewing your sleep-tracking chart. Based on your findings, is there anything that you want to investigate or try, to improve your sleep?

____

____

____

____

____

____

____

____

If you have difficulty sleeping at least three nights a week for one month, you need to reach out to your physician and seek expert help.

Day	Activities done last night in the hour prior to falling asleep	Time you went to bed	Approximate amount of time it took you to fall asleep	Approximate total number of hours slept	Approximate number of night awakenings and time spent awake	Time you woke and left bed	Other information about last night's sleep, as well as clues from yesterday (naps, exercise, food, stress) that may have impacted sleep	Insights about last night
1								
2								
3								
4								
5								
6								
7								

Figure 14-8. Sleep-tracking chart

MOSS

Answer the following questions on sleep, using the MOSS technique:

❑ Question (motivation):

Why are you motivated to improve your sleep habits?

❑ Question (obstacles):

What obstacles are you likely to encounter?

❑ Question (strategies):

What strategies can you use to overcome these obstacles?

❑ Question (strengths):

What strengths can you draw upon as you work toward your goal? Consider strengths that you've used to overcome previous challenges and your support system including your health care team, family, and friends.

SMART Goal

In order to take what you have learned about sleep and put it into action, create a SMART goal for yourself (refer to Chapter 4 page 55 for an overview of what a SMART goal entails).

❑ SMART Goal Time:

What is a SMART goal, focused on your sleep?

References

❑ Cited References

1. Merriam-Webster. www.mw.com.
2. National Institute of Neurological Disorders and Stroke (2014). Brain Basics: Understanding Sleep. Available: www.ninds.nih.gov/disorders/brain_basics/understanding_sleep.hrm#how_much?
3. Jessen NA, Munk AS, Lundgaard I, et al. (2015). The glymphatic system: a beginner's guide. *Neurochemical Research*, 40(12), 2583–2599.
4. Hirschkowitz M, Whiton K, Albert S, et al. (2015). National Sleep Foundation's sleep time duration recommendations: methodology and results summary. *Sleep Health,* 1(1), 40–43.
5. Williamson AM, Feyer AM (2000). Moderate sleep deprivation produces impairments in cognitive and motor performance equivalent to legally prescribed levels of alcohol intoxication. *Occupational and Environmental Medicine*, 57(10), 649–655.
6. Anxiety. American Psychological Association. https://www.apa.org/topics/anxiety. Accessed July 15, 2021.
7. Al Khatib HK, Harding SV, Darzi J, et al. The effects of partial sleep deprivation on energy balance: a systematic review and meta-analysis. *European Journal of Clinical Nutrition*. 2017 May;71(5):614-24.
8. Shechter A, Grandner MA, St-Onge MP. The role of sleep in the control of food intake. *American Journal of Lifestyle Medicine*. 2014 Nov;8(6):371-4.
9. CDC—About Our Program—Sleep and Sleep Disorders (2017, June 05). https://www.cdc.gov/sleep/aboutus.html. Accessed July 16, 2021.

❑ Book Resources:

- Colten HR, Alevogt BM. *Sleep Disorders and Sleep Deprivation: An Unmet Public Health Problem.* Washington, DC: National Academic Press; 2006.
- Gregory A. *Nodding Off: The Science of Sleep From Cradle to Grave*. London, England: Bloomsbury Sigma; 2018.
- Paul S, Benjamin H. *Sleep Essentials.* Monterey, CA: Healthy Learning; 2020.
- Walker M. *Why We Sleep: Unlocking the Power of Sleep and Dreams.* New York: Scribner; 2017.
- Williamson J. *Sleep Rituals: 100 Practices for a Deep and Peaceful Sleep.* Vero Beach, FL: Adams Media; 2019.
- Winter C. *The Sleep Solution*. New York: Berkeley; 2018.

❑ Other Resources:

- American Sleep Apnea Association—www.sleepapnea.org
- American Sleep Association—www.sleepassociation.org
- Drowsy Driving—www.sleepfoundation.org/drowsy-driving
- Harvard Medical School—healthysleep.med.harvard.edu
- National Sleep Association—sleepfoundation.org
- National Sleep Foundation—www.thensf.org

CHAPTER 15
SOCIAL SUPPORT

"Medicine and technology may fail us at times, but human connection grounded in love and compassion always heals."

—Dr. Vivek Murthy
19th Surgeon General of the United States

PAVING the Path to Wellness: Questions on Social Support

For each of the following five statements, choose the number on the frequency scale that best relates to you (frequency: 1= never, 2= rarely, 3= sometimes, 4= often, 5= routinely).

- I can name at least one person who brings me strength. ____
- I am involved with a group (activity, exercise class, art class, religious affiliation or the like). ____
- I visit with friends on the phone or in person at least five times a week. ____
- I have a healthy relationship with my spouse, partner, or best friend. ____
- I have a pet or plant that I can nurture and spend time with every day. ____

Subtotal—social support: ____

Lightspring/Shutterstock.com

According to American psychiatrist and author Dr. Edward Hallowell, social support through a five-minute conversation makes all the difference in the world, if the parties participate actively. To make it work, you have to bring your full attention to the other person by setting aside what you're doing, putting down the memo you were reading, disengaging from your laptop, or abandoning your daydream. Usually, when you do this, the other person (or people) will feel the energy and respond in kind, naturally.

Live and Learn: Dr. Amy Comander

During the COVID19 pandemic, physical distancing from others has been a cornerstone of preventive advice. During this challenging time, most everyone has faced difficulties with maintaining their social connections.

I am fortunate to be part of a group of friends who truly enjoy birthday celebrations that are always planned in advance. We will have dinner at a local restaurant, get together for Trivia Night at a local pub, or meet up at a friend's home for Sunday brunch. We have done some creative birthday outings as well. Last year, one of my friends, a yoga instructor, hosted a private yoga class for my birthday celebration! Another friend invited us to a private "spin class" at a nearby cycling studio. We have also met at a local studio for a "Paint Night."

How does one celebrate a birthday, surrounded by friends, during a pandemic? When faced with this challenge, we decided we needed to get creative, and that is where the "birthday hike" emerged. The first hike was in the winter—a walk in the woods on a nearby trail. It happened to be snowing, so we wore our winter gear—hats, scarves, winter coats, and snow boots—and trudged along the trail, admiring the magical trees with their snow-laden branches. We all enjoyed this activity together so much that we started to arrange "birthday hikes" for our other friends' birthday celebrations. We have now used the "birthday hike" as an opportunity to meet up at nearby parks, trails, and new destinations.

As people reflect on the pandemic, many individuals question what parts of "normal life" they missed and what they learned. I certainly look forward to hugging my friends; I miss sharing meals at restaurants in downtown Boston. However, I have really enjoyed the new tradition of the "birthday hike," which provides an opportunity for social connection, physical activity, and a "time-out" in the outdoors. I hope we will continue this tradition going forward.

Social Connection Timeline

❑ Reflection Time:

Write out or draw what comes to mind about your social connections during each of these phases of your life: childhood, high-school, young adulthood, middle age, older adulthood. Consider times when you met your partner a new friend, joined an organization that resulted in meaningful connections, or started a new career.

❑ Reflection Time:

After reflecting on social connections throughout your life in the above activities, what insight did you gain, patterns did you notice, or reflections do you have?

____

____

____

____

____

____

____

As people mature, so do their relationships. People come and go from your life. Sometimes, connections dissolve as you enter different phases of your life. Other separations may be more painful, such as a contentious divorce or the death of a loved one.

Social connection is key. It means so much, more than words can describe or research can verify. It's simple but complex. Its beauty and necessity are addressed in this chapter.

On a superficial level, social connection is connecting with others. Exchanging words, holding doors, smiling at people, following detour signs, and following people on social media are all forms of connection. They all represent different types of connections. There's connection with another person through verbal and non-verbal communication. There's connection with the community and neighborhood by following rules, guidelines, and laws designed for safety. There's connection through social media with strangers or people you've never met. Projects, community service, work, religious activities, education, classes, and ideas often connect people. Connection is vital to your health and happiness.

Definitions of Connection

According to the *Merriam-Webster Dictionary*,[1] connection is defined in several ways:

- Something that joins or connects two or more things
- The act of connecting two or more things or the state of being connected
- A situation in which two or more things have the same cause, origin, goal, etc.

Early in life, the act of connection manifests itself in a variety of ways. For example, children work with Lego bricks to form connections. They also play in sandboxes and classrooms forming social connections and friendships.

Social connections, a sense of belonging, and friendships play vital roles in people's lives. Maslow's Hierarchy of Needs places a sense of belonging in the third level of his pyramid, with physiologic needs and safety needs at levels one and two (Figure 15-1). After people have food and water, as well as a safe place to live and sleep, they desire love. In this instance, love entails a sense of belonging or a feeling of connection to others. As human beings, everyone longs to be loved and understood. People want to be supported by others and to offer support in return. This sense of belonging is a basic human need.

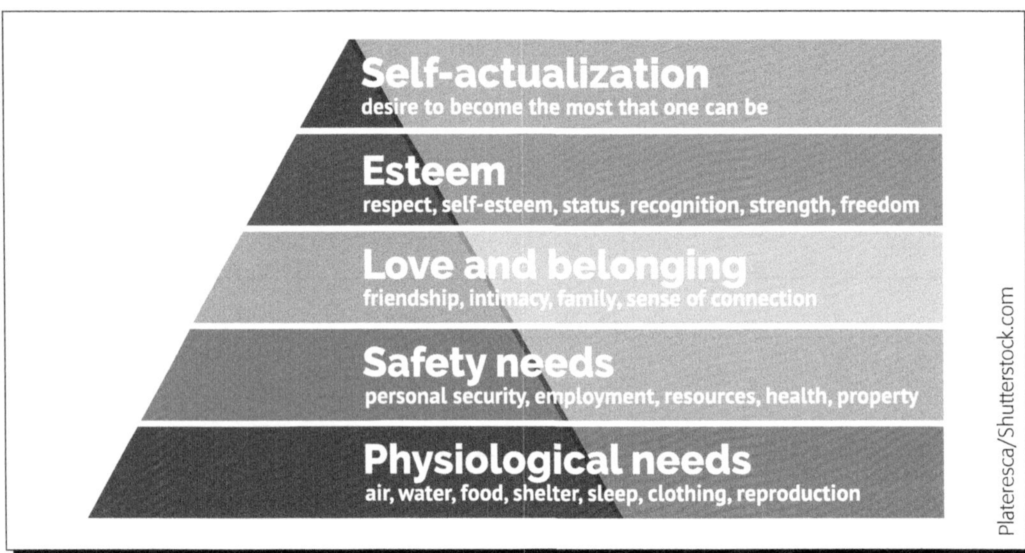

Figure 15-1. Maslow's original Hierarchy of Needs

You can enhance your sense of belonging and social connection in a variety of ways, including the following:

- Take the Social Network Index assessment. (www.psy.cmu.edu/~scohen/SNI.html).
- Be an advocate for health and wellness, e.g., be a pear-health coach.
- Connect–in the next month, make one new acquaintance or reconnect with an old friend.
- Hug–during the next week, hug someone at least once a day.
- Smile–within the next week, at least once a day, give a smile to someone.
- Talk and listen–meet up with a friend and have a good, long conversation.
- Help each other–help a friend with something.
- Help others–get involved in a volunteer experience.
- Help yourself.

Oxytocin = "Love Hormone" or "Bonding Hormone"

Not only is connection a basic human need, it is also a physiologic response, which starts as babies. The hormone oxytocin helps make the uterus contract, facilitating an infant's birth. Oxytocin is known as the bonding hormone or the love hormone. The word is derived from Greek—oxus, which means sharp and tokos, which means childbirth. This hormone also signals to the mammary glands to produce milk for a mother to feed her baby. Of historical note, Vincent du Vigneaud received the Nobel Prize for synthesizing oxytocin in 1953. Its power is undeniable.

Researchers are fascinated by the power of oxytocin. In a paper published in the journal *Nature*,[2,3] researchers looked at the brain's response to social interactions and found that they act as a reward, much like eating, kissing, or hugging. Oxytocin is pleasing and a "feel-good" hormone that works in concert with certain neurotransmitters, such as serotonin (some antidepressants work to increase the level of serotonin) and dopamine (which is intricately involved with the reward system in the brain), as well as the GABA system in the brain, to provide an "anti-anxiety" effect.[4]

In addition, research on oxytocin suggests that this hormone plays a role in increasing trust, reducing fear, improving emotional recognition, increasing eye gazing, and increasing the ability to read emotions behind facial expressions. All of these functions are important for facilitating connections among people and enabling them to express empathy and fully understand another person's verbal and non-verbal cues.[5]

A variety of activities have been found to increase oxytocin, including the following:[5]

- Making love
- Hugging
- Massaging
- Cuddling
- Holding hands
- Petting a dog

Connecting With a Pet Can Impact Your Health and Wellness

There are many benefits of living with a pet. One, a pet is loveable. Cats and dogs, for example, are often soft. Petting them is relaxing. Many people enjoy taking care of their cat or dog, and it gives them a sense of purpose when they wake up in the morning. Studies show that people with pets have significantly lower heart rates and blood pressure levels during resting baseline testing and significantly smaller increases from baseline levels during mental arithmetic testing, which many consider very stressful.[6]

People who have dogs as part of their family walk their dogs and thus get more physical activity than those who do not have dogs.[7] Walking the dog is a type of relaxing activity, bonding activity, and fun activity for both the dog and its owner. Dogs are great lifestyle coaches as they are fully present in the moment, playful, active, get their rest and sleep, and are often full of energy and positivity, especially when a family member comes home. Imagine being greeted in that excited and loving way by another human every single time you arrived home. The jumping up and down, the tail wagging, and the barking all make for a terrific greeting. It's no surprise that dogs are called "man's best friend." The bond is real!

Researchers have evaluated and examined this bond for decades. There is a physiologic effect of petting your dog, which involves a drop in blood pressure and sense of relaxation, as if reading a book. In addition, during the "greeting" response when your dog enters a room, your blood pressure likely raises slightly with excitement.[8] Interestingly, research demonstrates that interactions with dogs, especially those initiated by the dog's gaze, can increase the urinary oxytocin concentrations of their owners.[9] In fact, dogs may improve the health and sense of well-being of people in multiple ways. Bonding with animals provides humans with a special type of connection.

There are many benefits of living with a pet.

4 PM production/Shutterstock.com

Connection and Motivation at Home and Work

Oxytocin helps individuals feel connected which is a basic human need and an important component of sustaining motivation. Rich Ryan and Edward Deci's Self-Determination Theory[10] explains how people have three important needs to fill in order to sustain motivation for a task, job, project, or other aspect of their home or work life:

- Competence—the need to be effective in dealing with the environment
- Autonomy—the need to control the course of their life
- Relatedness—the need to have a close, affectionate relationships with others (bonding)

As such, relatedness or a sense of connection/belonging helps you stay on track and engaged in your work (at work and at home).

❏ Reflection Time:

Consider a project at home or work that you enjoyed or felt proud to complete. Did this project give you a sense of competence, autonomy, or relatedness to others? If so, describe this situation.

____

____

____

____

____

____

____

____

❏ Reflection Time:

When you have not felt motivated to complete a project or continue in a job or task, have you noticed the lack of one of these factors—competence, autonomy or relatedness? Explain.

____

____

____

____

____

____

____

____

Connection With a Wider Lens

Dr. Edward Hallowell is a practicing psychiatrist, the author of more than 20 books, an expert in attention-deficit/hyperactivity disorder (ADHD), and he operates several ADHD centers in the United States. Dr. Hallowell is known as a master of connection, as he has the ability to meet anyone and find some way to connect with them on a deep level, not just superficially. Dr. Hallowell's work is fascinating and enlightening. When speaking about connection, he urges his audience to consider many different types of connections. He details 12 vital ties:[11,12,13]

- Family of origin
- Immediate family
- Friends and community
- Work, mission, activity
- Pets and other animals (previously discussed in detail)
- Beauty
- The past
- Nature and special places
- Ideas and information
- Institutions and organizations
- Whatever is beyond knowledge
- Yourself

There are numerous powerful points in Hallowell's work. One is the importance of connecting with nature. Abraham Maslow appreciated this factor in the 1970s, when he revised his Hierarchy of Needs to include aesthetic needs, which included beauty, balance, and form, all of which are found in nature.

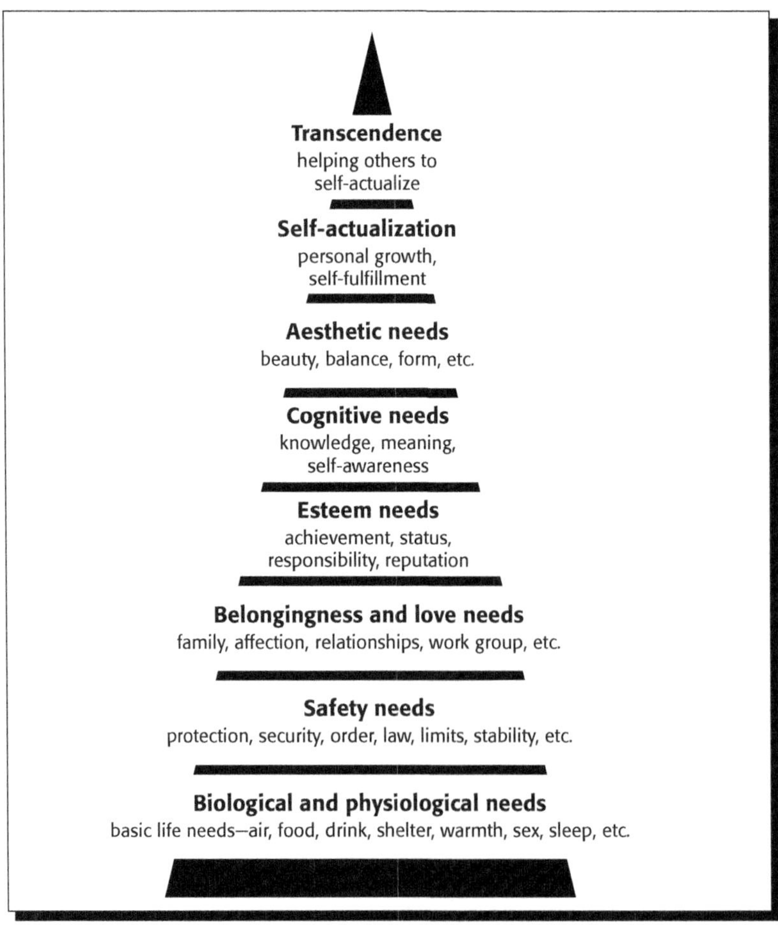

Figure 15-2. Maslow's revised Hierarchy of Needs

Connecting With Nature for Health

Interaction with and observing nature, such as landscapes, plants, animals, forests, and the wilderness have many positive effects on peoples' bodies and brains. Research shows that being in nature has beneficial physiologic effects. Not only does it foster recovery from mental fatigue and is restorative, it may also help people heal from previous hurt. In addition, spending time in nature increases positive outlook on life, enhances stress coping and recovery from illness, restores concentration, and improves productivity.[14]

The Japanese consider forest bathing as a type of therapy. Walking in the forest can be relaxing and soothing. Mounting evidence and research have led some professionals to recommend spending at least 120 minutes in nature each week.

Benefits of Social Support

Social connections offer numerous benefits for your physical and mental health. Sociologists Drs. Debra Umberson and Jennifer Montez summarized these in their paper titled, Public Policy: Social Ties and the Health of the Population.[15] The following is a summary of their research concerning the positive impact of having social ties (social connections):

- Social ties affect mental health, physical health, health behaviors, and premature mortality risk.
- Social ties are a potential resource that can be harnessed to promote population health.
- Social ties are a resource that should be protected as well as promoted.
- Social ties can benefit health beyond the target individuals by influencing the health of others throughout social networks.
- Social ties have both immediate (mental health, health behaviors) and long-term cumulative effects on health (physical health, mortality), and thus represent opportunities for short- and long-term investments in population health.
- Social ties—overburdened, strained, conflicted, or abusive—can undermine health.
- The costs and benefits of social ties are not distributed equally in the population, but vary based upon age, gender, socioeconomic status, and race.

Everyone was born to connect with others, and the hormone oxytocin enables them to form their first social bond with their mothers. As noted previously, oxytocin plays an important role in brain circuitry and through its actions, facilitates connections with others. Numerous studies have demonstrated the importance of social connections for health promotion. Unfortunately, social isolation can have negative implications for a person's mental and physical health. Social isolation can exacerbate underlying depression and low self-worth.

Research has demonstrated that socially isolated individuals have depressed immune function, disrupted sleep patterns, and higher levels of stress hormones. Furthermore, individuals who are socially isolated are also at increased risk for health conditions, such as high blood pressure, coronary heart disease, anxiety, and depression.

Social connections provide many benefits for your mental and physical health. In 1979, social epidemiologists Lisa F. Berkman and S. Leonard Syme did a landmark study that demonstrated the relationship between social and community ties, and mortality.[16] On review of data from the 1965 Human Population Laboratory survey of a random sample of 6928 adults in Alameda County, the researchers found that people who lacked social and community ties were more likely—2.3 times more likely for men, and 2.8 times more likely for women—to die in the follow-up period than those individuals who had more extensive contracts.

The key point to remember is that having social support can have a positive impact on your life, as the following lists from the work of Drs. Debra Umberson and Jennifer Montez indicate:

- Psychosocial Benefits:
  - ✓ Gives social support (reduces the impact of stress).
  - ✓ Offers personal control.
  - ✓ Provides symbolic meaning (belonging to a group).
  - ✓ Enriches coherence (fosters a sense of meaning).
  - ✓ Enhances mental health.
- Physiological Benefits:
  - ✓ Benefits the immune system.
  - ✓ Benefits the endocrine system.
  - ✓ Benefits the cardiovascular system.
  - ✓ Reduces physiological responses to both anticipated and existing stressors.
- Behavioral Benefits:
  - ✓ Influences health behaviors.
  - ✓ Provides information and create norms.
  - ✓ Enables a spouse to monitor, inhibit, regulate, or facilitate your health behaviors.

Volunteering Your Time Is a Good Way to Connect

Volunteering can take a number of forms, including spending your time at a local food pantry, helping to build houses for the homeless, teaching adults how to read, donating your gently worn clothes to shelters, serving at soup kitchens, as well as many other opportunities that are available for us to help make the world a little brighter for those who are suffering. By volunteering, you can connect with fellow volunteers, as well as those you are serving.

Research shows that connecting in this way gives you a reward in your brain and makes you feel good. It also has several other benefits. For example, one interesting study demonstrated that elderly female African American volunteers of low income, low education, and low Mini-Mental State Examination (MMSE) scores (indicative of some decline in cognitive function), who spent 15 or more hours mentoring students, assisting in a school library, or helping with conflict resolution, showed gains in executive function and increased activity in their brain in the pre-frontal cortex, compared to control subjects who did not volunteer.[17] In other words, older people, who volunteer helping students also help themselves retain their mental capacity, form connections and get a dose of dopamine for a reward. The takeaway point is that volunteering your time has numerous benefits.

Disconnection

The opposite of connection is disconnection. No one likes it when the phone disconnects. You are having a lovely conversation, and suddenly there's no one on the other line. Sometimes, this happens not only with your phone, but also in life. It hurts. When this occurs, it's important to reach out and form a new connection or engage with old, loyal, supportive people, who will provide you with reliable, steady social connections and comfort.

The COVID-19 pandemic put most everyone into a place of decreased social connection. In many cases, in-person connections were stripped away, especially for those who were elderly. The severity of this type of disconnection was highlighted globally. Figuring out creative ways to connect was of paramount importance. While using technology helped keep connections alive, they do not provide the same experiences as face-to-face, in-person connections. Individuals learned the value of these meaningful connections during their time in lockdown—while everyone was staying at home.

Due to this experience, most people are now exquisitely tuned in to social disconnection. As such, individuals must make every effort to stay connected and help those around them feel a sense of connection.

Strategies to stay connected with people when social distancing or at other times include the following:

- Call friends and family.
- Schedule Zoom meetings with friends and family.
- Facetime friends and family.
- Write letters to friends and family.
- Send care packages to loved ones.
- Use social media platforms to connect with friends and make new ones.
- Take walks while talking on the cell phone.
- Attend online educational classes or health workshops.
- Attend online (virtual) exercise classes, meditation classes, cooking classes, etc.

Among the strategies to connect with people when there are no social distancing limitations include the following:

- Invite people over for a healthy meal.
- Take walks and hikes with people.
- Go to the movies with people.
- Walk dogs together.
- Go to a dog park.
- Attend events at the local community center.
- Attend classes at the local YMCA.
- Attend religious services.
- Attend cooking classes.
- Join a book club.
- Go out to a restaurant with friends.

- Gather with relatives to celebrate a birthday.
- Join family members for a holiday.
- Visit a museum with a friend.
- Explore nature with someone.
- Go shopping.
- Attend community events.

Loneliness vs. Desired Solitude

Loneliness is a subjective mental state. When you are unable to connect or communicate with others, it is normal to feel lonely. Emotional, physical, and social factors contribute to loneliness. For example, during the COVID-19 pandemic, many people experienced loneliness due to separation from loved ones and social activities that they previously enjoyed.

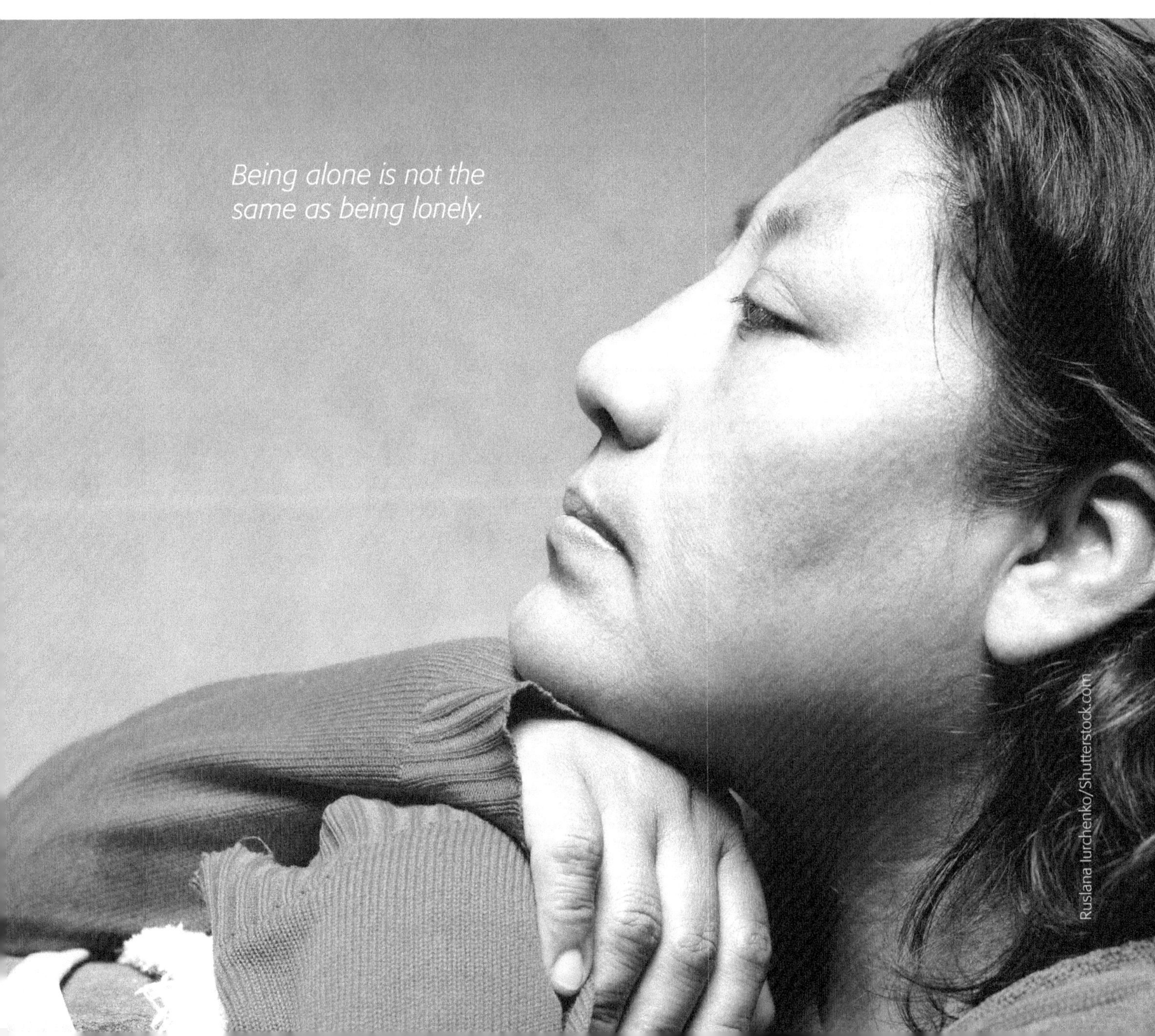

Social isolation is a physical state, which can be voluntary or involuntary. When you are socially isolated, you do not have contact with other individuals, and social relationships are absent. You are alone and are not necessarily enjoying being alone.

Experiencing a certain amount of solitude is desired for many people. Solitude gives them space to relax, reflect, and recharge, so that when they reengage with others, they are more fully present. Many people enjoy being alone. They crave alone time. Being alone is not the same as being lonely. When an individual is lonely, they crave time with others. They miss others. They want social interaction and connection. Most people know what it's like to feel lonely.

❏ Reflection Time:

Do you enjoy solitude or is being alone difficult for you? Explain.

____

____

____

____

____

____

____

____

Social Isolation

Social isolation research has shown that even among well-functioning individuals, social isolation eventually results in psychological and physical disintegration. In some cases, it can even result in death. For example, research on patients with cardiovascular disease found that socially isolated patients had 2.4 times the risk of cardiac death, when compared to their peers who were more socially connected.[15] In fact, social isolation—a low quality and quantity of social ties—is linked with a higher risk of cardiovascular disease, recurrent heart attacks, atherosclerosis, high blood pressure, cancer, delayed cancer recovery, slow wound healing, impaired immune function, and higher inflammatory markers.

Even when examining all age groups, for both men and women, risk of premature death was higher for people who had less social connection, which was measured by the number of close friends and relatives someone had, as well as how often they saw them. While everyone knows that smoking is bad for their health, most people don't realize that social isolation scores are as predictive of early death as is smoking cigarettes. Social isolation also rivals high blood pressure as a mortality risk factor. The medical literature clearly demonstrates the importance of high-quality connections for your health.[16,18]

State of the Art Review

The importance of social connection was highlighted by Dr. Beth Frates and her colleagues in an article on a state-of-the-art review that appeared in the *American Journal of Lifestyle Medicine.* Over the past several years, more research and a greater understanding of the importance of social connection has emerged. Lifestyle medicine is the field that advocates for the promotion of social connection as a tool for enhancing well-being and health.[19]

"A connection is the dynamic, living tissue that exists between two people when there is some contact between them involving mutual awareness and social interaction."

—Dr. Jane Dutton
Professor of Management at
the University of Michigan

Low-Quality Connections

Low-quality connections exist in toxic relationships. They can hurt you emotionally, mentally, or even physically. If you notice feeling anxious or irritable prior to connecting with someone, this may be a sign of a low-quality connection. Earlier in this workbook, the topic of leeches and lilies was discussed. If you are connected with a leech, someone whom you cannot trust or who drains your energy, that is a sign of a low-quality connection.

As such, some low-quality connections may eventually become high-quality connections. For this to occur, professional mental health support may be necessary. On the other hand, on occasion, you may not want to put effort into trying to improve a low-quality connection. Only you can determine whether a relationship is worth the investment.

According to Dr. Jane Dutton, in a low-quality connection, "a tie exists (people communicate, they interact, and they may even be involved in interdependent work), but the connective tissue is damaged."

Cultivating Quality Connections

Creating and maintaining high-quality connections takes effort, but the rewards are immense. In order for high-quality connections to be maintained, they must be nurtured. Jane Dutton's work on "fostering high-quality connections" suggests practices that support meaningful relationships.[20]

Phone calls, text messages, emails, and social media can often distract individuals from paying attention to the people who matter the most to them, those that are right in front of them. The next time you are with someone important to you, notice distractions that make it difficult to maintain your focus on the other person. If you value a relationship, strive to demonstrate presence through being mindful of your actions and your words. Dutton also encourages being genuine in your relationships through speaking and reacting honestly. Putting up fronts between yourself and others jeopardizes relationships.

Another strategy for encouraging quality connections is through affirming communication that highlights positive attributes of the other person. Connections are strengthened through this supportive communication. In addition to being mindful of your speech, high quality connections are also encouraged through empathetic, active listening. Try to listen at least as much as you speak. People undervalue the power of thoughtful, provocative questions that allow people to dig deep within the recesses of their brains to answer them. By thinking deeply, you are sharing deeply together. A deep question invites this deep thinking and connecting. It's often difficult to come up with thoughtful and inspiring questions. Here's one "If you could change one thing about your life right now, what would that be?" Here's another "What does it take for you to feel safe in a relationship?" And yet another "What makes you feel happy inside?"

❑ Reflection Time:

Think of a quality connection that you would like to strengthen. How can you use some of the strategies above to foster this important relationship?

____

____

____

____

____

____

____

Creating and maintaining high-quality connections takes effort, but the rewards are immense.

Relationships and Resilience

According to Dr. John Paul Stephens,[21] professor of organizational behavior at Case Western Reserve University, resilience is "the ability of individuals, groups, and organizations to absorb the stress that arises from these challenges and to not only recover functioning back to a 'normal' level but also learn and grow from the adversity to emerge stronger than before" (see Figure 10-4).

Dr. Stephens highlights two building blocks of resilience in relationships. The first involves the importance of expressing emotions, both positive and negative. This expression provides valuable information to the other person and fosters resilience. The second building block is the ability to constructively express emotions within a relationship. This expression allows individuals to become stronger by learning from their emotions.

Quality interpersonal relationships support resilience. Being surrounded by others who care about you and express their emotions will nurture the relationship and grow your resilience. In addition, being in relationships with people who have an orientation toward learning and improving supports resilience in times of stress.

❏ Reflection Time:

Who is someone in your life who supports you during times of intense stress? How does their emotional expression support your resilience?

____

____

____

____

____

____

____

____

Both coal and diamonds are formed through heat and pressure. Diamonds experience greater temperatures and more pressure than coal, during their formation. The additional stress that diamonds experience results in stronger connections (bonds) between its atoms. Stress leads to strong connections and eventually strength.

❏ Reflection Time:

Can you think of a relationship you have that was strengthened during a time of intense stress? Describe that relationship.

____

You are a diamond and are stronger because of the stress you have endured. Take time to foster the connections that help make you resilient.

High-Quality Connections

> *"Like a healthy blood vessel that connects parts of our body, a high-quality connection between two people allows the transfer of vital nutrients; it is flexible, strong, and resilient."*
>
> —Dr. Jane Dutton
> Professor of Management at
> the University of Michigan

Dr. Dutton's research connects positive psychology and organizational science. Her research has shown that when you experience a high-quality connection, you feel more alive, are filled with positive energy, and feel known or loved. In order for a high-quality connection to be experienced, it must be mutual where both participants feel safety in expressing their full range of emotions. This generativity and openness

Both coal and diamonds are formed through heat and pressure.

Joe Belanger/Shutterstock.com

to new ideas, and expression allows for both participants to bounce back when they experience setbacks. These people are the lilies in your life. Surrounding yourself with lilies, especially during difficult times, provides the emotional support needed to overcome adversity.

❏ Reflection Time:

List your most supportive relationships.

Strengthening High-Quality Social Connections Through MOSS

After reflecting on Dr. Hallowell's categories for connection that were discussed previously in this chapter, choose an area that you would like to focus on enhancing.

❏ Reflection Time:

In what domain do you want to strengthen connections?

MOTIVATORS

Consider your motivation for wanting to strengthen a connection in this area. Common motivators include wanting to experience friendship or love, have companionship, prevent loneliness, increase joy and happiness, decrease stress, or increase your sense of purpose.

❏ Reflection Time:

What is your motivation for wanting to establish or strengthen this connection?

____

____

____

____

____

____

____

____

OBSTACLES

When you establish or strengthen a connection, you sometimes experience obstacles. Common obstacles to fostering quality connections include a lack of time or confidence, not knowing how to initiate the relationship, technology, feeling insecure, a history of past negative experiences or overcoming the inertia of keeping things the same. The pandemic also created barriers to establishing connections.

❏ Reflection Time:

What obstacles may you experience when trying to establish or strengthen this connection?

____

____

____

____

____

____

____

____

____

STRATEGIES

To overcome obstacles, you must strategize how to move forward. Among the examples of how others have overcome common obstacles are the following:

- *Technology:* Technology can be a barrier or tool to establishing quality connections, depending on how it is used.

❑ Reflection Time:

How does technology interfere with your ability to have quality social connections?

____

____

____

____

____

____

____

❑ Reflection Time:

Do you want to make any changes to decrease technology's interference with your connections? Explain.

____

____

____

____

____

____

____

- *Reaching out:* Reaching out can be difficult, especially if you are introverted, have a history of negative past experiences, or struggle with initiating relationships. To overcome this, consider calling a friend or acquaintance to get to know them better, join a support group or organization, send an email or text to someone you want to connect with, join a club that aligns with your interests, or participate in a structured class where you will have opportunities to meet others. Remember, reaching out to someone can help the other person too, as they will benefit from connecting with you.

❑ Reflection Time:

Is there someone, an organization, or a group with which you would like to connect or reconnect? How can you take the next step to reach out?

- *Time inventory:* It's been said that your calendar shows what or whom you value most. If a lack of time is holding you back from establishing or maintaining quality connections, it may be time to take inventory of your time and see if there are changes that you wish to make.

❑ Reflection Time:

Examine your calendar to determine where and on what you are spending your time. What insight did you gain?

❑ Reflection Time:

Based on your time inventory, would you like to make any changes to how you use your time in order to strengthen quality connections?

❑ Reflection Time:

After reviewing your potential obstacles and the strategies above, what strategies do you want to try to help you overcome your obstacles?

STRENGTHS

Everyone possesses strengths that have helped them during difficult times in the past. Everyone has had struggles and obstacles that they have overcome. These strengths, knowledge, skills, wisdom, talents, and gifts can help you create and sustain high-quality connections.

❑ Reflection Time:

What personal strengths can you use to create or foster these quality connections?

SMART Goal

In order to take what you learned about social connection and put it into action, create a SMART goal for yourself (refer to Chapter 4 page 55 for an overview of what a SMART goal entails).

❑ SMART Goal Time:

What is your SMART goal, focused around social connection?

Connecting with nature is important.

Roman Zaiets/Shutterstock.com

References

❏ Cited References:

1. Merriam-Webster. www.mw.com.
2. Owen SF, Tuncdemir SN, Bader PL, et al. (2013). Oxytocin enhances hippocampal spike transmission by modulating fast-spiking interneurons. *Nature,* 600(7463), 458–462.
3. Dölen G, Darvishzadeh A, Huang KW, et al. (2013). Social reward requires coordinated activity of nucleus accumbens oxytocin and serotonin. *Nature,* 501(7466), 179–184.
4. Scheele D, Willie A, Kendrick KM, et al. (2013). Oxytocin enhances brain reward system responses in men viewing the face of their female partner. *Proceedings of the National Academy of Sciences*, 110(50), 20308–20313.
5. De Dren CK, Green LL, Van Kleef, et al. (2011). Oxytocin promotes human ethnocentrism. *Proceedings of the National Academy of Sciences*, 108(4), 1262–1266.
6. Allen K, Blascovich J, Mendes WB (2002). Cardiovascular reactivity and the presence of pets, friends, and spouses: the truth about cats and dogs. *Psychosomatic Medicine*, 64(5), 727–739.
7. Brown SG, Rhodes RE (2006). Relationships among dog ownership and leisure-time walking in Western Canadian adults. *American Journal of Preventive Medicine,* 30(2), 131–136.
8. Baun MM, Bergstrom N, Langston NF (1984). Physiological effects of human/companion animal bonding. *Nursing Research*, 33(3), 126–129.
9. Nagasawa M, Kikusui T, Onaka T, et al. (2009). Dog's gaze at its owner increases owner's urinary oxytocin during social interaction. *Hormones and Behavior*, 55(3), 443–441.
10. Deci EL, Ryan EM (eds.). *Handbook of Self-Determination Research*. Rochester, NY: University of Rochester Press; 2004.
11. Hallowell EM, Ratey JJ. *Driven to Distraction: Recognizing and Coping With Attention Deficit Disorder from Childhood Through Adulthood*. New York: Touchstone; 1995.
12. Hallowell EM. *The Childhood Roots of Adult Happiness: Five Steps to Help Create and Sustain Lifelong Joy.* New York: Ballantine Books; 2003.
13. Hallowell EM. *Connect: 12 Vital Ties That Open Your Heart, Lengthen Your Life, and Deepen Your Soul.* New York: Simon and Schuster; 2001.
14. Maller C, Townsend M, Pryor A, et al. (2006). Healthy nature healthy people: 'contact with nature' as an upstream health promotion intervention for populations. *Health Promotion International*, 21(1), 45–54.
15. Umberson D, Crosnoe R, Reczek C (2001). Social relationships and health behavior across the life course. *Annual Review of Sociology*, 36, 139–157.
16. Berkman LF, Syme SL (1979). Social networks, host resistance, and mortality: a nine-year follow-up study of Alameda County residents. *American Journal of Epidemiology*, 109(2), 186–204.
17. Carlson MC, Erickson KI, Kramer AF, et al. (2009). Evidence for neurocognitive plasticity in at-risk older adults: the experience corps program. *Journal of Gerontology Series A: Biomedical Sciences and Medical Sciences*, 64(12), 1275–1282.

18. Pantell M, Rehkopf D, Jutte D, et al. (2003). Social isolation: a predictor of mortality comparable to traditional clinical risk factors. *American Journal of Public Health,* 103(11), 2056–2062.
19. Martino J, Pegg J, Frates EP (2017). The connection prescription: using the power of social interactions and the deep desire for connectedness to empower health and wellness. *American Journal of Lifestyle Medicine*, 11(6), 466–475.
20. Dutton JE, Heaphy ED (2003). The power of high-quality connections. *Positive Organizational Scholarship: Foundations of a New Discipline*, 3, 263–278.
21. Stephens JP, Heaphy ED, Carmeli A, et al. (2013). Relationship quality and virtuousness: emotional carrying capacity as a source of individual and team resilience. *The Journal of Applied Behavioral Science*, 49(1), 13–41.

❑ Book Resources:

- Cain J (ed). *The Learning Curve.* Monterey, CA: Healthy Learning; 2021.
- Christakis N, Fowler JH. *Connection: the Surprising Power of Social Networks and How They Shape Our Lives.* New York: Little, Brown Spark; 2011.
- Corley J. *The Joy of Friendship: A Thoughtful and Inspiring Collection of 200 Quotations.* Hobart, NY: Hatherleigh Press; 2018.
- Deci EL, Ryan EM (eds.). *Handbook of Self-Determination Research.* Rochester, NY: University of Rochester Press; 2004.
- Dutton JE. *Energize Your Workplace: How to Create and Sustain High-Quality Connections at Work.* Hoboken, NJ: Jossey-Bass; 2007.
- Egger G, Binns A, Rossner S. *Lifestyle Medicine: Managing Diseases of Lifestyle in the 21st Century,* 3rd ed. Cambridge, MA: Academic Press; 2017.
- Hallowell EM. *Connect: 12 Vital Ties That Open Your Heart, Lengthen Your Life, and Deepen Your Soul.* New York: Simon and Schuster; 2001.
- Hallowell EM. *The Childhood Roots of Adult Happiness: Five Steps to Help Create and Sustain Lifelong Joy.* New York: Ballantine Books; 2003.
- Hallowell EM, Ratey JJ. *Driven to Distraction: Recognizing and Coping With Attention Deficit Disorder from Childhood Through Adulthood.* New York: Touchstone; 1995.
- Leaver K. *The Friendship Lure: Reconnecting in the Modern World.* New York: Harry N. Abrams; 2018.
- Murthy V. *Together: The Healing Power of Human Connection in a Sometimes Lonely World.* New York: Harper Wave; 2020.
- Ornish D, Ornish A. *Undo It: How Simple Lifestyle Changes Can Reverse Most Chronic Diseases.* New York: Ballantine Books; 2019.
- Schawbel D. *Back to Human.* Boston, MA: Da Capo Lifelong: 2018.
- Willet W, Wood M, Childs D. *Thinfluence: Thin-flu-ence (Noun) The Powerful and Surprising Effect Friends, Family, Work, and Environment Have on Weight.* Emmans, PA: Rodale Books; 2014.

❑ Other Resources:

- Take the Social Network Index assessment—www.psy.cmu.edu/~scohen/SNI.html
- Spread health and wellness—be a peer-health coach to somebody.

- Connect–the next month, make one new acquaintance or reconnect with an old friend.
- Hug–during the next week, give a hug at least once a day.
- Smile–within the next week, at least once a day, give a smile to a total stranger.
- Talk and listen–meet up with a friend and have a good, long conversation.
- Help each other–help a friend with something.
- Help others–get involved in a volunteer experience.
- Help yourself.

SECTION III
BEYOND THE BASICS

Matt Benoit/Shutterstock.com

CHAPTER 16
FINAL THOUGHTS

"Life is a journey filled with unexpected miracles."

—Unknown

PAVING the Path to Wellness is a journey. It's a process of exploration, self-awareness, challenge, compassion, and joy. Hopefully, you'll have that feeling as you look back at your time with the program and the workbook. The journey is ongoing. The joy is available each day.

Progress, rather than perfection, is the goal. You may have heard the expression that perfection is the enemy of progress. Perfection is also the best friend of procrastination. We hope that you feel empowered to investigate and try to put a wide variety of ideas into action each day. With time, making small changes leads to big rewards. Patience is key. Perseverance powers you along the way, and a growth mindset sets you free to be you and bring out your best self. In other words, this workbook is designed as a recipe for your success. Bon appetit!

APPENDIX A
RECOMMENDED REFERENCES

❏ Books:

Allen D. *Getting Things Done: The Art of Stress-Free Productivity*. Westminster, London, England. Penguin Books; 2002.

Amen D. *The Brain Warrior's Way*. New York: Penguin Random House; 2016.

American Heart Association. *The New American Heart Association Cookbook*, 9th ed. New York: Harmony Books; 2019.

Arloski M. *Wellness Coaching for Lasting Lifestyle Change*. Duluth, MN: Whole Person Associates; 2009.

Atkinson D. *You Still Got It Girl.* Monterey, CA: Healthy Learning; 2016.

Bean A. *The Runner's Cookbook*. London, England: Bloomsbury Sport; 2018.

Beiloch S. *Choke*. New York: Atria Paperbacks; 2010.

Ben-Shahar T. *Choose the Life You Want: The Mindful Way to Happiness.* New York: The Experiment; 2014.

Ben-Shahar T. *Happier: Learn the Secrets to Daily Joy and Lasting Fulfillment.* New York: McGraw-Hill Education; 2007.

Ben-Shahar T. *Happier: Learn the Secrets to Daily Joy and Lasting Fulfillment.* New York: McGraw-Hill Education; 2007.

Benson H. *The Wellness Book*. New York: Simon and Schuster; 1993.

Bittman M, Katz D. *How to Eat: All Your Food and Diet Questions Answered.* Boston, MA: Houghton Miffin; 2020.

Branden N. *The Six Pillars of Self-Esteem: The Definitive Work on Self-Esteem by the Leading Pioneer in the Field.* New York: Bantam; 1995.

Buettner D. *The Blue Zones Solution: Eating and Living Like the World's Healthiest People*. Washington, DC: National Geographic; 2015.

Burnett B, Evans D. *Designing Your Life: How to Build a Well-Lived, Joyful Life*. New York: Knopf; 2016.

Cain J (ed). *The Learning Curve*. Monterey, CA: Healthy Learning; 2021.

Christakis N, Fowler JH. *Connection: the Surprising Power of Social Networks and How They Shape Our Lives.* New York: Little, Brown Spark; 2011.

Colten HR, Alevogt BM. *Sleep Disorders and Sleep Deprivation: An Unmet Public Health Problem*. Washington, DC: National Academic Press; 2006.

Corley J. *The Joy of Friendship: A Thoughtful and Inspiring Collection of 200 Quotations.* Hobart, NY: Hatherleigh Press; 2018.

Cousins N. *Anatomy of an Illness: As Perceived by the Patient*. New York: W.W. Norton & Company; 2005.

Covey S. *The 7 Habits of Highly Effective People: Powerful Lessons in Personal Change*, revised ed. New York: Free Press; 2004.

Covey SR. *The 7 Habits of Highly Effective People: Powerful Lessons in Personal Change*. New York: Simon and Schuster; 2004.

Csikzentmihalyi M. *Flow: The Psychology of Optimal Experience*. New York: Harper Perennial Modern Classics; 2008.

Deci EL, Ryan EM (eds.). *Handbook of Self-Determination Research*. Rochester, NY: University of Rochester Press; 2004.

Drucker PF. *Managing Oneself.* Boston, MA: Harvard Business Press; 2007.

Drucker PF. *The Effective Executive: The Definitive Guide to Getting the Right Things Done*. New York: Harper Business; 2006.

Duhigg C. *The Power of Habit: Why We Do What We Do in Life and Business*. New York: Random House Trade Paperbacks; 2014.

Dutton JE. *Energize Your Workplace: How to Create and Sustain High-Quality Connections at Work*. Hoboken, NJ: Jossey-Bass; 2007.

Dweck CS. *Mindset: the New Psychology of Success—How We Can Learn to Fulfill Our Potential.* New York: Ballantine Books; 2007.

Eckmann TF, Eckmann KL. *101 Mindfulness and Meditation Practices*. Monterey, CA: Healthy Learning; 2018.

Eckmann TF. *101 Brain Boosters*. Monterey, CA: Healthy Learning; 2013.

Editors of America's Test Kitchen. *The Complete Mediterranean Cookbook: 500 Vibrant, Kitchen-Tested Recipes for Living and Eating Well Every Day*. Boston, MA: America's Test Kitchen; 2016.

Egger G, Binns A, Rossner S, *Lifestyle Medicine: Managing Diseases of Lifestyle in the 21st Century*, 3rd ed. Cambridge, MA: Academic Press; 2017.

Fabritias F. *The Leading Brain*. New York: TarcherPerigee; 2017.

Frankl VE. *Man's Search for Meaning*, 4th ed. Boston, MA: Beacon Press; 2000.

Frederickson B. *Love 2.0: Finding Happiness and Health in Moments of Connection*. New York: Plume; 2013.

Freudenberger H, Richelson G. *Burnout: The High Cost of Human Achievement.* Norwell, MA: Anchor Press; 1980.

Greger M, Stone G. *How Not to Diet.* New York: Flatiron Books; 2015.

Greger M, Stone G. *The How Not to Diet Cookbook.* New York: Flatiron Books; 2017.

Greger M. *How Not to Diet.* New York: Flatiron Books; 2019.

Gregory A. *Nodding Off: The Science of Sleep From Cradle to Grave.* London, England: Bloomsbury Sigma; 2018.

Grimley D, Prochaska JO, Velicer WF, et al. The Transtheoretical Model of Change. In TM Brinhaupt and RP Lipka (eds) *Changing the Self: Philosophies, Techniques, and Experiences* (pp. 201–227). Albany, NY: State of New York Press; 1994.

Hahn TN. *How to Relax.* Berkeley, CA: Parallax Press; 2015.

Hallowell EM. *Connect: 12 Vital Ties That Open Your Heart, Lengthen Your Life, and Deepen Your Soul.* New York: Simon and Schuster; 2001.

Hallowell EM. *The Childhood Roots of Adult Happiness: Five Steps to Help Create and Sustain Lifelong Joy.* New York: Ballantine Books; 2003.

Hallowell EM, Ratey JJ. *Driven to Distraction: Recognizing and Coping With Attention Deficit Disorder from Childhood Through Adulthood.* New York: Touchstone; 1995.

Hanley K. *How to Be a Better Person: 400+ Simple Ways to Make a Difference in Yourself—And the World.* Avon, MA: Adams Media; 2018.

Harris D. *10% Happier: How I Tamed the Voice in My Head, Reduced Stress Without Losing My Edge, and Found Self-Help That Actually Works—A True Story.* New York: Day Streets Books; 2014.

Hart A. *Jar Salads: 52 Happy, Healthy Lunches to Make in Advance.* Collingwood, Victoria, Australia: Smith Street Books; 2016.

Heller M. *The Everyday Dash Diet Cookbook.* New York: Grand Central Life & Style; 2013.

Hensrud DD. *The Mayo Clinic Diet*, 2nd ed. Rochester, MN: Mayo Clinic Press; 2017.

Kabat-Zinn J, Hanh TN. *Full Catastrophe Living: Using the Wisdom of Your Body and Mind to Face Stress, Pain, and Illness.* New York: Bantam; 2013.

Kabat-Zinn J. *Mindfulness for Beginners.* Chicago: Sounds True, Inc.; 2007.

Kabat-Zinn J. *The Healing Power of Mindfulness: A New Way of Being.* New York: Hachette Books; 2018.

Katz D. *The Truth About Food: Why Pandas Eat Bamboo and People Get Bamboozled.* Independently Published; 2018.

Katzen M. *Moosewood Cookbooks*, 40th ed. Berkeley, CA: Ten Speed Press; 2014.

Laforet M. *The Vegan Holiday Cookbook.* Toronto, Canada: Robert Rose; 2017.

Lauger EJ. *Mindfulness*, 2nd ed. Boston, MA: Da Capo Lifelong Books; 2014.

Leaver K. *The Friendship Lure: Reconnecting in the Modern World.* New York: Harry N. Abrams; 2018.

Leider RJ. *The Power of Purpose: Creating Meaning in Your Life and Work.* Oakland, CA: Berrett-Koehler Publishers; 2005.

Lianov L. *Roots of Positive Change.* Middletown, DE: HealthType LLC; 2019.

Loehr, J, Loehr, JE, Schwartz T. *The Power of Full Engagement: Managing Energy, Not Time, is the Key to High Performance and Personal Renewal.* New York: Simon and Schuster; 2005.

Mariotti F (ed.) *Vegetarian and Plant-Based Diets in Health and Disease Prevention.* Cambridge, MA: Elsevier Academic Press; 2017.

Matthews J. *The Professional's Guide to Health and Wellness Coaching.* San Diego, CA: ACE; 2019.

McGonigal K. *The Upside of Stress: Why Stress is Good for You and How to Get Good at It.* New York: Avery; 2016.

Milkman K. *How to Change: The Science of Getting From Where You Are to Where You Want to Be.* New York: Portfolio Books; 2021.

Miller WR, Rollnide S. *Motivational Interviewing: Helping People Change.* New York: Guilford Press; 2012.

Miralles F, Garcia H. *Ikigai: The Japanese Secret to a Long and Happy Life.* Westminster, London, England: Penguin Life; 2017.

Moore M. *Coaching Psychology Manual*, 2nd ed. Philadelphia, PA; 2016.

Moran D. *Beating Osteoporosis*. Newnan, GA: Green Tree; 2019.

Murthy V. *Together: The Healing Power of Human Connection in a Sometimes Lonely World.* New York: Harper Wave; 2020.

Naidoo U. *This is Your Brain on Food: An Indispensable Guide to Surprising Foods That Fight Depression, Anxiety, PTSD, OCD, ADHD, and More*. New York: Little, Brown Spark; 2020.

Neff K. *Self-Compassion: The Proven Power of Being Kind to Yourself.* New York: William Morrow Paperbacks; 2015.

Neston J. *Breath: The New Science of a Lost art.* New York: Riverhead Books; 2020.

Nolan A, Schumann K, Callahan S. *Mothers Need Time-Outs Too: It's Good to Be a Little Selfish—It Actually Makes You a Better Mother.* New York: McGraw-Hill Education; 2008.

Nöteberg S. *Pomodoro Technique Illustrated: The Easy Way to Do More in Less Time.* Raleigh, NC: Pragmatic Bookshelf; 2009.

Ornish D, Ornish A. *Undo It: How Simple Lifestyle Changes Can Reverse Most Chronic Diseases*. New York: Ballantine Books; 2019.

Ottolenghi Y. *Plenty: Vibrant Vegetable Recipes From London's Ottolenghi.* San Francisco, CA: Chronicle Books; 2011.

Palmer S. *The Plant-Powered Diet: The Lifelong Eating Plan for Achieving Optimal Health, Beginning Today.* New York: Experiment Publishing; 2012.

Paul S, Benjamin H. *Sleep Essentials.* Monterey, CA: Healthy Learning; 2020.

Payne D. *Time-Out: Adult Coloring Book.* Scotts Valley, CA: CreateSpace Independent Publishing Platform; 2015.

Perlmutter LT. *The Heart and Science of Yoga: The American Medication Association's Empowering Self-Love Program to a Happy, Healthy, Joyful Life.* New York: AMI Publishers; 2017.

Peterson C, Seligman ME. *Character Strengths and Virtues.* American Psychological Association/Oxford Press; 2004.

Quach D. *Calm Clarity.* New York: TarcherPerigee; 2018.

Rama S. *The Art of Joyful Living.* Honesdale, PA: Himalayan Institute Press; 1989.

Ratey J. *Spark. The Revolutionary New Science of exercise and the Brain.* New York: Little, Brown Spark; 2008.

Rath T. *Strengths Finder 2.0.* Washington, DC: Gallup Press; 2007.

Richmond M. *The Physiology Storybook*, 3rd ed. Monterey, CA: Healthy Learning; 2011.

Rippe J (ed). *Lifestyle Medicine*, 3rd ed. Boca Raton, FL: CRC Press; 2019.

Rose S. *Whole Beauty: Meditation and Mindfulness—Rituals and Exercises for Everyday Self-Care.* New York: Artisan; 2019.

Ryan MJ. *The Happiness Makeover: How to Teach Yourself to Be Happy and Enjoy Every Day.* New York: Harmony; 2005.

Sapolsky RM. *Why Zebras Don't Get Ulcers*, 3rd ed. New York: Holt Paperbacks; 2004.

Schawbel D. *Back to Human.* Boston, MA: Da Capo Lifelong: 2018.

Schwartz SY, Goldstein D. *Unplug: A Simple Guide to Meditation for Busy Skeptics and Model Soul Seekers.* New York: Harmony; 2017.

Seale S. *The Full Plate Diet: Slim Down, Look Great, Be Healthy!* Austin, TX: Bard Press; 2010.

Seligman ME. *Authentic Happiness: Using the New Positive Psychology to Realize Your Potential for Lasting Fulfillment.* New York: Atria Books; 2004.

Seligman ME. *Flourish: A Visionary New Understanding of Happiness and Well-Being.* New York: Simon and Schuster; 2012.

Shah R, Davis B. *Nourish: The Definitive Plant-Based Nutrition Guide for Families—With Tips & Recipes for Bringing Health, Joy, & Connection to Your Dinner Table.* Boca Raton, FL: Health Communications; 2020.

Sharf-Hunt D, Hait P. *Studying Smart: How to Do Your Work and Do It Well, How to Survive the Pressure…and Still Have Time for Fun*. New York: Harper Paperbacks; 1990.

Sherzai D, Sherzai A. *The 30-Day Alzheimer's Solution: The Definitive Food and Lifestyle Guide to Preventing Cognitive Decline.* San Francisco, CA: HarperOne; 2021.

Shiue L. *The Spicebox Kitchen.* New York: Hachette Books; 2021.

Sood A. *Mayo Clinic Guide to Stress-Free Living.* Boston, MA: Da Capo Lifelong books; 2013.

Sood, A. *The Mayo Clinic Handbook for Happiness: A 4-Step Plan for Resilient Living.* Boston, MA: De Capo Lifelong Books; 2015.

Soojung A, Pang K. *Rest: Why You Get More Done When You Work Less.* New York: Basic Books; 2016.

Sortun A. *Spice: Flavors of the Eastern Mediterranean.* New York: William Morrow; 2006.

Stern B. *HeartSmart: The Best of HeartSmart Cooking.* Toronto, Canada: Penguin Random House Canada; 2006.

Storoni M. *Stress-Proof: The Scientific Solution to Protect Your Brain and Body—And Be More Resilient Every Day*. New York: TarcherPerigee; 2017.

Urban H. *Life's Greatest Lessons*. New York: Fireside; 2003.

Velasquez L. *Dare to Be Kind: How Extraordinary Compassion Can Transform Our World.* New York: Hachette Books; 2017.

Walker M. *Why We Sleep: Unlocking the Power of Sleep and Dreams.* New York: Scribner; 2017.

Wei M, Groves JE. *The Harvard Medical School Guide to Yoga: 8 Weeks to Strength, Awareness, and Flexibility.* Boston, MA: Da Capo Lifelong Books; 2017.

Westcott W. *Building Strength and Stamina*, 3rd ed. Monterey, CA: Healthy Learning; 2016.

Whitworth L, Kimsey-House K, Kimsey-House H, Sandahl P. *Co-active Coaching—New Skills for Coaching People Towards Success.* London, England: Breasley Publishing; 2007.

Wikgren S, Scott C, Rinaldi A. *Health and Wellness for Life.* Champaign, IL: Human Kinetics; 2010.

Willet W, Wood M, Childs D. *Thinfluence: Thin-flu-ence (Noun) The Powerful and Surprising Effect Friends, Family, Work, and Environment Have on Weight.* Emmans, PA: Rodale Books; 2014.

Williamson J. *Sleep Rituals: 100 Practices for a Deep and Peaceful Sleep.* Vero Beach, FL: Adams Media; 2019.

Winter C. *The Sleep Solution.* New York: Berkeley; 2018.

Yoke M, Kennedy C. *Functional Exercise Progressions.* Monterey, CA: Healthy Learning; 2004.

Yoke M. *101 Nice-to-Know Facts About Happiness.* Monterey, CA: Healthy Learning; 2015.

Zander RS, Zander B. *The Art of Possibility: transforming Professional and Personal Life,* rev. ed. Westminster, London, England: Penguin Books; 2002.

❏ Journal Articles:

Allen K, Blascovich J, Mendes WB (2002). Cardiovascular reactivity and the presence of pets, friends, and spouses: the truth about cats and dogs. *Psychosomatic Medicine*, 64(5), 727–739.

Ariga A, Lleras A (2011). Brief and rare mental "breaks" keep you focused. Deactivation and reservation of task goals preempt vigilance decrements. *Cognition.* 118(3), 439–443.

Bamia C, Trichopoulou A, Trichopoulas D (2008). Age at retirement and mortality in a general population sample: the Greek EPIC study. *Am J Epidemiol,* 167(5) 561–569.

Baun MM, Bergstrom N, Langston NF (1984). Physiological effects of human/companion animal bonding. *Nursing Research*, 33(3), 126–129.

Berkman LF, Syme SL (1979). Social networks, host resistance, and mortality: a nine-year follow-up study of Alameda County residents. *American Journal of Epidemiology*, 109(2), 186–204.

Blażek M, Kaźmierczak M, Besta T (2015). Sense of purpose in life and escape from self as the predictors of quality of life in clinical samples. *J Relig Health*, 54(2), (517–523).

Boyle PA, Buchanan AS, Barnes LL, et al. (2010). Effect of a purpose in life on risk of incident Alzheimer's disease and mild cognitive impairment in community-dwelling older persons. *Archives of General Psychiatry*, 67(3), 304–310.

Brown SG, Rhodes RE (2006). Relationships among dog ownership and leisure-time walking in Western Canadian adults. *American Journal of Preventive Medicine*, 30(2), 131–136.

Carlson MC, Erickson KI, Kramer AF, et al. (2009). Evidence for neurocognitive plasticity in at-risk older adults: the experience corps program. *Journal of Gerontology Series A: Biomedical Sciences and Medical Sciences*, 64(12), 1275–1282.

De Dren CK, Green LL, Van Kleef, et al. (2011). Oxytocin promotes human ethnocentrism. *Proceedings of the National Academy of Sciences*, 108(4), 1262–1266.

Dölen G, Darvishzadeh A, Huang KW, et al. (2013). Social reward requires coordinated activity of nucleus accumbens oxytocin and serotonin. *Nature*, 501(7466), 179–184.

Dutton JE, Heaphy ED (2003). The power of high-quality connections. *Positive Organizational Scholarship: Foundations of a New Discipline*, 3, 263–278.

Fredrickson. BL (2004). The broaden-and-build theory of positive emotions. *Philosophical Transactions of the Royal Society of London. Series B: Biological Sciences*. 359(1449), 1367–1377.

Frudenberge H (1974). Staff burnout. *Journal of Social Issues*. 30(1), 159–165.

Hirschkowitz M, Whiton K, Albert S, et al. (2015). National Sleep Foundation's sleep time duration recommendations: methodology and results summary. *Sleep Health*, 1(1), 40–43.

Jean-Louis G, Zizi F, Clark LT, et al. (2008). Obstructive sleep apnea and cardiovascular disease: role of the metabolic syndrome and its components. *J Clinical Sleep Medicine*, 4(3), 261–272.

Jessen NA, Munk AS, Lundgaard I, et al. (2015). The glymphatic system: a beginner's guide. *Neurochemical Research*, 40(12), 2583–2599.

Knowles, MS (1978). Andragogy: Adult learning theory in perspective. *Community College Review*. 5(3) 9–20.

Landrigan CP, Rothschild JM, Cronin JW, et al. (2004). Effect of reducing interns' work hours on serious medical errors in intensive care units. *The New England Journal of Medicine*, 351, 1838–1848.

Maller C, Townsend M, Pryor A, et al. (2006). Healthy nature healthy people: 'contact with nature' as an upstream health promotion intervention for populations. *Health Promotion International*, 21(1), 45–54.

Martino J, Pegg J, Frates EP (2017). The connection prescription: using the power of social interactions and the deep desire for connectedness to empower health and wellness. *American Journal of Lifestyle Medicine*, 11(6), 466–475.

Nagasawa M, Kikusui T, Onaka T, et al. (2009). Dog's gaze at its owner increases owner's urinary oxytocin during social interaction. *Hormones and Behavior*, 55(3), 443–441.

Owen SF, Tuncdemir SN, Bader PL, et al. (2013). Oxytocin enhances hippocampal spike transmission by modulating fast-spiking interneurons. *Nature*, 600(7463), 458–462.

Pantell M, Rehkopf D, Jutte D, et al. (2003). Social isolation: a predictor of mortality comparable to traditional clinical risk factors. *American Journal of Public Health*, 103(11), 2056–2062.

Scheele D, Willie A, Kendrick KM, et al. (2013). Oxytocin enhances brain reward system responses in men viewing the face of their female partner. *Proceedings of the National Academy of Sciences,* 110(50), 20308–20313.

Smith BW, Tooley EM, Montague EQ, et al. (2009). The role of resilience and purpose in life in habituation to heat and cold pain. *J. Pain*, 10(5), 493–500.

Sofi F, Cesari F, Abbate R, et al. (2008). Adherence to Mediterranean diet and health states: meta-analysis. *British Medical Journal*, 337.

Steger MF, Kawabata Y, Shimai S (2008). The meaningful life in Japan and the United States: levels and correlates of meaning in life. *Journal of Research in Personality*, 42(3), 660–678.

Stephens JP, Heaphy ED, Carmeli A, et al. (2013). Relationship quality and virtuousness: emotional carrying capacity as a source of individual and team resilience. *The Journal of Applied Behavioral Science*, 49(1), 13–41.

Steptoe A, Deaton A, Stone, AA (2015). Subjective well-being, health, and ageing. *The Lancet*, 385(9968), 640–648.

Umberson D, Crosnoe R, Reczek C (2001). Social relationships and health behavior across the life course. *Annual review of Sociology*, 36, 139–157.

Umberson D, Karas Montez J (2010. Social relationships and health: a flashpoint for health policy. *Journal of Health and Social Behavior*, 51 (1_suppl), 554–566.

Webber D, Guo Z, Mann S (2015). Self-care in health: we can define it, but should we also measure it? *Selfcare Journal*, 4(5), 98–114.

Whillans AV, Dunn EW, Smeets P, et al. (2017). Buying time promotes happiness. *Proceedings of the National Academy of Sciences*, 114(32), 8523–8527.

Williamson AM, Feyer AM (2000). Moderate sleep deprivation produces impairments in cognitive and motor performance equivalent to legally prescribed levels of alcohol intoxication. *Occupational and Environmental Medicine*, 57(10), 649–655.

❑ Online Resources:

5 Foods Linked with Better Brainpower. https://www.health.harvard.edu/healthbeat/foods-linked-to-better-brainpower

CDC—About Our Program—Sleep and Sleep Disorders (2017, June 05). https://www.cdc.gov/sleep/aboutus.html

Centers for Disease Control and Prevention (CDC) (2016). Insufficient Sleep is a Public Health Problem. https://www.cdc.gov/features/dssleep

Czeisler C. Drowsy Driving (video file). http://healthysleep.med.harvard.edu/healthy/matters

Drowsy Driving. https://www.sleepfoundation.org/drowsy-driving

Glass K. Transportation and Sleep: A Hypnotically Dangerous Relationship (2010). http://www.end-your-sleep-deprivation.com/transportation-and-sleep.html

Group EW. Dirty Dozen: The Fruits and Vegetables with the Most Pesticides. https://www.ewg.org/foodnews/dirty-dozen.php

Harvard Health Publishing. www.health.harvard.edu

Healthy Eating Plate. https://www.hsph.harvard.edu/nutritionsource/healthy-eating-plate

HENRY FORD: Why I Favor Five Days' Work With Six Days' Pay. Wikisource. https://en.wikisource.org/wiki/HENRY_FORD:_Why_I_Favor_Five_Days%27_Work_With_Six_Days%27_Pay

Hoeller SC (2015, July 3). 8 reasons why Americans should take their vacation days. *Business Insider.* https://www.businessinsider.com/why-americans-should-take-their-vacation-days-2015-6

Johns Hopkins Medicine E-Newsletters. https://www.hopkinsmedicine.org/news/e-newsletters

National Institute of Neurological Disorders and Stroke (2014). Brain Basics: Understanding Sleep. https://www.ninds.nih.gov/Disorders/Patient-Caregiver-Education/Understanding-Sleep

National Sleep Foundation. Drowsy Driving: Facts and Stats (2016). http://drowsydriving.org/about/facts-and-stats

Redmond BF (2009). Need Theories—PSYCH 484: Work Attitudes and Job Motivation. Confluence. https://wikispaces.psu.edu/display/PSYCH484/2.+Need+Theories

Robert Emmons. Profile. Greater Good Magazine. https://greater good.berkeley.edu/profile/robert_emmons

USDA. What's Cooking? USDA Mixing Bowl: A Collection of Recipes for Schools and Child Care Centers. Blog series. https://www.usda.gov/media/blog/2015/02/23/whats-cooking-usda-mixing-bowl-collection-recipes-schools-and-child-care

Web MD. Sleep Disorders. Healthy Sleep Health Center. https://www.webmd.com/sleep-disorders

Wolf CR. Virtual platforms are helpful tools but can add to our stress. *Psychology Today.* May 14, 2020. https://www.psychologytoday.com/us/blog/the-desk-the-mental-health-lawyer/202005/virtual-platforms-are-helpful-tools-can-add-our-stress

World Health Organization. Physical activity. https://www.who.int/news-room/fact-sheets/detail/physical-activity

World Health Organization. Self-care interventions for health. https://www.who.int/news-room/fact-sheets/detail/self-care-health-interventions#:~:text=What%20is%20self%2Dcare%3F,support%20of%20a%20health%20worker

❑ Organizations:

Alzheimer's Association—www.alz.org

American Academy of Sleep Medicine—www.sleepeducation.org

American Cancer Society—www.cancer.org

American College of Lifestyle Medicine (ACLM)—www.lifestylemedicine.org

American College of Sports Medicine (ACSM)—www.ACSM.org

American Council on Exercise (ACE)—www.acefitness.org

American Heart Association (AHA)—www.heart.org

American Medical Association (AMA)—www.ama-assn.org

American Public Health Association (APHA)—www.apha.org

American Sleep Apnea Association—www.sleepapnea.org

American Sleep Association—www.sleepfoundation.org

Arthritis Foundation—www.arthritis.org

Benson-Henry Institute—www.bensonhenryinstitute.org

Centers for Disease Control and Prevention (CDC)—www.cdc.gov

Cleveland Clinic—www.clevelandclinic.org

Department of Health and Human Services (HHS)—www.hhs.gov

Food and Drug Administration (FDA)—www.fda.gov

Food and Nutrition Information Center (FNIC)—www.nal.usda.gov

Gluten Intolerance Group—www.gluten.org

Harvard Medical School (Health and Medical Information)—health.harvard.edu

Health Resources and Services Administration—www.hrsa.gov

Institute of Lifestyle Medicine—www.instituteoflifestylemedicine.org

International Osteoporosis Foundation—www.osteofound.org

Livestrong Foundation—www.livestrong.org

National Cancer Institute—www.cancer.gov

National Center for Health Statistics—www.cdc.gov/nchs

National Center on Sleep Disorders Research—www.nhlbi.nih.gov

National Council on Aging—www.ncoa.org

National Institute of Allergy and Infectious Diseases—www.niaid.nih.gov

National Institute of Diabetes and Digestive and Kidney Diseases—www.niddk.nih.gov

National Institute of Mental Health—www.nimh.nih.gov

National Institute on Aging—www.nia.nih.gov

National Institutes of Health, Office of Dietary Supplements—www.ods.od.nih.gov

National Institutes of Health, Office of Research on Women's Health—www.orwh.od.niv.gov

National Osteoporosis Foundation—www.nof.org

National Sleep Association—www.sleepfoundation.org

National Sleep Foundation—www.thensf.org

Obesity Medicine Association—www.obesitymedicine.org

Office of Disease Prevention and Health Promotion—www.health.gov

Pancreatic Cancer Action Network—www.pancan.org

Parkinson's Foundation—www.parkinson.org

Prostate Cancer Foundation—www.pcf.org

Robert Wood Johnson Foundation—www.rwjf.org

Skin Cancer Foundation—www.skincancer.org

Society for Vascular Medicine—www.vascularmed.org

Susan G. Komen for the Cure—www.komen.org

T.H. Chan School of Public Health—www.hsph.harvard.edu

U.S. Anti-Doping Agency—www.usada.org

Women's Heart Foundation—www.womensheart.org

APPENDIX B
Joining or Leading a PAVING the Path to Wellness Program—Online or In-Person Groups

At some point, you may decide to extend or expand your involvement with the PAVING the Path to Wellness program. In that instance, consider the following:

- If you are not part of a PAVING the Path to Wellness online or in-person program but are interested in potentially joining a group or learning more, visit www.bethfratesmd.com.
- Opportunities to participate in online or in-person PAVING groups are available through visiting the website.
- Health professionals who have been trained by Dr. Frates, Dr. Comander, and/or Dr. Tollefson facilitate PAVING the Path to Wellness groups. They are committed to providing high-quality training to other facilitators, so that every participant can be empowered, educated, and supported during their PAVING program.
- If you are interested in becoming a PAVING the Path to Wellness facilitator and are a health professional, visit www.bethfratesmd.com to learn more.
- Even if you have completed this workbook, you are welcomed, indeed encouraged, to join one of the PAVING the Path to Wellness groups that meet online or in-person. Being part of a community of people committed to advancing their well-being through the PAVING process is very powerful.

fizkes/Shutterstock.com

APPENDIX C
Blank PAVING Wheel Form

PAVING the Path to Wellness

Measuring your Overall Wellness Using the PAVING Wheel

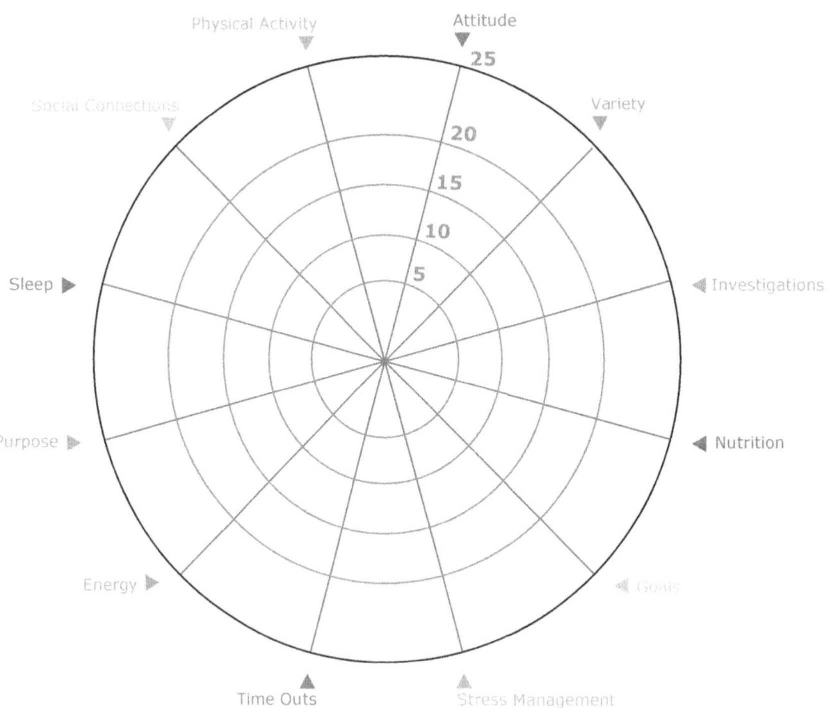

HOW TO USE THIS PAVING WHEEL

SCORE Plot your total scores for each component of the PAVING Wheel.

CONNECT Connect your scores.

EVALUATE Use the resulting PAVING Wheel (see example to the right) to evaluate areas where you may want to improve and consult the corresponding Module for more guidance.

RE-EVALUATE regularly by re-using this PAVING Wheel whenever you want to gauge your overall wellness and areas where you may want to improve.

EXAMPLE

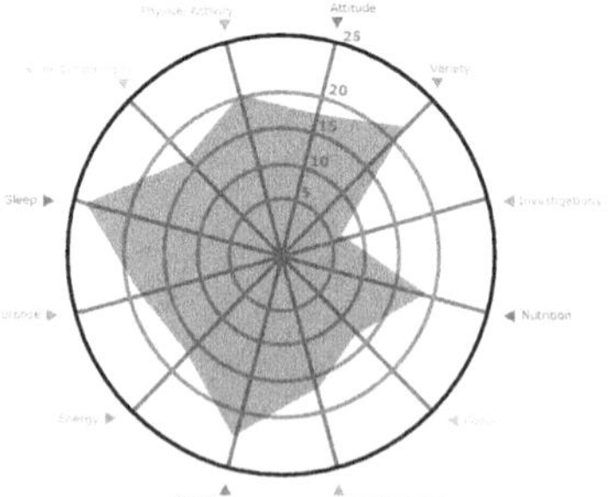

"There are no right or wrong answers. No scores are good or bad. Using the PAVING Wheel is for you alone to assess your Wellness and identify areas to improve your own personal Wellness."

1

INSTRUCTIONS Rank each item on a scale of 1-5. The Key is below. Calculate the subtotal of each of the 12 sections and plot them on the PAVING Wheel on page 1.

1 **Never** do this **2** Only **rarely** do this **3** **Sometimes** do this **4** **Often** do this **5** Do this regularly as **part of my routine**

MODULE 1 Physical Activity	
	I exercise 5 days in the week for about a half an hour.
	I enjoy myself when I exercise.
	I perform strength training exercises twice a week.
	I perform flexibility exercises routinely.
	I perform balance exercises routinely.
Physical Activity Total:	

MODULE 1 Stress	
	I have learned about stress and its effect on the mind and body.
	I am familiar with stress reduction techniques, and I use at least one when I feel that I am anxious, annoyed, or worried.
	I know about stress resiliency, and I practice enhancing my resiliency on a regular basis.
	I don't get angry easily.
	I meditate, take deep breaths, practice yoga, or do mindfulness based stress reduction (MBSR) regularly.
Stress Total:	

MODULE 2 Attitude	
	I use mistakes as opportunities to learn and grow.
	I write thank you notes or express my gratitude verbally.
	I celebrate success when it happens.
	I concentrate on the task at hand fully without distraction.
	I am optimistic about the day.
Attitude Total:	

MODULE 2 Time outs	
	If I sit for over an hour, I stand up and take a break for five minutes each hour.
	If I feel frustrated and annoyed, I take a few deep breaths to calm down.
	I take my vacation every year.
	When I am at home, I make sure to turn off my computer and put my work projects away at least for an hour at dinner time.
	After working on the same project for a few hours, I step away from it to get perspective on it.
Time Outs Total:	

MODULE 3 Variety	
	I do a variety of different exercises.
	I try to have a rainbow of colors on my plate.
	I enjoy a variety of fruits and vegetables.
	I like to try new activities.
	I spend time and connect with a wide range of friends.
Variety Total:	

MODULE 3 Energy	
	I have a friend who I know energizes me.
	I have identified at least one activity that brings me joy and energy.
	I am able to avoid situations and people that drain my energy.
	I only drink two cups of coffee a day.
	I don't rely on sugar/sweets or cookies for a quick energy fix.
Energy Total:	

MODULE 4 Investigations	
	I perform mini experiments on myself regularly.
	I am curious as to what foods are good for my body.
	I am curious as to what effect physical activity has on my body.
	I read about the latest research findings in medicine, nutrition, sleep, stress management, and/or exercise.
	I talk about health with family and friends.
Investigations Total:	

MODULE 4 Purpose	
	I feel that I have a clear purpose in life.
	I am able to prioritize my activities and projects easily.
	I make sure that my activities and projects are in alignment with my values.
	I have identified the people and activities that are most important to me.
	I am using my strengths to fulfill my purpose.
Purpose Total:	

MODULE 5 Nutrition	
	I eat 4 fruits a day.
	I eat 5 or more vegetables a day.
	I know proper portions for protein, carbohydrates, and fats, and I eat those portions.
	I think about the food that I eat and ask myself if it is good for my body.
	I view food as fuel, as medicine, and enjoyment too.
Nutrition Total:	

MODULE 5 Sleep	
	I sleep 7-8 hours a night.
	I don't drink coffee after noon time.
	I have a bedtime routine in which I relax before bed.
	I don't sleep with my phone on in the bedroom.
	I take 20 minute naps when I am over tired.
Sleep Total:	

MODULE 6 Goals	
	I set long-term goals for myself, share them with someone, and review them.
	I set three-month goals for myself, share them with someone, and work toward them.
	I set monthly goals and share them with someone.
	I set weekly goals and share them with someone.
	I set daily goals for myself and keep myself accountable for them.
Goals Total:	

MODULE 6 Social	
	I can name at least one person who brings me strength.
	I am involved with a group (activity, exercise class, art class, religious affiliation or the like)
	I visit with friends on the phone or in person at least 5 times a week.
	I have a healthy relationship with my spouse, partner, or best friend.
	I have a pet or plant that I can nurture and spend time with every day.
Social Total:	

ABOUT THE AUTHORS

Beth Frates, MD, FACLM, DipABLM, is a trained physiatrist and a health and wellness coach, with expertise in lifestyle medicine. She is an award-winning teacher at Harvard Medical School, where she is an assistant clinical professor. A pioneer in lifestyle medicine, Dr. Frates developed and first taught a college Lifestyle Medicine course at the Harvard Extension School in 2014, which is still one of the most popular courses offered at the school. In 2020, she was voted president-elect of the American College of Lifestyle Medicine (ACLM).

Dr. Frates also authored a syllabus on lifestyle medicine, which instructors and professors can download through the ACLM website as a template for their curriculum. In addition, Dr. Frates co-authored the *Lifestyle Medicine Handbook: An Introduction to the Power of Healthy Habits*, which Book Authority ranked in the top 20 medical books released in 2018. To accompany the syllabus and handbook, she also co-created Lifestyle Medicine 101, a full college curriculum, with 12 weeks of PowerPoints and a teacher's manual, both of which are free and accessible through the ACLM website. Most recently, Dr. Frates co-authored *The Teen Lifestyle Medicine Handbook*, published in October 2020, with corresponding slide-decks for faculty use.

As Director of Wellness Programming at the Stroke Institute for Research and Recovery at Spaulding Rehabilitation Hospital, a Harvard Medical School affiliate, Dr. Frates has created and implemented a 12-step wellness program, PAVING the Path to Wellness for patients and health care practitioners. At the present time, she serves as the Director of Lifestyle Medicine and Wellness for the Department of Surgery at Massachusetts General Hospital. In addition, Dr. Frates has her own consulting/coaching practice in lifestyle medicine, where she sees patients 1:1 and in groups.

Michelle Tollefson, MD, FACOG, DipABLM, FACLM, is an obstetrician-gynecologist in Denver, Colorado, and a professor in the Health Professions Department at Metropolitan State University of Denver, where she created and oversees the Lifestyle Medicine Program and the Wellness Coaching and Lifestyle Medicine Pathway.

Dr. Tollefson is a graduate of Creighton University, where she received both her Bachelor of Science and Doctor of Medicine degrees. She is board certified in obstetrics and gynecology and completed her residency at the University of Missouri in Kansas City. She is also board certified in lifestyle medicine and is a fellow of the American College of Lifestyle Medicine).

As an ACLM member for over a decade, she founded and co-chaired the Women's Health Member Interest Group, as well as the Pre-Professional Lifestyle Medicine Education Member Interest Group. She currently serves as the ACLM Executive Board Secretary and is on the Education and Membership Committees.

Most recently, Dr. Tollefson co-edited *Improving Women's Health Across the Lifespan*, which is part of Dr. James Rippe's Lifestyle Medicine book series. In addition, Dr. Tollefson leads workshops and speaks at national conferences on Lifestyle Medicine and women's health topics.

Dr. Tollefson is also a breast cancer survivor and thriver. In addition, she facilitates PAVING the Path to Wellness online lifestyle medicine groups for breast cancer survivors (thrivers) and women who want to optimize their health during and beyond menopause

Amy Comander, MD, DipABLM, is a breast oncologist and Director of Breast Oncology and Survivorship at the Massachusetts General Hospital (MGH) Cancer Center in Waltham and at Newton Wellesley Hospital. She is co-medical director of the MGH Cancer Center in Waltham, and an instructor in medicine at Harvard Medical School.

Dr. Comander is a graduate of Harvard University, where, as an undergraduate, she developed a passion for understanding the biological basis of behavior. Subsequently, she studied neurobiology and psychology as part of the multidisciplinary Mind, Brain, and Behavior Initiative. She then received her Doctor of Medicine at Yale University School of Medicine. She completed her internal medicine residency training and hematology-oncology fellowship training at Beth Israel Deaconess Medical Center and Harvard Medical School. She is board certified in hematology, medical oncology, and Lifestyle Medicine.

As a breast oncologist, Dr. Comander has witnessed the struggles her patients face during and following completion of primary cancer treatment, and she is passionate about improving the overall health and well-being of breast cancer survivors through lifestyle interventions. She is the founding co-chair of the American College of Lifestyle Medicine Breast Cancer Committee. In collaboration with Dr. Frates, she launched the PAVING the Path to Wellness Program lifestyle medicine group for breast cancer survivors. She trains other colleagues at the MGH Cancer Center to run PAVING groups, so that this transformational experience can be offered to a larger group of breast cancer survivors. Dr. Comander practices what she preaches, having run marathons, including seven consecutive Boston Marathons to date. She views running marathons as a metaphor for life, and her favorite running mantra is "Every mile out there is a gift and every finish line is a gift" (Amby Burfoot, winner of the 1968 Boston Marathon).